*The destiny of every human being
depends upon his relationship
to Jesus Christ.
It is not on his relationship to life,
or on his service or his usefulness,
but simply and solely on
his relationship to Jesus Christ.*
—OSWALD CHAMBERS

ENCOUNTER

FACE 2 FACE ➙ ← WITH JESUS

SKIP HEITZIG

BRIDGE
LOGOS
FOUNDATION

Alachua, Florida 32615

Bridge-Logos
Alachua, FL 32615 USA

Encounter: Face to Face With Jesus
by Skip Heitzig

Printed in the United States of America.

Library of Congress Catalog Card Number: 2009927064
International Standard Book Number 978-0-88270-978-9

Scripture quotations in this book are from the *New King James Version.* Copyright © 1979, 1980, 1982 by Thomas Nelson, Inc. Used by permission. All rights reserved.

Scripture quotations marked NLT are taken from the *Holy Bible, New Living Translation,* copyright © 1996. Used by permission of Tyndale House Publishers, Inc., Wheaton, Illinois 60189. All rights reserved.

Scripture quotations marked NIV are taken from the *Holy Bible, New International Version*®. NIV®. Copyright © 1973, 1978, 1984 by International Bible Society. Used by permission of Zondervan. All rights reserved.

Scripture quotations marked AMP are taken from *The Amplified Bible* edition identified as Copyright © 1984 by Zondervan Publishing House.

Scriptures marked NCV are taken from the *Holy Bible, New Century Version,* copyright © 1987, 1988, 1991 by Word Publishing, Dallas, Texas 75039. Used by permission.

Cover design copyright © 2000 Rome & Gold

Author photo copyright © 2009 Fred Roybal

G616.316.N.m907.35240

*This book is dedicated to my wife, Lenya, and son, Nathan,
who have helped me to see Jesus in fresh new ways and
to discover His presence in their personalities.*

*It is also dedicated to my mother, Agnes Heitzig,
who kept the fires of encouragement burning brightly
when things grew dark and cold.*

Contents

Acknowledgments

This book comes out of both an examination of the New Testament Scriptures and a personal exploration of their relevancy to human life. I would like to acknowledge the help of a few who have deepened that process and made this book possible. Dr. G. Campbell Morgan's fine volume *The Great Physician* was an early inspiration to me. Special thanks to Dr. Billy Graham, who introduced me to Jesus in 1973, and to Chuck Smith, who unfolded the character of Jesus through teaching and who modeled it through his life.

Thanks also to my editor, Lynn Vanderzalm, for providing professional creativity in editing and giving me a grid to help focus the writing of this book.

My secretary, Holly Ropes, assisted me greatly by not allowing other things to rob me of the time to devote to this project. Laura Sowers aided me in the early preparation of this book. Thanks to the congregation at Calvary for making my role as pastor so fun and rewarding.

A special thanks to my wife, Lenya, who always believed in me and cheered me on from beginning to end, even through the late-night writing and rewriting.

And, finally, I want to express my deep gratitude to Jesus himself, who graciously invaded my life and left His magnificent impression on it, rendering me eternally awed at His ways.

Foreword

Knowing Jesus Christ is the central issue of life. Not merely knowing about Him, not simply studying about Him, not just analyzing, critiquing, or debating Him—but knowing Him. Knowing Him personally. Knowing Him intimately. Knowing Him as He is revealed in the Scriptures, in a way that transforms our lives not only here and now but also for eternity.

In this book my friend Skip Heitzig—pastor of one of America's premier churches and a gifted Bible teacher whose ministry extends around the world—will help you to know Jesus Christ up close.

My own relationship with Jesus Christ began when, at twenty-two years of age, I got down on my knees in a Jerusalem hotel room, repented of my sins, and invited Christ to be my Lord and Savior. Growing up in the home of Billy and Ruth Graham, I had heard about Christ all my life. But I had never acted on what I had heard. I had not personally placed my trust in Him. When I finally did, my life began to change. Peace and fulfillment replaced the emptiness that had become my constant companion. I found that through Christ I could overcome old habits and live God's way. I discovered that He had a purpose for my life, a purpose that far surpassed any plans or ambitions that I had ever dreamed for myself. I began to experience what Christ himself spoke about in John 17:3: "Now this is eternal life: that they may know you, the only true God, and Jesus Christ, whom you have sent" (NIV).

As Skip relates in the following pages, he and many others have also encountered Jesus Christ and have been unforgettably changed by His love and power. The great news is that you can meet Jesus up close too; He is willing and able to transform you just where you are. Whoever you are, whatever you've done, no matter what your past—Jesus Christ loves you. He died on the Cross, then rose from the grave so that your sins could be forgiven and you could receive new life, eternal life. All it takes is a sincere desire on your part to turn from living your way and trust in Him.

As you read this book, I pray that you will grow in knowing Jesus. Whether you're just beginning in a relationship with Him or whether you've known Him for a long time, you'll find that the insights in this book will enrich your walk with Him. And anything that does that deserves priority attention.

Franklin Graham
Chairman and CEO, Samaritan's Purse

Will the Real Jesus Please Stand Up?

Socrates taught for forty years, Plato for fifty, Aristotle for forty, and Jesus for only three. Yet the influence of Christ's three-year ministry infinitely transcends the impact left by the combined one hundred and thirty years of teaching from these men who were among the greatest philosophers of all antiquity. —ANONYMOUS

What was Jesus like—really like? Some of us grew up with the portrayal the film industry gave us. I was raised seeing my fair share of movies about the life of Jesus Christ. Every Easter and sometimes at Christmas, Hollywood would make a creative concession and "get spiritual" by showing a few films about Jesus. But many portrayed Him as either a soft, almost effeminate loner or as a mystical, glow-in-the-dark caricature. I always came away from such movies thinking that Jesus was either untouchable or not relevant—or both.

What *was* Jesus like? That question has been pondered and debated since He first walked this Earth thousands of years ago. Even during His brief thirty-three-year time on Earth, people were not sure what to make of Him. Some called Him a prophet, sensing the resemblance between His teachings and those of past spiritual leaders (Matthew 16:14). Others insisted that He was a madman because of His radical claims and unconventional behavior (John 10:20). Those who met Him and got to know Him up close, however, had a different view of Him. To them He was God's unique Son, Israel's Messiah, the world's Savior, and their Lord and God (Matthew 16:16; John 1:41; 4:42; 20:28).

Even today the controversy continues. Jesus has been reinterpreted through the lens of selective history and revised by the prejudices of jaded men and women. Some worship Him intensely. Some respect Him standoffishly. And some hate Him passionately. Some Jews dare to respect Him as a first-century reformer calling His people back to the God of the Old Testament. Muslims still admit to admiring Him as a unique prophet for His own time. Hindus acknowledge Him as a promoter of nonviolence and as a person who had achieved a high level of consciousness.

Many people believe that nothing good came from Jesus. To them He was an impostor-messiah who was, at best, a renegade clergyman. More modern voices decry Jesus as a low caste artisan who was illiterate and may or may not have been a carpenter. They insist that His "miracles" never happened and that most of the words attributed to Jesus were not His. So the jungle of controversial opinions thickens with the mists of time.

We don't really know what Jesus looked like, although many artists have attempted to paint His likeness. Millions have come to believe that Jesus looked like the figure in Warner Sallman's painting *Head of Christ*, while others opt for the stern countenance given by Leonardo da Vinci in the *Last Supper*. The 1925 Bruce Barton classic, *The Man Nobody Knows*, casts Jesus as the strong "outdoor man," hearty through years of toil and one who enjoyed life to the full.[1]

The people who met Jesus up close were profoundly transformed.

While the New Testament is virtually silent about Jesus' outward appearance, it clearly describes the many one-on-one encounters that Jesus had with a wide variety of people. People met Him, ate lunch with Him, walked long distances with Him, shot questions at Him, and engaged in long conversations with Him. They saw Him up close. They were face-to-face with God in flesh.

xiv

And everyone who met Jesus was somehow changed by the encounter. No one remained the same afterward. The people who met Jesus up close were profoundly transformed.

That's the focus of this book. It is not an attempt to paint a full theological portrait of Jesus Christ. It rather offers glimpses of His life as He met and interacted with people.

What was it like to meet Jesus? What did people think about Jesus once they met Him? What was their initial reaction to Him? Did their opinions change over time? Did Jesus approach each person in the same way? What were His purposes in His interactions with people? How did He treat them? Did He favor certain people over others? What made people like Him—or hate Him?

I hope that you will see Him as a gracious, loving, and compassionate man whose approach to each person He met was as unique as the individuals themselves, whether they were lunatics or lawyers, prostitutes or priests.

These are the questions this book aims to answer. Moreover, as you place yourself in each story, I hope you can answer two deeper and more profound questions: *How can I meet Him in a similar way? How can I allow Jesus to transform my life?*

As we explore the New Testament stories of men and women who met Jesus up close, we will gain insight into Him as a *person*. What made Him tick? What drove Him? Why did He act a certain way with one person and an entirely different way with another? We'll also examine His *power*. His powerful acts made people both love Him and fear Him. Finally we will glimpse His *glory*. Some saw His glory close up and not only lived to tell about it but were forever motivated by it. Using these three divisions, we will watch as He interacts with people from different social, economic, and spiritual backgrounds. We'll see how He handled the privileged and the poor, the deeply religious as well as determined skeptics. We will relate more easily to some characters than to others. But each of them will teach us something about Jesus, ourselves, and people we know.

I also hope that you will see Jesus far differently than you have ever seen Him before. I hope that you will see Him as a gracious, loving, and compassionate man whose approach to each person He met was as unique as the individuals themselves, whether they were lunatics or lawyers, prostitutes or priests. I pray that as you watch person after person be transformed by the power of Jesus Christ, you will be encouraged and think, *If Jesus could have that effect on that person, imagine what He can do in my life or the lives of people I love.*

When my son was still a toddler, I remember coming home from work and calling out to him to let him know that I was home. Nathan would respond to my voice and come to find me. He would cock his tiny head as far back as it could reach to look up at me. I could tell he was pleased to see me, but he also seemed a bit overwhelmed by the sheer size difference between us. One day I tried a different approach. Instead of expecting him to come to find me, I strolled into his bedroom, and I got down on the floor at his level to talk and play with him. I was on his turf and in his world, and he related to me in a whole new way. I was no longer a six-foot-plus figure in the doorway; I was a more manageable eyeball-to-eyeball daddy. I was "dad up close," and it made a huge difference.

Essentially that's what God did in Jesus Christ. Coming down to our level and living on our turf for thirty-three years, Jesus was God stooping to meet humanity.

Once during a summer thunderstorm a young boy woke up to an earsplitting clap of thunder. Darting into his parents' bedroom, he put a death grip on his dad's neck. "Hey!" his father cried. "Haven't I told you that when you hear those noisy old storms it'll be all right? God will protect you, and you can trust Him."

The boy's response was classic. "Yeah, I know that," he countered, "but when the lightning is that close and the thunder is that loud, I want *someone with skin on!*"

That's what Jesus was to those who met Him—God with skin on. As we stand next to those who met Jesus up close, as we hear the words exchanged and see the transformation that takes place, I pray that a yearning develops within us—a yearning to meet the same Jesus—the *real* Jesus.

part one

The Person of Jesus

ONE

A Messenger in the
Middle of Nowhere

A Man with a Purpose

*In those days John the Baptist came, preaching in the Desert of
Judea and saying, "Repent, for the kingdom of heaven is near."
This is he who was spoken of through the prophet Isaiah: "A voice of
one calling in the desert, 'Prepare the way for the Lord, make straight
paths for him.'" John's clothes were made of camel's hair, and he had
a leather belt around his waist. His food was locusts and wild honey.
People went out to him from Jerusalem and all Judea and the whole
region of the Jordan. Confessing their sins, they were baptized by him
in the Jordan River.*

*But when he saw many of the Pharisees and Sadducees coming
to where he was baptizing, he said to them: "You brood of vipers!
Who warned you to flee from the coming wrath? Produce fruit in
keeping with repentance. And do not think you can say to yourselves,
'We have Abraham as our father.' I tell you that out of these stones
God can raise up children for Abraham. The ax is already at the root
of the trees, and every tree that does not produce good fruit will be
cut down and thrown into the fire.*

*"I baptize you with water for repentance. But after me will
come one who is more powerful than I, whose sandals I am not fit
to carry. He will baptize you with the Holy Spirit and with fire. His
winnowing fork is in his hand, and he will clear his threshing floor,
gathering his wheat into the barn and burning up the chaff with
unquenchable fire."*

*Then Jesus came from Galilee to the Jordan to be baptized by
John. But John tried to deter him, saying, "I need to be baptized by
you, and do you come to me?"*

*Jesus replied, "Let it be so now; it is proper for us to do this to
fulfill all righteousness." Then John consented.*

1

As soon as Jesus was baptized, he went up out of the water. At that moment heaven was opened, and he saw the Spirit of God descending like a dove and lighting on him. And a voice from heaven said, "This is my Son, whom I love; with him I am well pleased" (Matthew 3:1-17, NIV).

— —

John saw Jesus coming toward him and said, "Look, the Lamb of God, who takes away the sin of the world!" (John 1:29, NIV).

— —

Sixty miles northwest of Detroit, Michigan, is the city of Flint, the heart of the American automobile industry. Many years ago automakers in Flint kept hundreds of dies—or molds—they used for making various models of cars so that for a ten-year period, the manufacturer could reproduce the same model for thousands of buyers. That meant that your car could be identical to your neighbor's car.

God does not work with molds. When He creates a man or a woman, He makes no reproductions, no replicas. That was certainly true of John the "Baptizer." John was one of a kind. No die was cast for him. He stood out from the crowd.

One of the unique things about John was that he had an unusual mission. In fact, John's personal mission statement was delivered to him before he was born! An angel announced John's assignment and made it clear that he was to be a special child.

A Divine Calling

John's father, Zechariah, was one of the many Jewish temple priests who served on a yearly schedule. During his turn to perform the priestly duties he caught a glimpse of God's plan. He and his wife, Elizabeth, were childless, a stigma regarded in that culture as a sign of divine disfavor. But one day in the temple, Zechariah was startled when an angel appeared with a delightfully surprising message: "Don't be afraid, Zechariah! For God has heard your prayer, and your wife, Elizabeth, will

2

bear you a son! And you are to name him John. You will have great joy and gladness, and many will rejoice with you at his birth, for he will be great in the eyes of the Lord. He must never touch wine or hard liquor, and he will be filled with the Holy Spirit, even before his birth. And he will persuade many Israelites to turn to the Lord their God. He will be a man with the spirit and power of Elijah, the prophet of old. He will precede the coming of the Lord, preparing the people for his arrival. He will turn the hearts of the fathers to their children, and he will change disobedient minds to accept godly wisdom" (Luke 1:13-17, NLT). What a sense of joy and responsibility Zechariah and Elizabeth must have had when they thought about the angel's words.

We can imagine that as John grew, his parents had lengthy conversations with him, reinforcing the angel's words. We can almost hear Zechariah and Elizabeth saying, "God has special plans for you, John. You must prepare yourself. As our prophet Elijah once did, you will persuade people to turn to God again and you will prepare them to receive the Messiah."

Sometime during his upbringing, John gravitated toward the writings of the prophet Isaiah, who predicted a heralding voice that would speak to Israel. "A voice of one calling: 'In the desert prepare the way for the Lord; make straight in the wilderness a highway for our God'" (Isaiah 40:3, NIV). In response to that prophecy, John, probably as a teenager or young adult, went to live in the barren wilderness near the Dead Sea in order to prepare the way for the Lord—whatever that would mean. In an age when the spiritual light had dimmed in the Jewish nation, John was to be a divine flashlight enabling people to walk on God's righteous path.

The Wilderness Pulpit

At first glance many people probably thought John was an odd fellow, an eccentric. He wore strange clothing. He lived a simple, secluded life in the wilderness. Eating off the land, he foraged for wild honey common to the area as well as for protein-rich locusts, one of the few insects not forbidden by the ancient Jewish dietary laws.

3

People were curious about who John was and what he was doing. When priests and Levites were sent out from Jerusalem to ask John if he was the Messiah, he clearly told him that he was not. (See John 1:20-23.) When they pressed him about who he was, he replied with the prophetic words from Isaiah: "I am the voice of one calling in the desert, 'Make straight the way for the Lord.'"

His audience knew what those words meant. In ancient times, when a king came into a province, a herald would precede him, proclaiming, "Get ready! The king is coming!" Preparations were then made for the monarch's arrival: people would repair the roads, clearing debris, patching holes, and making crooked paths straight.

One of the ways John was preparing the path for people to meet Jesus was to preach and baptize. With the rocky wilderness as his backdrop, John baptized people and spoke of coming judgment, following the example of the Old Testament prophets such as Joel, Ezekiel, and Jeremiah. John didn't preach milky, sweet sermons but went directly to the point, regardless of whether his message might offend. John went for the jugular: "Repent, for the kingdom of heaven is at hand!" (Matthew 3:2). No opening illustration. No alliterated points. No fluff. He delivered truth as simply as he lived his life.

And the people responded. The Scripture tells us that people from Jerusalem, all Judea, and all the region around the Jordan went to hear John, to confess their sins, and to have him baptize them in the Jordan (Matthew 3:5-6).

John never minced words. When the Pharisees and Sadducees came to him, he called them a brood of snakes and confronted them about their hypocrisy, reminding them that they were not spiritually secure just because they were descendants of Abraham. With fearless courage, John preached his uncompromising message.

Why was John so harsh? Why the strong denunciations? Because John hadn't yet encountered Jesus. John was taking all his cues so far from the written word; he had not yet met the living Word.

John's message was accurate, of course. Judgment of sin was coming, and it would be administered by the very

4

Lord he was heralding. John had every right to make strong denunciations against those who repeatedly broke God's laws and misrepresented God to the nation. But that was only part of the truth. The rest of the picture would be seen only after John met Jesus.

The Messenger Meets the Messiah

John's encounter with the Messiah occurred when Jesus, John's cousin, journeyed from His hometown at Nazareth to John's desert parish, where the Jordan River flows into the Dead Sea. But Jesus caught John off guard by doing a surprising thing. When Jesus arrived, He deliberately stepped into the muddy waters of the Jordan, made His way toward John, and waited His turn to be baptized. John was confused because he knew that baptism was something only sinners needed to do, demonstrating their need for forgiveness of sins. John was resistant.

He was not ready to baptize Jesus. *It doesn't make sense; it just isn't right,* John must have thought. Jesus didn't need to repent of any sin. Why was He standing around all these sinners as if He were one of them?

John protested, saying, "I am the one who needs to be baptized by you ... so why are you coming to me?"

But Jesus firmly replied, "It must be done, because we must do everything that is right" (Matthew 3:14-15, NLT). So John submitted to his Lord's command and baptized Him.

Jesus was saying in essence, "My baptism is important, John, because by it I'm identifying with sinful people. John, you denounce sin, and that's good, but that will never cure sin. Righteousness needs to be fulfilled, and that's why I've come—to do what no one else could ever do—to make people right with God." (See Matthew 3:15, NKJV.) John the Baptist was learning in that instant that Israel's long awaited Messiah had come to identify with broken, fallen humanity. He wanted to launch His ministry among the common people, the sinful ones, those who knew they needed God to do a new work in their lives.

Although John balked at first because of his traditional understanding of the Messiah's role, he was growing in that understanding. John had been proclaiming a conquering king

5

who would judge the sinful world and set things in order. As true as that would one day be, John was also beginning to learn that Jesus would come first to identify with that sinful world. John had seen Jesus through the lens of His *final* act of judging people for their sin, not His *intermediate* act of rescuing people *from* their sin. All that was changing now that John met Jesus, and there was more to follow.

*John had seen Jesus through the lens of His **final** act of judging people for their sin, not His intermediate **act** of rescuing people from **their sin**.*

As soon as Jesus rose up, still dripping from the Jordan's waters, an amazing sign appeared. The heavens opened up, and John saw the Holy Spirit appear overhead in the form of a dove. To the Jewish mind, a dove was associated with sacrifice: Rich people sacrificed bulls, while poor people used doves.[1] John's understanding was broadened that day. He saw clearly that the Messiah was anointed by God to *be* a sacrifice—a sacrifice for all classes of society.

Then John heard an unmistakable voice say, "This is My beloved Son, in whom I am well pleased" (Matthew 3:17). It was as if God was giving His endorsement of Jesus' uniqueness among men and His oneness with God the Father. This announcement made it clear that Jesus was far more than a son of God in a general sense or in a spiritual way. This title was closely associated with Jesus' royal position as Israel's Messiah. (See Luke 1:32-33.) John got the message—*this* One was *the* One!

Encounter with the Lamb

John's next encounter with Jesus happened several weeks later, after Jesus had emerged victorious from a forty-day wilderness confrontation with Satan.[2] Again, Jesus came to the Jordan River to meet John. When John saw Him, he made an announcement that seemed to emerge from his newfound awareness of who Jesus was: "Behold! The Lamb of God who takes away the sin of the world!" (John 1:29).

6

Did you notice the difference? Before John's first encounter with Jesus, he had seen Him as the judge of sinners; the lion who would pounce on His prey. (See Genesis 49:9.) And John had shaped his message accordingly. But this time, rather than making a strong denunciation against the sinners, John made a strong proclamation affirming the Savior. John was beginning to realize that while Jesus was the lion, He must first become God's sacrificial Lamb sent to atone for the world's sins. What accounted for this staggering change in John's perception?

It was, no doubt, a number of things. First, the baptism encounter had an incredible impact on John. Seeing Jesus stand in the river to identify with sinners showed him that Jesus' activity was *relational*—He was identifying with common, sinful humanity. Seeing the Holy Spirit in the form of a dove revealed that Jesus' activity was to be *sacrificial*—He who identified with such people would somehow be involved in atoning for their sins.

John perceived that the Messiah was to be not only the judging One but also the saving One, bearing the sins John had so passionately denounced.

Second, I can imagine that after the baptism, John retreated to the familiarity of Scripture to try to understand why Jesus had acted as He had at the Jordan River. Very likely John searched through the scrolls of Isaiah's prophecy—the very prophet who had predicted his own mission as forerunner. John would have read passages predicting the Messiah's future judgment of the Earth (Isaiah 24) as well as His righteous reign as king (Isaiah 32). But he also would have studied Isaiah 53, where he would have read, "He was led as a lamb to the slaughter. And as a sheep is silent before the shearers, he did not open his mouth" (Isaiah 53:7, NLT).

John's baptismal encounter with Jesus readied him for this encounter. John's perception of who Jesus was blossomed into a mature realization that Jesus would act the part of the familiar atonement lamb used on Yom Kippur, the Jewish high holiday. John perceived that the Messiah was to be not only the *judging One* but also the *saving One*, bearing the sins John had so passionately denounced.[3]

This realization helped John draw a bigger circle, this time not just around a nation but around the world. This Lamb would take away not only Israel's sins but also the sins of the whole world.

What Can We Learn from John's Encounters with Jesus?

Have you met Jesus? Really met Him? Or have you merely heard about Him or read about Him or studied about Him?

If you have met Jesus, how have you been affected? What were your preconceptions about Him? Were those preconceptions supported when you met Him, or were they shattered? What difference did it make that you met Jesus? How did you grow?

Meeting Jesus made a huge difference for John the Baptist. He had studied about the man whose life would play such a major part in his own life. But until John met Jesus and saw Him act, his view of Him was very clouded. Jesus surprised John, changed him, and solidified his purpose.

Meeting Jesus May Surprise You

Meeting Jesus shattered John's preconceptions of what He would be like. Jesus did not act like a king. He did not act like a judge. Instead He acted like a lamb who would take on himself the sins of the whole world.

Meeting Jesus may shatter your preconceptions too. He may not act the way you thought **Be open to the ways** He would. Jesus may surprise you **in which Jesus may** as you learn about His openness to sinners or His anger at religious **want to shape you.** snobbery or His indifference toward people's status. He may surprise you with His willingness to enter your world or to forgive your sin or to give you a second chance.

When He does surprise you, don't be resistant, as John was initially. Instead be open to the ways in which Jesus may want to shape you.

8

If you have faulty ideas of who Jesus is, ask yourself where those misconceptions originated. Have you adopted other people's perspectives of who Jesus is? Have you bought into the culture's view? How can you meet Jesus and discover for yourself who He is?

One obvious way is to immerse yourself in the Bible, the written revelation of who Jesus is. As you discover more of His character on the pages of Scripture, allow Him to speak to you and direct you. Begin your reading with the Gospels (Matthew, Mark, Luke, and John)—the eyewitness accounts of Jesus' life on Earth. As you gain new insights into His style, His promises, and even His challenges and rebukes, your relationship with Him will grow. Someone once noted that "God is never greater than our present understanding of Him." In other words, we will relate to God only at the level that we know Him.

But also make sure that you meet the living Word. Spend time with His people. Meet Him in worship. Be where He is active, where He brings healing to broken people, or where He rescues people from the darkness of their sin.

Then let Him surprise you.

Meeting Jesus Will Change You

Meeting Jesus changed John in two significant ways: his understanding and his message.

Understanding. When John met Jesus at the Jordan River, he began to get insight into His character. He saw Jesus' compassion as He stood in the same water as sinners, the people John knew really needed to be there. As a result John saw into the heart of God. He saw God's matchless love as Jesus descended to the level of sinful humanity.

Every time John discovered more about Jesus, his understanding and faith grew.

When we first encounter Jesus, we usually gain an understanding of some of the fundamentals: Jesus loves me, He forgave my sins, and one day I'm going to be with Him in Heaven forever. Those are great truths. They are transforming truths. But there's much more to the Christian life than stopping right there. Christianity isn't about just one encounter. The more you meet with Jesus, the more deeply

9

you will get to know Him. And the more you know Him, the more you will love Him and want to serve Him.

Discovering Jesus is what brings a thrill to the Christian life. I can still remember the drudgery that going to church was for me when I was growing up. It was an enforced event. I *had* to do it, but I really didn't want to do it. I didn't go to church to encounter Jesus. I wasn't expecting to meet Him in the experience of attending a church service. Years later, when I got serious about following Jesus, a sense of expectancy developed. I grew more open to discovering truths that had been kept hidden for years because I simply wasn't open to them.

The more you meet with Jesus, the more deeply you will get to know Him.

Now that I have encountered Jesus and have felt the joy of discovery, I long for a deeper understanding. I am eager to place myself in situations where I will grow.

Seminary professor Howard Hendricks tells the story of his daughter, Bev, who when she was young was deeply interested in her own growth.

> She promised me she would grow while I was gone on a ministry trip for a couple of weeks. When I returned and stepped off the plane, she greeted me with, "Daddy, come home quick! We gotta see how much I growed!" So we went home to the closet door and measured. It couldn't have been more than a few millimeters, but she jumped up and down. "Daddy, I told you, I did grow!" Then we went into the living room for a special time of talking, and she asked me one of those questions you wish kids wouldn't ask: "Daddy, why do big people stop growing?"[4]

Searching question, isn't it? I think if we were honest with ourselves, we would probably have to admit that we stop growing spiritually whenever we stop welcoming discovery.

Be open to discovery. Allow Jesus to change your understanding of who He is.

Message. As you discover who Jesus is and grow in your understanding, you will find that you will speak of Him differently to others.

As we have already seen, that was the case with John. John became a signpost for the people who came to see him in the barren desert. He gave aimless hearts spiritual direction. "Get back to God" was John's heart cry. "Follow Him and do what He requires." It was exactly as the angel had predicted concerning John: "And he will turn many of the children of Israel to the Lord their God" (Luke 1:16).

When the crowds came to John, he pointed people to the source of life. He saw himself as nothing but an intermediary. He never allowed himself to become the focus of the attention. When people suggested that he might be the Messiah, he set them straight and told them that he wasn't even worthy to tie the Messiah's sandal strap! In fact, John said of his own ministry and that of Christ's, "He must increase, but I must decrease" (John 3:30). Turning the creation back to their Creator, turning the sinners back to their Savior, turning the hopeless back to the source of hope became the mark of John's message.

When you meet Jesus, allow Him to change your message too. If He has met you in your discouragement, proclaim Him to be the gentle encourager. If He has met you in the depths of your sin, proclaim Him to be the faithful forgiver. If He has met you in your confusion, proclaim Him to be only truth.

As you discover who Jesus is, tell others what you see and experience. Invite them to meet Jesus too. Be a signpost that leads them to Jesus.

Meeting Jesus Will Direct You

Why were you born? What is the purpose of your life? What direction are you traveling?

John's purpose was clear from the beginning: His divine calling was to point people to God. For that reason John was born. For that reason he was effective. For that reason he was great. John lived to see others encounter the living Word, and that gave him a sense of fulfillment.

If you are like most people, you long to know that your life counts for something, that you have a purpose for being on

11

Earth. How will you know what that purpose is, and how will you fulfill that purpose?

Unlike John, you did not have an angel announce your calling before you were born. But you do have two of the resources John had available to him: the Scriptures and the Holy Spirit.

John learned about his purpose by reading the Scriptures, and you can too. As you immerse yourself in the Word, as you see what God requires of His children, and as you see how Jesus interacted with people, you will find direction. The Bible reveals a God who takes a personal interest in the lives of His children, equipping them with abilities and arranging opportunities for them to use those abilities. The Holy Spirit— God's presence in us—will then equip you to fulfill your God-given purpose. The Spirit will lead you into truth and tell you what God wants you to know. (See John 16:13-15.)

The Bible reveals a God who takes a personal interest in the lives of His children, equipping them with abilities and arranging opportunities for them to use those abilities.

Everyone whom God calls has a purpose. There is a part of God's program on Earth that only you can fulfill. One of life's greatest pursuits is to discover what that purpose is and to live within its flow, even though you may feel as if you are going against how culture says you should live.

In the icy waters off the coast of Greenland are innumerable icebergs of varying size. Even a casual observation reveals that the small ice floes move in one direction while the massive ones flow in another. The reason for this is simple. Surface winds drive the little bergs while deep ocean currents move the larger masses of ice along according to their routes. Likewise, people carried by an awareness of God's will for their lives are pulled by a deeper current than the surface winds of trends or societal pressures.

Sometimes you may feel conflicted about the purpose you believe God has given you. In the movie *Chariots of Fire*, the Scottish runner Eric Liddell had a decision to make. He was scheduled to leave for the mission field, but he felt called to run in the Olympic Games in Paris. His sister tried to convince him that if he ran in the Olympics, it would indicate that he put sports above Christ. In a discussion with his sister, Eric Liddell responded, "I know God made me for a purpose. But He also made me fast! And when I run, I feel His pleasure!" Liddell knew that being a missionary was God's plan for his life, but he also believed that running in the Olympics was a part of that grand design.

John the Baptist knew God had made him for a purpose, and he lived to be obedient to that design. When John preached in the desert, he could feel God's pleasure. When he met Jesus Christ and learned of His mission, he could feel God's pleasure. Being the voice in the wilderness gave John the sense of fulfilling the plan of God in his own life.

When we live with a firmly developed sense of purpose, we care more about quality than quantity. One morning in 1888, Alfred Nobel, the inventor of dynamite, opened the daily newspaper and was stunned to find an article about his own death. Alfred's brother had died, but some careless reporter had confused Alfred with his brother and had written the obituary about Alfred! But the mistake made Alfred think. He realized that the world perceived him as simply the "Dynamite King." His legacy was that he was a successful industrialist who had amassed a fortune from explosives. There was no mention of his efforts for world peace. He would be remembered only for being a "merchant of death."

Alfred made an immediate decision. He determined to do something to make sure the world would remember him for the values to which he had devoted his life. He decided that this could be accomplished by the way he disposed of his vast wealth in his last will and testament. That's the reason why today we have the prestigious award given to someone who has contributed significantly to the cause of world peace—the Nobel Peace Prize.

How Can You Meet with Jesus?

The whole concept of "meeting with" or "encountering" Jesus may still seem a bit fuzzy. After all, how can you meet someone who no longer lives in a physical body on Earth? What does

13

it mean for you to meet Jesus? It's not as complicated as you may think.

Introduce yourself. When you first meet a person, you generally speak. You exchange names and basic information about yourself. This is a good place to begin with Jesus, even though He already knows all about you. Tell Him that you want to have a relationship with Him. Confess that you are not quite sure about how to go about it but that you are willing to learn. Don't worry about how good your words sound to Him. He isn't interested in the form as much as the attitude and motivation behind the form. It may feel awkward at first to speak words into empty air. But trust that He hears you. Tell Him that you are interested in finding out who He really is and that you are willing to act in response to what you find out.

Learn about Him. The Bible reveals what Jesus is like and what He desires from us. Just as two people can get to know each other through their correspondence, you can encounter Jesus by reading about Him—what He said about himself, what He said about God, what He said about how He wants you to live, and how He related to others. These interactions will serve as touch points for you to learn how He wants to relate to you as well.

Enjoy Him. As you learn more about Jesus, you will learn to trust Him more. As you watch Him forgive people, you will be encouraged to confess your sins to Him and to find the same forgiveness. As you observe His holy nature, you will grow in your desire to stay away from activities that would offend or hurt Him. Your relating to Him will develop into your enjoyment of Him.

— —

FOR DISCUSSION AND REFLECTION

1.   In what ways has Jesus surprised you? What responses, statements, or revelations in Scripture have you found to be surprising? Have you found that Jesus sometimes acted differently from what you anticipated?

2. How has your understanding of Jesus changed from your first encounter with Him? What specific things about the character of Jesus have you learned by experience? What have you learned by reading the Bible? How has your message about Jesus changed?

3. What is your God-given purpose in life? What makes you feel God's pleasure? How did God call you to that purpose? How is He equipping you to fulfill that purpose? If you do not know what your purpose is, how can you meet with Jesus and discover His plan for you? Who can help you do that?

4. John said of Jesus, "He must increase, but I must decrease" (John 3:30). What do you think John meant by that statement? How would you change if you lived out this verse in your personal life, in your home, in your business dealings, and in your relationships?

5. Write your own obituary. Ask a friend to help you. Include the things other people feel are important about you. Is this the legacy you would like to leave? If not, how will you change that?

Religion Gets a Makeover

A Religious Person Meets Jesus

There was a man of the Pharisees named Nicodemus, a ruler of the Jews. This man came to Jesus by night and said to Him, "Rabbi, we know that You are a teacher come from God; for no one can do these signs that You do unless God is with him."

Jesus answered and said to him, "Most assuredly, I say to you, unless one is born again, he cannot see the Kingdom of God."

Nicodemus said to Him, "How can a man be born when he is old? Can he enter a second time into his mother's womb and be born?"

Jesus answered, "Most assuredly, I say to you, unless one is born of water and the Spirit, he cannot enter the Kingdom of God. That which is born of the flesh is flesh, and that which is born of the Spirit is spirit. Do not marvel that I said to you, 'You must be born again.' The wind blows where it wishes, and you hear the sound of it, but cannot tell where it comes from and where it goes. So is everyone who is born of the Spirit."

Nicodemus answered and said to Him, "How can these things be?"

Jesus answered and said to him, "Are you the teacher of Israel, and do not know these things? Most assuredly, I say to you, We speak what We know and testify what We have seen, and you do not receive Our witness. If I have told you earthly things and you do not believe, how will you believe if I tell you heavenly things? No one has ascended to heaven but He who came down from heaven, that is, the Son of Man who is in heaven. And as Moses lifted up the serpent in the wilderness, even so must the Son of Man be lifted up, that whoever believes in Him should not perish but have eternal life.

For God so loved the world that He gave His only begotten Son, that whoever believes in Him should not perish but have everlasting life" (John 3:1-16).

Over half of all Americans believe that religion is important in their lives. That may sound like encouraging news, but that number signals a steady decline from early baby-boom years of the 1950s, when the figure was 75 percent.[1] The truth is, we Americans have been grappling with the relevance of religion in our society since our country was founded over two hundred years ago.

But two thousand years ago things were different. In ancient Israel, people considered religion the dominating force of life. But for some people religion just wasn't enough. Nicodemus was one who felt the need for more.

On the surface Nicodemus appeared to have it all. Tradition indicates that Nicodemus belonged to a distinguished and wealthy Jerusalem family. His family heritage was part of the "old money" of Jerusalem's ruling class. Some have even identified him as the wealthy brother of the illustrious Jewish historian Josephus.[2]

Besides being rich and famous, Nicodemus was a Pharisee, one of the elite scholars of his day. Some think he was among the most famous teachers in Jewish theological circles of his world. If people had a Bible question, they would go to see Professor Nicodemus. He had the answers. As a Pharisee, Nicodemus had pledged to be righteous, to separate himself from any and all sin. He had taken an oath to spend his days striving to keep all the details of the law, not only the Ten Commandments but the hundreds of do's and don'ts the Pharisees had added to the Mosaic law. Like all Pharisees, Nicodemus believed that keeping the rules perfectly would be his ticket to Heaven.

Soon the rules began to rule, and people lost sight of the One who rules.

But such zeal exacted its toll. Soon the rules began to rule, and people lost sight of the One who rules.

Background, bucks, and brains—a powerful combination. But it wasn't enough for Nicodemus. He had a hole in his soul, and he didn't know how to fill it. Even after drinking long at the well of religion, Nicodemus knew his soul was parched. It was that thirst that drove him to find Jesus.

Nicodemus sensed something exceptional and singular about this man from Nazareth. What made hordes of people follow Him? Nicodemus had most likely heard that virtually everywhere Jesus went, He confronted death, disease, and depression but left behind Him life, health, and joy. Could this be the coming Messiah the prophets told about?

A Face-to-Face Encounter

Nicodemus had to find out for himself. Driven by his curiosity and his thirst to fill his soul, Nicodemus seized the opportunity to meet Jesus of Nazareth.

Nicodemus arranged to meet Jesus alone, at night. It was too risky to meet during the day, when others would see them. He would have too much explaining to do to his fellow Pharisees, who were distrustful of Jesus.

Nicodemus tried to keep the tone of the meeting on a professional level. His opening line was polite: "Rabbi, we know that You are a teacher come from God; for no one can do these signs that You do unless God is with him" (John 3:2). The use of the word we is telling. Nicodemus wanted to make it clear that he was acting as part of a spiritual team.

Jesus wasn't just a teacher come from God; He was God come to teach.

He came representing the Jews, or perhaps the Pharisees in particular. He didn't want the visit to be interpreted as anything but a courtesy extended to Jesus by the religious ruling class.

While Nicodemus may have wanted to have a theological discussion about the source of miraculous power, Jesus wanted something different. Nicodemus would soon learn that Jesus wasn't just a teacher come from God; He was God come to teach.

And Jesus had one goal for Nicodemus: getting him into the Kingdom of God. (See John 3:2-5). So His response to Nicodemus' opening comment was a startling one. Jesus

19

didn't say, "Yes, Nicodemus, I'm glad that you recognize that I am from God. You obviously have studied the Scriptures thoroughly."

No. He moved quickly from pleasantries to eternal verities. This man was hungry for truth, and Jesus knew it.

Jesus looked Nicodemus in the eye and said, "I assure you, unless you are born again, you can never see the Kingdom of God" (John 3:3, NLT). In that sudden transition Jesus moves right to the core of the man's greatest need. Unimpressed by Nicodemus' clout, Jesus sees Nicodemus not as a heavyweight theologian but as a person with a weighty need.

A Mind-to-Mind Encounter

No doubt Nicodemus was disturbed by Jesus' statement. After all, he and his colleagues, the Pharisees, had already solved the question of how to get into the Kingdom. It was simple: Obey the law and keep the rules.

It was a matter of balancing one action with another: righteous deeds outweighed sin. If people did enough good deeds, they could earn rewards, like getting an upgrade into the first-class section of God's Kingdom. He had it all figured out.

Who was this man to say that he had to be born again? What kind of talk was that?

Nicodemus engaged his mind and entered the discussion on a cognitive level. Like a news reporter, Nicodemus probed Jesus with questions: "How can a man be born when he is old? Can he enter a second time into his mother's womb and be born?" (John 3:4).

Nicodemus had already been born. That was obvious. What could this compelling rabbi mean by being "born again"?

On some level Nicodemus knew that Jesus was speaking figuratively. He knew that theological ideas are not always logical. As a distinguished instructor among the Jews, Nicodemus was accustomed to the use of spiritual allegory. But how could a person experience the power of a new life— especially the older a person becomes? How can people change who they are? How do they become recast once the cement of their own habits has hardened? How could Nicodemus personally go through such a metamorphosis?

A Heart-to-Heart Encounter

Nicodemus' questions prompted Jesus to move matters straight to the heart. "Most assuredly, I say to you, unless one is born of water and the Spirit, he cannot enter the Kingdom of God. That which is born of the flesh is flesh, and that which is born of the Spirit is spirit" (John 3:5-6). Nicodemus wanted to get an answer to a question; Jesus wanted to get the questioner into God's Kingdom. Nicodemus opens with formalities; Jesus moves the conversation to fundamentals. Nicodemus wrestles with this truth mentally; Jesus takes it from being an issue of the mind to one of the heart. He makes it clear that the Kingdom of God can't be entered with an upgrade. No amount of points scored by good works will cut it.

Just as Nicodemus came into this world because of a physical birth, he could gain entrance into the next world, God's Kingdom, by another birth—a spiritual one. "That which is born of the flesh is flesh, and that which is born of the Spirit is spirit," Jesus insisted (v. 6). Human life reproduces human life, but it cannot produce spiritual life. Nothing done by human effort could ever generate the transformation Nicodemus knew he needed. So many of his contemporaries were attempting to do the impossible—bring life out of lifeless ritual.

Something Jesus said helped Nicodemus understand how this transformation was possible. He used words Nicodemus would have recognized: "unless one is born of water and the Spirit." As a teacher of the Old Testament, Nicodemus remembered the pledge God made through the prophet Ezekiel: "Then I will sprinkle clean water on you, and you will be clean. Your filth will be washed away ... and I will give you a new heart with new and right desires, and I will put a new spirit in you. I will take out your stony heart of sin and give you a new, obedient heart" (Ezekiel 36:25-26, NLT).

Those ancient expressions began to take on fresh meaning as Jesus framed them anew for Nicodemus. Nicodemus needed a new heart, not another animal sacrifice made in the Jewish temple. Nicodemus needed the purification that comes from God's Holy Spirit. That's the cleansing that would make life in God's Kingdom possible.

And Nicodemus wanted it.

21

He had spent his whole life in the business of cleansing and purification, but he had never felt satisfied. There were always more sacrifices and more holy days, and their effects were only temporary. As soon as one ritual ended, he needed to make preparations for another. What Nicodemus needed was something that lasted! But how could he be sure?

As if reading the teacher's mind, Jesus further pressed on Nicodemus' heart. "The wind blows where it wishes, and you hear the sound of it, but cannot tell where it comes from and where it goes. So is everyone who is born of the Spirit" (John 3:8). Wind cannot be seen or controlled. It is intangible, but its effects are unmistakable. Just as the traces of a breeze can be observed in the movement of leaves, the movement of God's Spirit in a person's life is undeniable.

Still Nicodemus was unclear about it all. "How can these things be?" he asked.

Jesus gently challenges Nicodemus. "You're Israel's teacher, right? This shouldn't be beyond your scope, Nicodemus." Then Jesus raises the issue of the necessity of faith. The real problem for this learned Pharisee wasn't so much a problem of intellect as a deeper issue of unbelief. "If I have told you earthly things and you do not believe, how will you believe if I tell you heavenly things?" (John 3:12). Nicodemus' heart was now laid bare.

The Jesus Nicodemus Never Knew

Nicodemus didn't get what he expected from this teacher who came from God. He encountered much more.

Nicodemus found that Jesus spoke about Heaven with absolute authority. "No one has ascended to heaven but He who came down from heaven, *that is*, the Son of Man who is in heaven" (John 3:13). Heaven was Jesus' hometown. If anyone would know about Heaven, it would be Jesus. Heaven was His point of origin, and it would be His place of return. Someone who was simply "a teacher come from God" couldn't have come down from Heaven. Nicodemus' eyebrows must have risen a bit at this point in the conversation. This isn't what he expected to encounter when he went out to meet Jesus. He thought he was going to interview a controversial new rabbi.

Instead he was face-to-face, mind-to-mind, and heart-to-heart with someone who came down from Heaven itself.

Not only did Jesus have the divine *authority* to talk about Heaven, but He also had the *ability* to get Nicodemus there. Jesus hinted of things to come, pointing to His future sacrificial death on a Roman cross: "And as Moses lifted up the serpent in the wilderness, even so must the Son of Man be lifted up, that whoever believes in Him should not perish but have eternal life" (John 3:14-15). Just what did Jesus mean by *that*?

Nicodemus recognized the allusion to an incident that happened while the Israelites wandered in the desert for forty years on the way to the Promised Land. The people had complained to Moses, blaming him for their discomfort. As a result, God had sent snakes into the camp, and many people died from the bites. But God in His mercy provided a solution to their deadly problem. God told Moses to make a brass snake, put it on a pole, and lift it up in plain view of the people. Anyone who looked at the serpent would be healed instantly.

Nicodemus was familiar with the story, but what did it have to do with Jesus? What did He mean when He said that He would be "lifted up" and that anyone who believed in Him would have eternal life?

As the questions bounced around in his mind, Nicodemus was discovering much more about Jesus—and about himself. Not only did Jesus speak about Heaven with *authority*, not only did He have the *ability* to get people there, but he found out that God was willing to take *anybody*! This was a shock to Nicodemus, who had spent his whole life making clear distinctions as to who was qualified or disqualified for God's favor.

But Jesus pointedly revealed that anyone can have everlasting life—if that person believes in Him. He clearly stated, "For God so loved the world that He gave His only begotten Son, that whoever believes in Him should not perish but have everlasting life" (John 3:16). Who could have such life? *Whoever* is willing to believe. *Whoever* will obey the mandate to be born again.

Faith would be the key that would unlock the door to God's Kingdom. Those words rested heavily on Nicodemus' heart.

23

Jesus' Impact on Nicodemus

The meeting Nicodemus had with Jesus provided one of the clearest insights into Jesus' redemptive work. Jesus laid out the plan of salvation for Nicodemus and for all those who would read the story for years to come.

But whatever happened to Nicodemus? Did anything change in his life? Did his encounter with Jesus transform him in any way? Would Nicodemus spend his life asking questions, or would he live out the answers Jesus gave him?

We don't know many details about what happened to Nicodemus, but Scripture does give us two small glimpses into his life after his late-night meeting with Jesus. The first glimpse comes in the midst of a critical meeting. The Jewish religious leaders were becoming increasingly hostile toward Jesus. They were threatened by His power, and they had determined to arrest Him. They dispatched a group of thugs to grab Him and bring Him to their court. Not only did their attempt fail, but the men who had been hired to arrest Jesus came back very impressed by what they had heard Him say.

The Pharisees reacted with anger. They looked out over the assembly of religious leaders and asked a somewhat rhetorical question: "Have any of the rulers or the Pharisees believed in Him?" (John 7:48). The room was thick with tension when that question was posed.

In a moment of courageous support, Nicodemus spoke up. "Does our law judge a man before it hears him and knows what he is doing?" (John 7:51).

That statement may not sound too impressive on the surface, but keep in mind the context. Nicodemus was with his colleagues, and they were obviously angry with Jesus. For Nicodemus to have said anything was remarkable. For him to have voiced support for Jesus was unthinkable. What a risk for him!

What led Nicodemus to this point? Maybe his encounter with Jesus had left a deep impression on him. Maybe he was a tentative disciple of Jesus at this point. While Nicodemus' stand wasn't a strong one, he did confront his peers, risking his position of influence among them. The curious inquirer had matured into a tentative supporter. Signs of new life were beginning to show in Nicodemus.

The most dramatic evidence of Jesus' impact would come later on when Nicodemus shows up again, this time after Jesus' death. The Cross had claimed the life of this controversial Messiah. He had been "lifted up" as He said he would. Now it was time to take Him down and give Him a proper burial. Nicodemus came again to Jesus, this time to care for His body.

And this time Nicodemus was not alone. Accompanying him was Joseph, a fellow Pharisee and also a member of the elite Jewish Sanhedrin. "After this, Joseph of Arimathea, being a disciple of Jesus, but secretly, for fear of the Jews, asked Pilate that he might take away the body of Jesus; and Pilate gave him permission. So he came and took the body of Jesus. And Nicodemus, who at first came to Jesus by night, also came, bringing a mixture of myrrh and aloes, about a hundred pounds. Then they took the body of Jesus, and bound it in strips of linen with the spices, as the custom of the Jews is to bury" (John 19:38-40).

Why is that noteworthy? Because Joseph's relationship to Jesus was one of faith, and Nicodemus was with him.

Joseph was described as a secret disciple. He believed in Jesus' claims but was afraid to express his commitment. This demonstrates that Jesus' influence had made it to the upper echelons of Judaism. Joseph was a disciple. Could that mean that Nicodemus was one too—since they were together?

It's hard to say for sure, but we can give Nicodemus credit for the way he honored Jesus after the Crucifixion. In this act both men were risking public scorn, and, even more serious, they risked their own lives. It's quite possible that Nicodemus had mulled over what Jesus had told him and was now ashamed of his own cowardice and came to render belated service to Jesus. That's pretty significant spiritual growth—from inquirer to supporter to servant. The wind was blowing, and the effects were being seen and felt.

What About You?

The Jesus who met with Nicodemus that night also wants to meet with you. Jesus' words are timeless. He said to Nicodemus, "For God so loved the world that He gave His only begotten Son, that whoever believes in Him should not perish but have everlasting life." Although He pointed the finger of application at Nicodemus, He opened His hands to everyone—including you.

What will you do with this invitation?

Like Nicodemus, we are by nature very curious and unsatisfied creatures. We're born asking questions about life. That's where the journey begins. We want to know what makes things tick and why they are the way they are. We want to know why we were created. That's one of the reasons so many religions exist. People search for a framework in which to find answers to their questions.

Personal interest demands a personal encounter. We all have some measure of curiosity, and such curiosity should awaken our spiritual senses as it did for Nicodemus. His questions led him on a search to meet the One about whom he had studied. What about you? What path has your curiosity led you down? Has your journey led you to Him?

I'll applaud anyone whose spiritual curiosity compels him or her to "check it out" in person. Nicodemus wasn't content to accept other people's word about who Jesus was. Personal interest demands a personal encounter. Have you gone straight to the Source to address your spiritual curiosity? Far too many people are content to live with someone else's theological or philosophical views.

Basing your eternity on what a teacher, or pastor, or friend tells you rather than meeting with Jesus yourself is at best presumptuous and at worst eternally foolish. Curiosity opens the door to encounter the living God.

Nicodemus did what we all should do; he searched out the answers for himself. When you come directly to Jesus and discover who He really is, He will make an unmistakable impact on your life. You will discover that even the best religious framework cannot compete with the life change that results from being born again.

My friend Roy Gustafson put it this way:

Religion is man-made. The gospel is God-given. Religion is what man does for God. The gospel is what God has done for man. Religion is good views.

The gospel is good news. Religion can become a farce. The gospel is always a force of the power of God unto salvation![3]

Part of your spiritual journey will include not just curiosity but growth. Nicodemus grew from a polite inquirer to a hesitant supporter and then to a humble servant. His journey progressed, and so should yours. Don't be content to stop with formalities. The right progression will be to allow your curiosity to create a thirst to know Him more deeply.

Too many people start and stop with a formal face-to-face relationship. The soul's longing can never be satisfied with a superficial encounter. Commit to meeting mind-to-mind and heart-to-heart with Jesus.

For God So Loves That He Responds

Just as Jesus had a goal in His meeting with Nicodemus, He has good plans and objectives for your life as well. God loves you so much that He wants to meet you personally, to bring you into His Kingdom, and to help you change.

Jesus Wants to Meet You Personally

As a Pharisee, Nicodemus had heard about Jesus. But he had never met Jesus up close until that night. When Nicodemus took the initiative to meet Jesus, he discovered a person who was far more than just a "teacher come from God." He found a person who loved him enough to respond to him.

That same Jesus wants to respond to you and show you His love for you.

Jesus responds to those with curious hearts. God will never force His way into your life. He comes by your invitation. You must open the door. And opening the door isn't limited to a single event. I have found that I must regularly take the initiative to meet with Jesus. Come to Him with your questions. Don't allow your curiosity to fade. Deeper probing develops deeper living.

Jesus is available to those who seek Him. Seeking God simply means setting time aside to make Him your priority. Again, seeking God is not a one-time occurrence, and it should not be relegated to a Sunday-only experience. Commit to meeting with Jesus daily. If that means that you get out of bed earlier or go to bed later, do it. Seeking Him personally and passionately will keep your spiritual life refreshed.

Jesus will take "whoever," but He asks you to believe in Him. Whoever you are, wherever you are, whatever you have done, you can come to Jesus. Come to Him just as you are, but come ready to believe that He loves you and that He died for your sins. Then be prepared to become part of His Kingdom.

Quite a package, wouldn't you say? When you meet Jesus, you will never again be content with "religion." You will want the real thing.

I'll never forget the afternoon I met Jesus. It was toward the end of a long and jobless summer, when time seemed to crawl. I was on my own in life for the first time. As a recent high school graduate I was trying desperately to "get a life," but nothing seemed to work out.

Like Nicodemus I had questions. I'm not sure I wanted to hear truthful answers at the time, but I remember trying to wrestle with them as a brash seventeen-year-old. I was pretty smug. I reasoned, *I'm good enough. My religion is sufficient.*

Then one late-summer afternoon I met Jesus. Alone in my oldest brother's apartment in San Jose, California, I was looking for meaning. I turned on the TV and found myself watching an evangelistic crusade. My heart was like wet cement. Not totally aware of what was happening at the time, I released my questions and empty heart to Jesus.

It was a strange but liberating experience, a feeling of cleansing and relief. Though my journey had begun long before this point, it was this life-changing encounter that opened up the path before me. I was beginning to understand clearly that "everlasting life" wasn't something I had to wait until I arrived in heaven to enjoy. The Kingdom of God was already beginning to blossom in my life because I had encountered the King.

Jesus Wants to Bring You into His Kingdom

Making us a part of His family is God's prime objective for us. That's why Jesus said it's a must to be born again. He doesn't want anyone to perish eternally.

Don't skip over the first two words in Jesus' statement to Nicodemus. He said, "Most assuredly, I say to you, unless one is born again, he cannot see the Kingdom of God" (John 3:3). Jesus didn't say, "In my opinion the new birth would be a good thing," or, "I feel that the born-again experience is an attractive one." No! He was absolute and categorical. The new birth is essential for Kingdom living. Spiritual transformation is a must in order to relate to the King.

Listen again to Jesus' uncompromising mandate: "You must be born again." He is not opening up lanes in the cosmic freeway of religious experiences. He's being exclusive, very exclusive.

But Jesus also lovingly makes it possible for us to be born again. Through the Holy Spirit, He reaches into our lives, accepts our fragile belief, and transforms us into His children.

Chuck Colson knows the power of that transformation. He once occupied a place of notoriety as Richard Nixon's "hatchet man." When Colson's world caved in with the Watergate scandal, he was ready to listen to the truth about his need for God. One lonely night he drove to a friend's home, where his friend told him the simple truth about God. That night a profound change occurred. Colson tells his own story:

> With my face cupped in my hands, my head leaned forward against the wheel, I forgot about my machismo, about pretenses, about fears of being weak, and as I did, I began to experience a wonderful feeling of being released. Then came the strange sensation that water was not only running down my cheeks, but surging through my whole body as well, cleansing and cooling as it went. These were not tears of sadness or remorse, nor of joy—but somehow, tears of relief. And then I prayed my first real prayer. "God, I don't know how to find you, but I'm going to try. I'm not much the way I am now, but somehow I want to give myself to you." I didn't know how to say more so I just repeated over and over the words: Take me.[4]

A few days later Colson experienced more:

Strength and serenity, a wonderful new assurance about life, a fresh perception of myself and the world around me. In the process, I felt old fears, tensions, and animosities draining away. I was coming alive to things that I'd never seen before; as if God was filling the barren void that I'd known for so many months, filling it to the brim with a whole new kind of awareness.[5]

By the way, as you might have guessed, he titled his conversion story *Born Again*. His riveting book describes the radical changes that took place in his life.

Nicodemus needed a new birth. Chuck Colson needed a new birth. And so does everyone else. Background and upbringing are never enough to give anyone an "extra push" into Heaven.

Ask Franklin Graham, the son of the famed evangelist Billy Graham. Talk about having spiritual connections! Talk about having a holy edge! But Franklin will be the first to tell you that it wasn't enough. Raised in the spiritual greenhouse of the Graham home, Franklin, like Nicodemus, went through all the right motions. Baptism, regular church attendance, and a steady diet of the gospel were familiar stuff for this southern son of the world's most renowned preacher. But deep inside, Franklin knew he was hollow.

One evening in Switzerland Billy Graham had a pointed confrontation with his son. "Your mother and I sense that you are struggling in your heart, Franklin. You need to face the truth, and you need to make your own decision. Until you do, you will not have peace."

Angered by his father's words, Franklin decided he would run rather than face the truth. He ran to several countries in the Middle East trying to fill his life without committing his life to Christ. Then one night in a hotel room in Jerusalem, the very place where Jesus had that conversation with Nicodemus, Franklin Graham decided Jesus Christ was right. He prayed and received Him into his life and was born again. At that moment he was more than the son of a world-renowned preacher. He was a child of the living God.

What about you? Are you born again? If not, then you are not yet a citizen of God's Kingdom. Rather than hiding behind the walls of your family background or a secondhand theology, step into the light of real change by believing in Jesus and allowing Him to give you a new birth.

Jesus Wants to Help You Change

When Nicodemus first came to Jesus, he was a deeply religious man, but his religion was external; it had not touched his heart. Deep change came for Nicodemus only after he had a heart-to-heart encounter with Jesus and heard the challenge to be born again.

Are you like Nicodemus? Is your "religion" external? Maybe you regularly attend church and have involvement there. You give of your financial resources. You sing with the rest of those who gather. Great. Keep it up.

But don't stop there. Don't be content with the outward form. Move through the layers. Aim at nothing less than heart-to-heart communion with the living Christ. We need to be outwardly active and we need our minds to be engaged in what we believe, but the most important thing is that our hearts are deeply changed and fully surrendered to the lordship of Jesus Christ.

If you sense that your core is hollow, as Franklin Graham did, don't make the same mistake he did by running and trying to find an external solution. Despite what our culture would want us to believe, we can't change inner problems by changing our outward circumstances. We will not find redemption or peace through fame or wealth or prestige or science or politics. True redemption comes only when we believe in the Lord Jesus Christ and are born again by the Spirit of God. That's when the real change begins—from the inside out.

When communism spread throughout the Soviet Commonwealth of Independent States and Eastern Europe, a spokesman traveled from town to town, evangelizing crowds of people with this new doctrine. One evening a crowd gathered in a large city and was mesmerized by all the promises of this new way of life. The spokesman thundered the party dictums to an increasingly enthusiastic crowd. Rounds of applause broke out. Sensing that the people were concerned about the future of the economy, he proclaimed, "Communism will put a new coat on every man!" Just then a man in crowd shot to

31

his feet and yelled back, "But only Jesus can put a new man in the coat!" Superficial change will never satisfy the cravings of the soul.

When we invite Jesus Christ to come and give us new life, nothing remains the same. Our status before God is changed for eternity. Our relationship to our society, friends, and family also changes. Even our personality and lifestyle begin to change and continue to change until we've crossed the threshold of eternity—where we'll really change!

The apostle Paul summed it up best when he said: "Therefore, if anyone is in Christ, he is a new creation; old things have passed away; behold, all things have become new" (2 Corinthians 5:17). Allow Jesus to make you a new creation. Allow Him to change you deep within so that your spirituality becomes authentic. Don't settle for anything less.

FOR REFLECTION AND DISCUSSION

1. Think about your own spiritual/religious journey. If you have already met Jesus heart-to-heart and have been born again, what factors led to that experience? What changes have you seen in your life? Have you shared with others the story of your journey to the new birth?

2. If you have not been born again, what are you going to do about it? What initiative will you take to meet with Jesus?

3. In what ways is your spiritual life superficial or limited to the external? What keeps you from moving closer to Jesus? What will you do to change that?

4. What have you been spiritually curious about lately? In what ways will your curiosity motivate you to encounter Jesus more deeply?

5. Have you engaged your mind in your relationship to Jesus? Why is critical thinking helpful to understanding spiritual issues? How can it lead you to deeper appreciation of Jesus? How is it limiting?

6. In what ways does Nicodemus' spiritual growth from inquirer to supporter to servant reflect your own development since you first met Jesus?

7. Study these three passages about being born again. What can you learn from the third passage about the effect of your new birth on your relationship to other people?

But to all who believed him and accepted him, he gave the right to become children of God. They are reborn! This is not a physical birth resulting from human passion or plan—this rebirth comes from God (John 1:12-13, NLT).

All honor to the God and Father of our Lord Jesus Christ, for it is by his boundless mercy that God has given us the privilege of being born again. Now we live with a wonderful expectation because Jesus Christ rose again from the dead (1 Peter 1:3, NLT).

Now you can have sincere love for each other as brothers and sisters because you were cleansed from your sins when you accepted the truth of the Good News. So see to it that you really do love each other intensely with all your hearts. For you have been born again. Your new life did not come from your earthly parents because the life they gave you will end in death. But this new life will last forever because it comes from the eternal, living word of God (1 Peter 1:22-23, NLT).

Mender of Broken Hearts

Jesus and the Broken People

Jesus left Judea and departed again to Galilee. But He needed to go through Samaria.

So He came to a city of Samaria which is called Sychar, near the plot of ground that Jacob gave to his son Joseph. Now Jacob's well was there. Jesus therefore, being wearied from His journey, sat thus by the well. It was about the sixth hour.

A woman of Samaria came to draw water. Jesus said to her, "Give Me a drink." For His disciples had gone away into the city to buy food.

Then the woman of Samaria said to Him, "How is it that You, being a Jew, ask a drink from me, a Samaritan woman?" For Jews have no dealings with Samaritans.

Jesus answered and said to her, "If you knew the gift of God, and who it is who says to you, 'Give Me a drink,' you would have asked Him, and He would have given you living water."

The woman said to Him, "Sir, You have nothing to draw with, and the well is deep. Where then do You get that living water? Are You greater than our father Jacob, who gave us the well, and drank from it himself, as well as his sons and his livestock?"

Jesus answered and said to her, "Whoever drinks of this water will thirst again, but whoever drinks of the water that I shall give him will never thirst. But the water that I shall give him will become in him a fountain of water springing up into everlasting life."

The woman said to Him, "Sir, give me this water, that I may not thirst, nor come here to draw."

Jesus said to her, "Go, call your husband, and come here."

The woman answered and said, "I have no husband."

Jesus said to her, "You have well said, 'I have no husband,' for you have had five husbands, and the one whom you now have is not your husband; in that you spoke truly."

The woman said to Him, "Sir, I perceive that You are a prophet. Our fathers worshiped on this mountain, and you Jews say that in Jerusalem is the place where one ought to worship."

Jesus said to her, "Woman, believe Me, the hour is coming when you will neither on this mountain, nor in Jerusalem, worship the Father. You worship what you do not know; we know what we worship, for salvation is of the Jews. But the hour is coming, and now is, when the true worshipers will worship the Father in spirit and truth; for the Father is seeking such to worship Him. God is Spirit, and those who worship Him must worship in spirit and truth."

The woman said to Him, "I know that Messiah is coming" (who is called Christ). "When He comes, He will tell us all things."

Jesus said to her, "I who speak to you am He."

... The woman then left her waterpot, went her way into the city, and said to the men, "Come, see a Man who told me all things that I ever did. Could this be the Christ?" Then they went out of the city and came to Him (John 4:3-30).

Finding happiness has become an obsession in our culture. The guaranteed rights of life, liberty, and the pursuit of happiness are so sacred that they are written into the Bill of Rights of our Constitution. But the business of making ourselves happy has become an increasingly complex pursuit. For example, a hundred years ago the average American could produce a list of *seventy* things he or she needed. Things have changed since then. It is now estimated that the average person has about *five hundred* personal needs. Happiness is a never ending pursuit—especially if we are looking for it in all the *wrong* places.

One day on the streets of the ancient town of Sychar, in the region of Samaria, a woman who had been looking in all the wrong places was about to be surprised.

At the Well, Dying of Thirst

Life wasn't easy for this woman. Rigorous work and limited social activities kept most Middle Eastern women remote and cut off. Women were not valued very highly in this patriarchal culture. Men saw them as objects to be owned or as an essential part of the workforce, much as an ox was part of the workforce. Even in this passage, the woman remains a nameless person. She is referred to by the writer as merely "a woman of Samaria."

We know that she was from the poorer class because she went out to draw water from the local well. The rich would never carry their own water; that was the job of the hired servants. But this woman was responsible for all the activities that every woman of her class faced: feeding the men first before being allowed to eat, walking while the men rode the family donkey, fetching water, and washing all the clothes.

But that's not all—this woman was a Samaritan. This meant she, along with her people, was the brunt of racial hatred. Samaritans were despised by their Jewish neighbors, who saw them as half-breeds because the Jews who lived in the region of Samaria had once intermarried with the ancient Assyrian pagans. Animosity had intensified between these two groups ever since that time. The final blow came when the Jews refused to let the Samaritans help rebuild the temple in Jerusalem. As a result, the offended Samaritans built their own temple on nearby Mount Gerizim. The rivalry was etched in stone. From that point on the Jews and Samaritans hated each another—in the name of God.

The Jews hated the Samaritans so much that no self-respecting Jew would even travel through the region of Samaria. Under their breath the Jews cursed them. They even spouted derogatory remarks such as, "He who eats the bread of a Samaritan is as he who eats swine's flesh!" "No Samaritan shall be made a proselyte!" "[Samaritans] have no share in the resurrection of the dead!"[1]

We know one other significant thing about this woman. The passage later tells us that she had been married five times. We aren't told why she was divorced by five different men, but it doesn't take much to imagine that she was a disillusioned, discouraged woman. Like most young women, she had probably dreamed of marrying and having a happy family. But somewhere along the way, those dreams were shattered. Her past was littered with the debris of failed relationships.

We can imagine that with each divorce came more broken dreams. With each broken dream came more bitterness. With each bitter experience came more distrust.

So here she was at the well. Dispirited and brokenhearted. Thirsty for hope.

The Stranger at the Well

This helps to understand the woman's mind-set when she found a man sitting at the well when she arrived to draw water. She knew she didn't trust men, especially *Jewish* men.

What she didn't know was that this day's walk to the well was a divine appointment. The man who was sitting there had come a long way to be at that specific place, at that specific time.

The fact that Jesus was there at all was a marvel in itself. People could travel through the land of Israel by one of three routes, the most direct being straight up through Samaria. But hardly any Jews took the direct route because it would take them through enemy territory. Most would usually walk *around* Samaria, choosing one of the two longer routes to avoid it altogether.

But Jesus went out of His way to get to the Samaritan village. He was following a divine itinerary. "He left Judea and departed again to Galilee. But He *needed* to go through Samaria" (John 4:3-4, emphasis added). He needed to go? Why would any Jew need to go there? Even the Gospel writer explains, "Jews have no dealings with Samaritans" (v. 9).

But that's where Jesus was different. He didn't care about expectations and customary dealings, especially when the expectations were based on prejudice. Jesus came to the well and waited there for the woman to arrive. He knew the deep seated hatred between the two rival groups. He knew that zealous Pharisees prayed that not a single Samaritan would be raised in the resurrection. He also knew that the woman He would meet at the well that day could become the key to unlocking that entire region. He knew she was thirsty for much more than water. Because of that, Jesus "needed" to go through Samaria.

An Appeal to Human Kindness

Jesus initiated the interaction with a polite request: "Give Me a drink" (John 4:7). The woman was startled. His words breached social protocol. It was never customary for a Jewish man, especially a spiritual leader, to publicly address a woman, much less a Samaritan woman. In fact, a rabbi was forbidden to speak even to his wife or daughter in public. Jesus knew those rules.

So did she. "How is it that You, being a Jew, ask a drink from me, a Samaritan woman?" was her bewildered response (v. 9). Jews kept their distance from Samaritans. Men kept their distance from women.

But Jesus wasn't interested in what was customary; he was concerned with what was compassionate.

But Jesus wasn't interested in what was customary; he was concerned with what was compassionate. To Him men and women were on the same level and had the same spiritual need. In His eyes this woman was not less than a man; she was a thirsty soul in need of refreshment. Jesus did what most were unwilling to do; He leveled the playing field. Anyone could talk to Him. Anyone could encounter Him. Anyone could come!

But Jesus' straightforward approach was met with skepticism. What was this Jew doing here talking to her? What did He want? Just a drink? She even may have wondered if His request was just an opening line to get something more. She had been around a lot of men in her time. She was wary and uncertain. It's quite possible that she saw Jesus at first as just another man with just another verbal fishing line trying to reel her in. But Jesus had simply appealed to her kindness. It was so basic and plain: He just wanted a drink! It was the kind of appeal that any local would respond to with open hospitality. It was a statement meant to disarm and pave the road for further dialogue.

But she didn't take it that way. Instead of meeting the request with kindness, she responded with sarcasm. "Why do you want a drink from me?"

An Appeal to Lifelong Hope

She bristled at His request, so Jesus probed deeper. He touched the nerve of hope.

Here she was, drawing water from a well dug by an ancient patriarch. At the same time she lived in a spiritual and emotional desert. She was dying of thirst inside. She needed to have her hope revived. She needed a drink from God's well. "If you knew the gift of God, and who it is that says to you, 'Give Me a drink,' you would have asked Him, and He would have given you living water" (John 4:10).

Talk about a leading statement, this is it! A gift? A gift from God? Living water? What's that supposed to mean? And what's this stuff about, "If you only knew who I am"? Who does He think He is?

Though His statement was mysterious, she still wanted to hear more. So she rolled off a few curt questions that reveal her skeptical interest.

"Sir, You have nothing to draw with, and the well is deep. Where then do You get that living water? Are you greater than our father Jacob, who gave us the well, and drank from it himself, as well as his sons and his livestock?" (v. 11-12).

If she even realized that Jesus was speaking figuratively, she didn't let on. She quickly brought the conversation that was going in a spiritual direction back on a purely physical track. The ancient well was probably 150 feet deep. This stranger didn't have a rope or a bucket. He should be more careful about making grandiose promises and acting like such an expert! What could He do that the great patriarch Jacob was unable to do? Whatever this Jewish riddle maker was up to, she didn't quite understand yet.

An Appeal to Spiritual Thirst

Unphased by an appeal to her kindness and by an extraordinary promise, the woman of Sychar was still spiritually parched. She was craving something deeper than what she would allow herself to admit. She either didn't comprehend what Jesus meant or was unwilling to go there. If it was simple misunderstanding, it would be cleared up by Jesus' next statement of contrast. "Whoever drinks of this water will thirst again, but whoever drinks of the water that I shall give him will never thirst. But the water that I shall give him will become in him a fountain of water springing up into everlasting life" (John 4:13-14). She finally knew that Jesus was not talking about the water that was in the well. This was a statement of comparison meant to draw a distinction between something physical and something spiritual.

Jesus' statements began to percolate inside of her. She knew the water deep inside the ground was never enough. She made it part of her routine to go there and fetch it every single day. She had been there the day before, and she would be back the next. Her need would never end.

But this man was talking about a deeper thirst. Living water. Everlasting life. He was talking about spiritual thirst. She replied to Jesus' invitation to enjoy living water with another flippant comeback. "Sir, give me this water, that I may not thirst, nor come here to draw" (v. 15). In essence she said, "I come here every day and haul water just to survive. You've got some pretty tall promises. Show me what you've got. If you can keep me from ever needing to make the trek to this well again, I'm all ears." There seems to be a mixture of both spiritual thirst and practical pessimism in her voice.

An Appeal to a Guilty Conscience

Up to this point Jesus was indulging this woman's cynicism. He knew that her words were expressions of a pain-filled life. Her past experiences dulled her spiritual sensitivity. She had been defensive and flippant while Jesus remained gracious and full of promise. If an appeal to kindness, hope, and inner thirst didn't daunt her, then it was time to get a bit more personal. With the precision of a sharpshooter, Jesus targeted her personal life and appealed to her conscience.

Jesus said to her, "Go call your husband, and come here" (John 4:16). Jesus wasn't intending to embarrass her; no one else was around to hear it. He wanted to awaken her.

Her reply was swift and terse: "I have no husband." At that moment she had no clue just how well-informed this man was.

Her entire marital history was well in view as Jesus continued, "You have well said, 'I have no husband,' for you have had five husbands, and the one whom you now have is

41

not your husband; in that you spoke truly" (v. 17-18). With one stroke of a phrase, her entire life was laid bare before this strange man who seemed to know more about her than anyone else she had ever met.

How did He know that? How did He know there were exactly five? Maybe He had been around town and had spoken to the townspeople. Such thoughts may have tumbled around in her mind as she stood before this unusual guest. He had opened the closet that contained skeletons of sin and hurt—skeletons she thought she had locked away. Her mind was probably flooded with memories of a string of hopes that had all ended in failure.

Why did Jesus do this? Why tear open a scab that concealed such a deep wound? Because for her to be able to drink and appreciate what Jesus had to offer, she must first admit her thirst. The mask of self-sufficiency had to come off. If other appeals wouldn't generate a response, this certainly would. She now stood looking in the mirror of her own painful past while she stood in the presence of someone who could help her face that past and change her future.

With abrupt change in demeanor she responds with respect, "Sir, I perceive that You are a prophet" (v. 19). Who else but a prophet could know so much about her? Who else but a prophet could move her so quickly from physical things to spiritual things? Who else but a prophet could get past the calloused exterior and into her painful heart to offer her an end to her thirst?

If He was a prophet, then He could answer a religious question that Jews and Samaritans had debated for decades—which temple was God's preference for worship. She tested Him further: "Our fathers worshiped on this mountain, and you Jews say that in Jerusalem is the place where one ought to worship" (v. 20). Both groups believed that God had commanded their forefathers to worship in a special place. The question was, which place? Was it Jerusalem, where Jews worshiped, or was it Samaria, where Jews avoided going? Such a question could potentially be divisive and end the conversation.

An Appeal to Future Deliverance

With a balance of truth mingled with love, Jesus explained that locale was irrelevant and that temples would become unnecessary. Jesus said to her, "Woman, believe Me, the hour is coming when you will neither on this mountain, nor in Jerusalem, worship the Father. You worship what you do not know; we know what we worship, for salvation is of the Jews. But the hour is coming, and now is, when the true worshipers will worship the Father in spirit and truth; for the Father is seeking such to worship Him. God is Spirit, and those who worship Him must worship in spirit and truth" (John 4:21-24). An encounter with an almighty God went much deeper than geography. It was all about authenticity in experience.

What a wonderful thought—God was on the lookout for true worshipers, not just Jewish or Samaritan worshipers. He helped her see that ethnicity wasn't as important as authenticity. It was all about the heart, not the art. *Where* one worships wasn't as important as *that* one worships. Not only did she see it, but she also wanted it.

As a result of their short conversation, this woman was now in the mood to discuss spiritual truth with Jesus. No longer hiding behind curt remarks, she expressed her deepest hopes that might have kindled within her since she was young. Her hope that God had a plan for the world, which included her, was being revived. She expressed it clearly: "I know that Messiah is coming" (who is called Christ). "When He comes, He will tell us all things" (v. 25).

Where *one worships* wasn't as *important* as that *one worships.*

Jesus didn't dwell on her past failures. He was glad to speak of the future. The woman had given her statement of faith: a deliverer was coming. It was the dream of divine interruption, that God's Messiah would one day enter time and space and explain everything that needed an explanation. "One day," she reasoned, "the Messiah everyone is talking about will come. When He does, things will change; life will get better when He's here."

If she was shocked when Jesus uncovered her past failure, she was even more so when He introduced Himself as her future hope. "I who speak to you am He" (v. 26). She was waiting for someone who would come "one day"—in the future. Jesus said to her, "That day is now. Hope is here. I who speak to you am the One!"

With each appeal Jesus was drawing her into a place of honesty and revealing to her who He was. She softened from a calloused and pessimistic water carrier to a candid seeker of spiritual truth. He opened Himself to her in successive layers until she realized exactly who He was.

1. He revealed himself as a thirsty man—"Give me a drink."

2. He revealed himself as a mystery man—"If you knew the gift of God and who it is who says to you, 'Give me a drink,'..."

3. He revealed himself as a source of refreshment—"Whoever drinks of the water that I shall give him will never thirst."

4. He revealed himself as an insightful prophet—"You have had five husbands, and the one whom you now have is not your husband."

5. He revealed himself as the object of her lifelong hopes, her Messiah—"I who speak to you am He."

Why Me, Lord?

Why her? Why did Jesus walk in the hot sun up the dusty hill for miles and miles to meet a woman who is not even named in the scriptural record? What reason could Jesus possibly have for revealing Himself to an outcast? Because Jesus came to redeem the outcasts. By meeting with people whom others would bypass, Jesus was sending a strong message that He didn't come just for the "high life" religious people down in Jerusalem. He was the King of restoration looking intentionally for people whom some considered to be "low-life" up in Samaria. No one else was doing that.

Jesus also came to mend this toughened woman's shattered dreams by healing her broken heart. He could show her how refreshing life really could become. He could prove to her that her dreams of living a satisfying life were possible. Unconditional love would awaken her dashed hope. The world she had been living in had jaundiced her view of God— especially any kind of merciful and loving God.

Jesus came to redeem the outcasts.

Her world had also distorted her view of men. Five attempts at marriage had a way of darkening her optimism. But this strange Jewish man at the well wasn't like all the rest. He wasn't another taker. Though He asked for a drink from the local well, He offered a quenched thirst from the eternal spring. Her goal was merely to survive the heat of the summer, to bring a jug of water home until the next day. He had plans that reached much further—both for the woman as well as her city.

Revival in Samaria

This woman's response to meeting Jesus was dramatic. When she finally realized who He was, she ran to tell the townspeople her experience. "Come, see a Man who told me all things that I ever did. Could this be the Christ?" (John 4:29).

It was the beginning of something wonderful for the whole area. Her change would spark fires of further change.

When the woman shared her story, many of the Samaritans of that city believed Jesus. They convinced Him to stay for two more days, and during that time even more people believed in Him. They said to the woman, "Now we believe, not because of what you said, for we ourselves have heard Him and we know that this is indeed the Christ, the Savior of the world" (v. 42).

From Samaria to Our Area

How does the story of an obscure woman at a well in the Middle East two thousand years ago relate to you and me? You probably can't relate to her marital history. And her lifestyle probably doesn't connect with yours. But her encounter with

Jesus reveals some truths that apply to men and women of all ages and from all backgrounds.

We All Have a Past

Each one of us has a "life package." Within that parcel are experiences, dreams, plans, successes, and failures that make us who we are. We each have a personal history filled with discouragements as well as joys. The woman at the well had a personal inventory of past failures that overshadowed the hope she may have once had.

Most of us have a similar package. It is varied and colorful. We are pleased to have people know about some parts of our package, but we are very careful to keep other parts hidden. The truth is, the skeletons in our closets probably aren't much worse than those in hers. We are ashamed of many of them, and though they make us blush, we want them to count for something. How is that possible?

1. Face the past honestly. Facing up to who we are and what we have done is known in the Bible as confession (see 1 John 1:9 and James 5:16). Confession is essential if we are to receive God's forgiveness. The Samaritan woman found out that Jesus already knew her deepest sin and yet He loved her. You can experience that same love and forgiveness. Tell God about your sin. Your secret is safe with Him. He already knows everything—every thought, word, and act. Your past doesn't surprise Him. Rather than thinking of God's omniscience (allknowingness) as a frightening thing, learn to see it as comforting. He knows about you completely, yet He loves you unconditionally. Facing the past by honest confession isn't for God's benefit; it's for yours. It brings you into alignment with His view of your sin and keeps the channels of communication with Him open.

2. Use the past beneficially. Once the woman discovered that Jesus not only knew her but also accepted her, she became secure. She was able to be open to others about her sinful past. Once we deal honestly with God about our "life package," we come away with a cleansed conscience. Once we have been honest with God, it's easier to become honest with other people. The past must never become a hitching post to keep us bound but rather a guidepost to keep us moving forward. Learn from your past mistakes. Ask Jesus to transform the skeletons in your closet so the past no longer haunts you but helps you. Pray to understand the depth of God's love in seeking you out. A great old hymn of the church celebrates such seeking love in one of its stanzas:

> *The love of God is greater far,*
> *Than tongue or pen can ever tell.*
> *It goes beyond the highest star,*
> *And reaches to the lowest Hell!*[2]

We All Have a Place

So much of the Samaritan woman's life was lived in the mundane. Daily trips to the local well outside her city and back perhaps became a tedious routine, but it was her life. Jesus came to her in the context of her everyday life. He didn't appear to her while she was on a pilgrimage to a faraway land. She hadn't seen a mysterious apparition in the skies above Sychar. She heard no special voice or sign that compelled her to visit the well that day. She did it every day. It was while she was going about her chores, during the tedium of daily life, that Jesus sought her out.

1. Jesus will meet you in your present place in life. Right where you are, within the walls of your home or the schedule of your occupation, you can meet Jesus. I once dramatically learned this lesson. After years of reading the Scriptures and yearning to travel to the Holy Land, I finally got my chance. I just knew it would be spectacular. To be where Jesus lived and spoke, to walk where He walked would have to be an awesome experience. To be sure, that first trip to Israel was exciting. Things I had only read about vividly came to life before my eyes. Places like Jerusalem, Galilee, and the Jordan River became etched in my memory forever. But the trip also was somewhat anticlimactic for me. I had heard stories of people who sat in the Garden of Gethsemane and were overcome with God's presence. I had heard people say that God met them in extraordinary ways at some of the sacred sites.

So I came as a pilgrim fully expecting the same to happen to me. I remember sitting in the Garden of Gethsemane, where Jesus had suffered in prayer, with my eyes closed and palms up—waiting. I sang and prayed and breathed softly—and I waited. Nothing happened. *What's wrong?* I wondered. *Why isn't this working? Something is supposed to happen!* It didn't, and I was disappointed. I let God know about it too. Maybe if I tried visiting a different spot things would be different. So I repeated the order of service while at the Garden Tomb, where Jesus is said to have risen from the dead. Surely God would meet me here. It was a special place, and I wanted a special "visitation." Again nothing happened—no voices, no apparitions, and no overwhelming feeling. So I returned home.

One evening back home in the States, I sat down with my Bible in my apartment after a busy day on the job. It was a routine I had followed many times before. I would read a passage and try to discover the application to my life. That night I sensed a deep satisfaction as I was communing with God. I sensed His presence in an unusually immediate sense. We enjoyed an encounter in which I knew I was accepted and cleansed as I confessed sin to God and worshiped Him. I found that Jesus came to meet me in my place of ordinary life rather than in a setting of extraordinary significance.

2. Jesus will use you in your present place in life. The woman of Samaria used her everyday routine, traveling back and forth from her town to the well, as a platform to touch others. She could have left her village and wandered throughout the countryside preaching with the disciples, but there is no record of such a move. No doubt she stayed in that place and continued her simple service to the townspeople. Similarly, the Lord can use you in the midst of the everydayness of life. Your routine can become an altar from which to serve. Your place may seem simple, even insignificant. Maybe you've struggled with your ability to serve God's purpose while you occupy such an average place in life. But Jesus will meet you there, and He will use you there. One busy housebound mother who understood this truth placed a sign over her kitchen sink: "Divine service rendered here three times daily!"

We All Have a Passion for More

The woman who met with Jesus by the well of Sychar never found the satisfaction she had always longed for—until that day. Her many attempts at marriage had failed to deliver

48

the happiness they initially promised. Her experiences never quenched her thirst; they merely intensified it. That's how life works. Every experience, relationship, hope, and dream is meant to whet the appetite for the "living water" of spiritual life.

True happiness lies only in a relationship with the Living Water, Jesus Christ. Every other thing leaves us empty and dry. We were created with a deep thirst for God. Like the body, which craves water to quench its physical thirst, the inner person can be satisfied only by spiritual water. Any time we look for refreshment elsewhere, we thirst again, and the thirst intensifies. The people of Israel found that out. God showed them the folly of looking for living water in all the wrong places. "For my people have done two evil things: They have forsaken me—the fountain of living water. And they have dug for themselves cracked cisterns that can hold no water at all!" (Jeremiah 2:13, NLT).

Western civilization is a good case study in unhappiness. While the search for happiness has become the obsession of our modern culture, few people are truly happy, even though some appear to have it all. Whether we go to the fountains of fame, money, pleasure, knowledge, gadgets, or sports, we will come back thirsty. The thirst only gets more intense because people keep drinking from the wrong well. The real problem isn't in the pursuit but in the source.

We All Have a Purpose

God's plan for us goes far beyond personal satisfaction. Jesus doesn't go out of His way to meet us merely to put a smile on our faces and a song in our hearts. His purpose is to make us people of influence. Once transformed, we must never become content merely to be a container for living water; we need to become conduits, allowing it to flow out to others. Thirsty people around us must see and feel what the living water has done for us. Jesus would speak of this later in the Jerusalem temple when He proclaimed, "If you believe in me, come and drink! For the Scriptures declare that rivers of living water will flow out from within" (John 7:38, NLT). Those who are receivers of this life-changing reality are to become transmitters as well.

The woman's encounter with Jesus gave her purpose. She left the well and told people what had happened to her. Her personal renewal led eventually to a citywide revival as well as a revival throughout the region. The Lord's impact on us can have an impact on our friends, family, schools, associations, cities, and states.

The British evangelist Gypsy Smith was once asked how to start a revival. I love his answer. He said, "Go home, lock yourself in your room, kneel down in the middle of your floor. Draw a chalk mark all around yourself and ask God to start the revival inside that chalk mark. When He has answered your prayer, the revival will be on!"[3] What a wonderful proposition to think of ourselves as becoming a catalyst to someone else's spiritual renewal. Our purpose for living should be born out of our passion for more in life. Allowing Jesus, the Living Water, to quench our thirst will motivate other people around us to come and drink at His well.

FOR REFLECTION AND DISCUSSION

1. Write a short biographical sketch of your life including your failures. What facts about yourself do you usually leave out when you are telling people about your life?

2. What painful experiences from your past need to be brought to God and confessed? Take the list, and ask God to help you learn from them and even use them for someone's benefit.

Example # 1: If you've become pregnant outside of marriage, seek God's healing touch and then get involved in counseling unwed mothers or those considering an abortion.

Example # 2: If you have a criminal background, consider getting involved with your church's outreach to the local jail or starting a discipleship group with inmates.

3. Which of the following describes your job?
Highly stimulating: You can't wait to get there.

Routine and monotonous: It pays the bills, but nothing ever changes.

Boring and uninteresting: You want to get out and change careers.

4. What difference would it make in your outlook if Jesus were waiting for you when you arrived at work? How could you cultivate His presence in your present occupation?

5. Consider Jesus' approach to the woman of Samaria: He appealed to her kindness, her lifelong hope, her spiritual thirst, her guilty conscience, and finally her hope for future deliverance. How could your approach to thirsty people around you be more effective if you used this model?

6. What things in life do you still dream about experiencing (marriage, a trip to Europe, owning a newer home, getting promoted)? How satisfied do you predict you would be if you could have or achieve these? How happy could you be without any of them?

7. How do you feel when you realize that God knows everything about you (every word, every thought, every action)? How does that feeling change when you realize that God loves you with an unconditional, everlasting love?

8. When was the last time you were spiritually renewed (at a retreat, emerging from a crisis, on a short-term mission trip, etc.)? What were the factors that made it happen for you? How could you use that experience to help other believers renew their spiritual commitment?

FOUR

A Tale of Two Sinners

A Spiritual Man and an Unspiritual Woman

*T*hen one of the Pharisees asked [Jesus] to eat with him. And He went to the Pharisee's house, and sat down to eat. And behold, a woman in the city who was a sinner, when she knew that Jesus sat at the table in the Pharisee's house, brought an alabaster flask of fragrant oil, and stood at His feet behind Him weeping; and she began to wash His feet with her tears, and wiped them with the hair of her head; and she kissed His feet and anointed them with the fragrant oil. Now when the Pharisee who had invited Him saw this, he spoke to himself, saying, "This Man, if He were a prophet, would know who and what manner of woman this is who is touching Him, for she is a sinner."

And Jesus answered and said to him, "Simon, I have something to say to you."

So he said, "Teacher, say it."

"There was a certain creditor who had two debtors. One owed five hundred denarii, and the other fifty. And when they had nothing with which to repay, he freely forgave them both. Tell Me, therefore, which of them will love him more?"

Simon answered and said, "I suppose the one whom he forgave more."

And He said to him, "You have rightly judged." Then He turned to the woman and said to Simon, "Do you see this woman? I entered your house; you gave Me no water for My feet, but she has washed My feet with her tears and wiped them with the hair of her head. You gave Me no kiss, but this woman has not ceased to kiss My feet since the time I came in. You did not anoint My head with oil, but *this woman has anointed My feet with fragrant oil. Therefore I say to you, her sins, which are many, are forgiven, for she loved much. But to whom little is forgiven, the same loves little."*

Then He said to her, "Your sins are forgiven."

And those who sat at the table with Him began to say to themselves, "Who is this who even forgives sins?"

Then He said to the woman, "Your faith has saved you. Go in peace." (Luke 7:36-50)

Opposites attract. Strong characters are often drawn to easygoing ones. Type A and Type B personalities often end up together. Playful personalities gravitate many times toward the more serious-minded.

In this story two very different people—a religious kingpin named Simon and an immoral woman—meet under the same roof. They were drawn together by mutual attraction—but not to each other. They were both drawn to the compelling person of Jesus. Yet their reasons for wanting to meet Him were as different as their individual temperaments.

Mealtime with the Messiah

The host for the meal was a man named Simon, whose name meant "hearing." And before the night was over, he would ask Jesus to speak to him, and he would get an earful.

It's not clear why Simon had invited Jesus to the gathering. Maybe Simon was genuinely curious about Jesus. Perhaps Simon wanted to add another feather to his cap by inviting a popular teacher to his home for a meal. But most likely Simon wanted to find out for himself what Jesus was up to. The religious leaders were already suspicious of this new rabbi in Israel and were observing His every move. "So the scribes and Pharisees watched Him closely, whether He would heal on the Sabbath, that they might find an accusation against Him" (Luke 6:7). Simon's meal was possibly their ploy designed to ensnare Jesus. What happened that night could perhaps be enough to level an accusation against Him. There was a scent of entrapment in the air.

Simon was a Pharisee, a member of the spiritual elite. In that, he was like Nicodemus. But unlike Nicodemus, Simon didn't go to meet Jesus; he asked Jesus to come to him, to his home, to his turf. Unlike Nicodemus, Simon had no pressing questions about Jesus' ministry or about eternal things. Unlike Nicodemus, Simon did not acknowledge Jesus' authority. Unlike Nicodemus, Simon did not readily open his heart; he kept it hidden behind the high walls of professionalism and skepticism.

Because Simon was a member of Israel's spiritual ruling class, we can assume that his home was fairly spacious, with room enough for a gathering. Eating styles and dinner arrangements in those ancient times were much different from what they are today. The dining table was low, surrounded on three sides by a couch called a *triclinium*. Guests would recline on the couch, with their left arms on the table and their feet extended away from the table toward the wall.

Guess Who's Coming to Dinner?

Simon and his other guests hadn't been at the dinner table long when a woman came in. It was not unusual for strangers to gather in the courtyard while the invited guests ate their meal. These strangers were allowed to listen to the wise words of invited rabbis and scholars.

But it was unusual for this particular woman to arrive on the scene. She was "a woman … who was a sinner" (Luke 7:37). And while the text does not mention any particular sin, most biblical scholars agree that she was a prostitute who was well known in the city. She spent many of her nights in immoral activity. But this night was different. With a heart full of guilt but longing for real love, she walked to Simon's house, and entered the courtyard gate. What a scene—the notorious sinner inside the home of the notable saint!

And the two people could not have been more different. Simon was a man of great reputation; she was a woman of ill repute. Socially and economically, they were on opposite ends of the spectrum. Yet both were in the presence of Jesus, the One for whom social status, gender, and money made no difference. What a dynamic—the host, the invited guest, and the uninvited intruder.

There most certainly was tension in the courtyard from the very moment she entered. It was a shock for such a woman even to be in an elite and spiritual setting. She slipped in among the "perimeter people" as they gossiped about this special Galilean guest named Jesus. Like others, this woman found herself attentive to every word Jesus spoke.

At first everything proceeded according to protocol. But then she did something that was not customary. She stood at Jesus' feet and wept. Loosing her hair, she used it to wash his feet with the moisture from her tears. Then she kissed his feet and anointed them with perfumed oil she carried in an ornate jar. What an intimate scene! What a potentially embarrassing scene!

The Scent of Forgiveness

Everyone noticed the woman's forward approach. How could this action not be interpreted as out of place? She was unorthodox, bold, and extravagant. There seemed to be an air of desperateness in her advance and lavishness in her expression to Jesus.

Her actions left her open to being misjudged by onlookers. And she was. As the sweet smell of the oil filled the Pharisee's home, so did the suspicions of the onlookers.

What prompted the woman to come to Simon's house that night? We don't know for sure, but she probably had heard about Jesus. Maybe she had even heard Him speak before. Had she been in the crowd the day He gave the powerful invitation? "Come to Me, all you who labor and are heavy laden, and I will give you rest. Take My yoke upon you and learn from Me, for I am gentle and lowly in heart, and you will find rest for your souls. For My yoke is easy and My burden is light" (Matthew 11:28-30). If we harmonize the four Gospel accounts, Jesus spoke these words shortly before He dined with Simon. Thus it's possible that she was there. She may have been on the fringes of that listening crowd as Jesus' words of rest and relief pierced her heart like an arrow. Maybe she thought, *If it's even possible for me to find forgiveness, it'll be from this One. I must find a way to be near Him.* So she came. She came boldly. She didn't care whether or not she was welcome. She somehow knew she would be accepted by the only One who could make all the difference.

Simon, obviously embarrassed by this emotional display, was angered by Jesus' nonchalance. Everyone in the local villages and throughout the countryside had been saying that this Jesus was a prophet. No way! No true prophet would have allowed himself to get into a physical encounter like this!

This display of emotion and physical touch most likely disgusted Simon because of the woman's reputation. He would never admit it out loud, but his heart was full of judgment. Simon had a wrong estimation of everyone involved in this scenario: A wrong estimation of Jesus: *He can't really be a prophet or He would know who this woman is!* A wrong estimation of the woman: *She's an outcast. She doesn't belong with Him!* A wrong estimation of himself: *Too bad not everyone can be as discerning as I am!*

Several factors may have kindled Simon's repulsion. Although perfume was quite acceptable, even among strictly orthodox Jews, the use of perfume in this woman's hands was different. Prostitutes used perfume as a tool of their trade in seducing men. In Simon's legalistic mind, Jesus' acceptance of the woman's gesture was tantamount to condoning the prostitute's lifestyle. Also, women in that day were expected to cover their heads and wear their hair bound in public. For a woman to expose her hair to public view was very offensive. Simon was incensed. First this woman taints his reputation by showing up in his home, and then she further sullies him by overtly offending his guests. How dare she embarrass Simon? Didn't she know who he was?

Pin the "Tale" on the Sinner

No sooner did those thoughts enter Simon's mind than Jesus addressed them. Simon was completely unaware that Jesus had been reading him like a familiar book. Jesus said, "Simon, I have something to say to you" (Luke 7:40).

Simon responded, "Teacher, say it" (v. 40). Simon may have been thinking, *Yes, go ahead and say what we are all thinking. Put this woman in her place. Condemn her actions. Defend yourself.*

But instead, Jesus told Simon a story. It was a simple anecdote of two people who owed different sums of money to the same person and were both forgiven. Jesus ended his tale with a question. "Which person loved the forgiving creditor the most?" Jesus asked rhetorically.

Simon knew the answer and gave it, "The person with the bigger debt." Simon was right but still needed to make the connection.

The point of Jesus' parable was obvious. It was a tale of two sinners—two people who both had incurred debt and both needed forgiveness. One debtor owed a huge amount—about two full years' worth of wages! He knew his liability would be nearly impossible to repay. The other debtor owed less and perhaps, like Simon, even justified the debt.

She was guilty of the outward sin of passion; Simon was guilty of the inner sin of pride. Jesus wanted to draw the parallel between the two debtors in the story and the two sinners in the room. It was very easy for Simon to see the woman's sin, but he was not willing to admit that he, too, was a sinner. Through the story Jesus was saying to Simon that both he and the woman were sinners. Both owed. Both needed forgiveness. But Simon had never thought this way.

Why was this woman so in touch with her shortcoming and Simon wasn't? Perhaps it was because of the nature of their offenses. She was guilty of the outward sin of passion; Simon was guilty of the inner sin of pride. Hers were sins of the flesh; his were sins of the spirit. Her sins were overt and known to all; his sins were inward and unknown to all but Jesus. Both were sinners of differing sorts.

The lesson Simon needed to learn is that a person's spiritual-need deficits can't be measured on the basis of *visible* debt. Just as the creditor in the parable was the only one who knew what both debtors owed, Jesus knew what both Simon and the woman owed.

They both needed the same experience—forgiveness. Jesus loved both kinds of sinners, and like the creditor in the parable, He was willing to "freely" forgive them both. It was merely their barriers that differed. Simon's barrier was his self-righteousness; the woman's was her self-consciousness. He was blinded *to* his need; she was blinded *by* her need. Simon was playing the part of the judge; she assumed the role of the guilty one under judgment. Simon, whose name meant "hearing," needed the parable in order to *hear* God's voice calling him to forgiveness.

Then Jesus leveled with this Pharisee. He made a clear and unmistakable application of His story to Simon's life. While looking into the eyes of the woman, Jesus spoke directly to Simon: "Look at this woman kneeling here. When I entered your home, you didn't offer me water to wash the dust from my feet, but she has washed them with her tears and wiped them with her hair. You didn't give me a kiss of greeting, but she has kissed my feet again and again from the time I first came in. You neglected the courtesy of olive oil to anoint my head, but she has anointed my feet with rare perfume. I tell you, her sins—and they are many—have been forgiven, so she has shown me much love. But a person who is forgiven little shows only little love" (Luke 7:44-47, NLT).

Now we have the complete picture of what happened that evening and how Simon had treated Jesus. Simon had shown no love to this guest. He had refused to give Jesus even the common tokens of Jewish hospitality: cool water to wash off the road dust, a kiss of greeting, and scented oil to welcome Him. Hospitality was a high value in the culture, yet Simon had ignored a foundational virtue. Simon's treatment of his guest was an insult.

It is ironic that the street woman—the uninvited guest—showed Jesus the hospitality that the "spiritual" host should have shown. She watered with her own tears and dried with her lengthy hair the very feet that Simon neglected. She lavishly offered what Simon selfishly refused. Simon, the "spiritual saint," was superficial and stingy. She, the "unspiritual sinner," was extravagant and generous. Her actions spoke louder than any words Simon may have said when Jesus entered the house that night.

The Wonder of It All

With a conclusion as unpredictable as the evening itself, Jesus stunned everyone in the room. To the woman now reddened from her tears, He said, "Your sins are forgiven.... Your faith has saved you. Go in peace" (Luke 7:48-50). The people hearing these words couldn't believe it. How could this dinner guest make such a bold claim as this? How dare He make this proclamation?

But she thought differently. She got what she had come for, and she left with what she needed. The love that she had not found in years of passionate encounters with other men, she now found in a single encounter with this unique man. She left forgiven.

Simon, on the other hand, remained surprised but enlightened. His heart had been exposed. He was able to glimpse his own lack of love as well as his own load of sin. She walked away with her burden lifted; Simon remained with his burden revealed.

He had also witnessed that night the natural expression of a woman who had been given a supernatural touch. This sinner insisted on showing her love and expressing her thankfulness.

Simon the Pharisee was also able to peer into the very heart of God—portrayed differently on that night than in any way he had seen before. In all his years of theological training Simon had never before encountered such a loving God so utterly willing to erase the debt of sin. But now he saw, and now he knew. It wasn't what he expected when he saw Jesus walk through his door that evening, but it certainly was what he needed.

He was now beginning to understand that faith, not faithfulness to a standard, was the necessary ingredient for forgiveness.

Even the rebuke that Jesus leveled at Simon was for his good. He needed the verbal jarring to shake his insensitive soul. That evening the grace of God interrupted his meal, confronted his manners, and challenged his smugness. He was now beginning to understand that faith, not faithfulness to a standard, was the necessary ingredient for forgiveness. Jesus' final words to the woman were penetrating. "Your faith has saved you. Go in peace." This unsuspecting Pharisee was now able to see firsthand the relationship between grace and peace.

If Simon had invited Jesus to be on trial that night, the tables were quickly turned. It wasn't Jesus who was the one being examined as much as it was Simon himself. Jesus was the only one qualified that night to play the role of judge. And the one who could read minds and respond to secret thoughts could also grant immunity through total forgiveness. Although temple priests could pronounce God's forgiveness after a sin offering had been made, Jesus promised forgiveness without the need for a sacrifice. Such a proclamation could only have left this Pharisee stunned.

Lessons from a Dinner Table

Simon learned that sin can wear many faces—even his own. What about you? With whom do you identify in this story? Are you like the woman, aware of your sin and seeking forgiveness from Jesus? Or are you like Simon, hiding your sin and convincing others that you are spiritual?

You must be willing to confront those dark areas of life that have been glossed over by reputation or by a thin veneer of outward actions. Stepping into the light of God's presence to evaluate your life honestly is one of the most liberating exercises you could ever undertake. Here are some helpful truths and corresponding actions to get you moving in the right direction.

Everyone Sins—Face It

The biblical word for *sin* originated from the idea of failing to hit a target or simply missing the mark. Not one of us has hit the target perfectly. We've all missed God's required mark, and thus we all are sinners. We've all fallen short. We've all gotten an F on life's test, and God doesn't grade on a curve. We may excuse our sin, but it's because our vision is tainted—*by the very sin we deny*. Some of the worst sinners think of themselves as the best people. Al Capone was once considered "public enemy number one" in America. He earned his place as one of this country's most notorious criminals. The amazing thing was, he didn't think he was all that bad. In fact, he believed he was just helping people to have a good time and was being persecuted for it. This hardened criminal saw himself as a hearty philanthropist!

We would all like to believe that the window to our hearts is stained glass. No one wants to admit that the glass is tainted, smeared, and even caked with the filth of sin, but it is. The sooner we admit it, the closer we are to having the window cleaned.

Sometimes we delude ourselves into thinking we aren't all that bad because we know people who have "sinned more" than we have. Maybe you think your spouse or children or even parents fall much shorter than you do, but the point is, we all fall short. You may get closer to the target than most, but don't kid yourself—yours is a far from perfect score!

Two of my high school buddies—Richard and Raymond—come to mind as an example. Richard was the kind of kid your parents warned you about. Mine did, and they were right. He was bad news! A manipulator and a liar, Richard took the stigma of "bad boy" to a new level. No one who knew him trusted him for very long. He worked hard to earn the reputation as the school troublemaker. He had "sinner" written all over him. After a string of felony convictions, Richard was found dead one morning—murdered after being released from prison on a drug conviction.

Then there was Raymond. This guy was the all-American kid next door—the kind any dad would want his daughter to date. Ray was at church every Sunday and dazzled everyone there with his winsome smile. He was polite. He was trustworthy. He was clever. And Ray was an actor—both in the drama club at school and in real life. He played the role of "good guy" so well that no one suspected his alcoholism and drug addition. It was hard for anyone to believe that he was capable of what was eventually uncovered. But in the end, the mask came off, and Raymond was exposed.

Richard and Raymond illustrate how we often cast the roles of "sinner" and "saint." On the celluloid of our minds we picture the cultural stereotypes of both kinds, and we are too often wrong.

Whether you're a Richard or a Raymond, the spiritual type like Simon or an obvious sinner like the prostitute, the sooner you admit your spiritual condition, the better off you will be.

Denying your sin may seem like an option, but doing so will only lead to further destruction. In ancient times conquering kings would prevent their prisoners' escape by strapping a dead body to each prisoner's back. With such hideous burdens, it was impossible for the prisoners to deny that they were captives. The smelly burden was its own proof. And the burden of sin is also accompanied by its own foul stench that manages to taint every element of our lives.

> *Our greatest need is forgiveness, and God's greatest gift is to grant it.*

We can respond to our own burden of sin in one of two ways: penitence or pride. We can face up to our sin and deal with it, or we can live in perpetual denial. We have seen what denial will do. The best choice is simply to agree with God's assessment—guilty! Everyone is guilty! "All have sinned" (Romans 3:23). This agreement with God's assessment is known as confession. It's simply owning up to our sin, identifying it.

We all know we are guilty. Only pride keeps us from saying the words, "God's right. I am a sinner." Many people never admit this, however, and it shows.

Call sin what it is. It's not just a hang-up or a quirk. It's more than an imbalance or idiosyncrasy. It's sin. Don't rename it. Don't whitewash it. Don't dress it up with politically correct speech. An old Yiddish proverb captures this truth well: "A scab is a scab, even if you smear honey on it."

God's Business Is Forgiveness—Seek It

Simon was at first unaware of his need, and he therefore was uninterested in forgiveness. He was blind to himself, blind to Jesus, and blind to the woman.

On the other hand, the uninvited woman understood her condition and sought a remedy. She knew two things that night: she was a great sinner, and Jesus was a great Savior. Those two truths compelled her to find forgiveness. Our greatest need is forgiveness, and God's greatest gift is to grant it.

Admitting sin is one thing; having it forgiven is another. Forgiveness is not automatic. We must seek it. The prostitute did precisely that.

63

I recently heard about a group of children who were undernourished. The cause of their problem was a mystery. Their mothers were giving them well-balanced and nourishing meals, but the children were still scrawny. What had gone wrong? It turns out that these children had unmet emotional needs that prevented them from having a normal appetite. Until their emotional needs were addressed, they would continue to be undernourished even though they had an abundance of good food available to them every day.

It's the same way in our spiritual lives. The world is infected with a terminal disease called sin. It's an epidemic. No one escapes it. And nothing cures it except forgiveness, available through Jesus Christ. But the medicine does no good sitting on the shelves of Heaven. Take it down and use it. *Ask* for God's forgiveness. Don't languish any longer without the flow of God's love. Think again of the woman. She came. She stepped forward. She didn't care if her reputation would be the subject of after-dinner gossip. She endured the looks of contempt, the staring eyes, the whispers, and still, *still* she came to Jesus. She knew the secret. She knew that God's greatest gift must be *received*.

God's Word Is True—Believe It

How did the sinful woman know she was forgiven? She knew because Jesus told her that she was. It was a simple promise, "Your sins are forgiven" (Luke 7:48). She didn't wait for an overwhelming feeling to give her assurance. She didn't look to the people around her to affirm it. His word carried enough weight so that when He spoke, she believed it. The outcome rested on the promise.

How do you know you're forgiven? Too many of God's children walk through life burdened, encumbered by failures, and without assurance of forgiveness. They run for refuge to churches and counselors and say, "I just don't feel it! I don't think I'm forgiven. I think God must be angry with me."

You can know that you are forgiven because God has told you that you are. God has given several such statements to those who have asked for pardon. For instance He said, "I, even I, am He who blots out your transgressions for My own sake; and I will not remember your sins" (Isaiah 43:25). Did you get that? It's an emphatic statement of remission. Not only did God say He would erase the transgression, He made a choice not even to remember it! Here's another statement. In the New Testament the apostles affirmed, "To Him all the prophets witness that, through His name, whoever believes in Him will receive remission of sins" (Acts 10:43). Notice that the promise is made to those who believe in Him. That's the real issue isn't it? It's all about believing in Jesus and His ability to erase our sins. Paul told the believers in Ephesus the same thing: "In Him we have redemption through His blood, the forgiveness of sins, according to the riches of His grace" (Ephesians 1:7). You know you're forgiven because He said you would be if you believe in Him and ask Him to forgive you.

The woman in the story went away believing what Jesus said, but Simon had difficulty accepting that He would forgive her. We are often like Simon; we think that some people don't deserve forgiveness. Those who don't understand the heart of God will always have difficulty believing that obvious sinners can be pardoned. When I first read about John DeLorean's conversion, I was skeptical. DeLorean, the automobile czar, had been indicted on charges of cocaine placement in the glove box of his signature cars. Charges were filed, and so were the news reports. It became the scandal of the year when it happened. Then I remember hearing that he had "changed," that he had become a Christian. *Yeah, right!* I thought. I had seen others conveniently convert when their necks were on the line. The finger of the law has a way of readjusting one's priorities in hopes of earning a lighter sentence. My skepticism—as well as my willingness to forgive—would soon be challenged.

It was a Sunday, and I was conducting the evening Bible study in a church that met in a rented facility in downtown Manhattan. The crowd was a bit different from the one I am used to addressing. A mixture of actors, artists, and models added color to this flock. One man in particular caught my attention. It wasn't his neatly groomed graying hair or his quiet manner. It was the way he listened. His whole being seemed to be engaged in every comment I made about the Scripture passage. He vigorously jotted down notes as if he were transcribing every word I said.

When the service was over and the people were leaving, I asked the pastor of the church, "Who's the older guy who takes all the notes?"

His answer floored me. "Oh, that's John DeLorean. He's the guy who made the cars and got into trouble over the drugs."

"Yeah, I heard of him," I mumbled, trying not to act totally ashamed of my previous attitude. Boy, did I feel like Simon the Pharisee that night! I realized just how difficult it is to overcome a bad reputation and to have others accept that sinners can be changed.

Jesus' Fellowship Is Available—Invite It

Simon invited Jesus to dine as a guest but not as a friend. He wanted Jesus' company but stopped short of wanting His companionship. Simon was content to live at the superficial level rather than go deeper.

Eating a meal together was considered one of the closest forms of fellowship in ancient times. Jesus even made use of this as a metaphor for spiritual intimacy. Jesus said to one New Testament church, "Behold, I stand at the door and knock. If anyone hears My voice and opens the door, I will come in to him and dine with him, and he with Me" (Revelation 3:20). Jesus will come as close as we allow Him to come, but He operates by invitation only. The woman in Luke 7 invited Jesus to a deeper spiritual relationship. Simon kept Him at a safe distance.

Just as Jesus didn't push Simon to go deeper than he was willing to go, He won't push you either. Jesus didn't insist on the hospitality that Simon overlooked. He didn't stand in the doorway with a basin of water saying, "Uh, Simon, didn't you forget something?" He didn't grab Simon's hand, put a bottle of oil in it, and blurt out, "Go ahead, Simon, anoint my head with this. It's your duty!" Jesus was a gracious guest. And when Jesus wanted to say something, He didn't announce it to the whole gathering by shouting out His message. Rather, Jesus asked politely and carefully, saying, "Simon, I have something to say to you." It was only after Simon invited Jesus to speak that the Lord got to deeper matters of the heart.

Jesus responds to us in the same way. His desire is to take us to deeper levels of fellowship, but He wants us to want it too. James reminded his readers, "Draw near to God and He will draw near to you" (James 4:8).

Jesus still responds to invitations.

I encourage you to face your sin, seek forgiveness, believe that you are forgiven, and invite Jesus to lead you into a deeper relationship with Him. Then take the next step. Do what the woman did. Unabashedly show Jesus your love for Him.

— ~

FOR REFLECTION AND DISCUSSION

1. Think back to when you discovered that you were a sinner and needed to do something about it. What things kept you from making that realization earlier?

2. What made you finally realize that you "missed the mark" and were a sinner? Circle one or more:

A special visit from an honest friend
A convicting sermon
A thoughtful self-examination
A book you were reading
The change you saw in someone else

3. How does self-righteousness keep a person spiritually aloof? In what ways do you battle self-righteousness?

4. Think back to the last time you offended someone and asked for that person's pardon. How did that person react when you asked for forgiveness? How did you react? How could you be sure that his or her word was enough? Do you treat God's promises the same way?

5. What three ways can you demonstrate your love to God because He has forgiven you?

FIVE

Voted Most Likely Not to Convert

A Radical Rabbi's Radical Encounter

Then Saul, still breathing threats and murder against the disciples of the Lord, went to the high priest and asked letters from him to the synagogues of Damascus, so that if he found any who were of the Way, whether men or women, he might bring them bound to Jerusalem.

As he journeyed he came near Damascus, and suddenly a light shone around him from heaven. Then he fell to the ground, and heard a voice saying to him, "Saul, Saul, why are you persecuting Me?"

And he said, "Who are You, Lord?"

Then the Lord said, "I am Jesus, whom you are persecuting. It is hard for you to kick against the goads."

So he, trembling and astonished, said, "Lord, what do You want me to do?"

Then the Lord said to him, "Arise and go into the city, and you will be told what you must do."

And the men who journeyed with him stood speechless, hearing a voice but seeing no one. Then Saul arose from the ground, and when his eyes were opened he saw no one. But they led him by the hand and brought him into Damascus. And he was three days without sight, and neither ate nor drank (Acts 9:1-9).

— —

After taking some food, he regained his strength.

Saul spent several days with the disciples in Damascus. At once he began to preach in the synagogues that Jesus is the Son of God. All those who heard him were astonished and asked, "Isn't he the man who raised havoc in Jerusalem among those who call on this

69

name? And hasn't he come here to take them as prisoners to the chief priests?" Yet Saul grew more and more powerful and baffled the Jews living in Damascus by proving that Jesus is the Christ (Acts 9:19-22, NIV).

— —

When was the last time you pulled out your high school yearbook and walked down memory lane? We cringe now when we look at the strange haircuts and clothing we thought were so cool. Remember the pages in the back of the yearbook—you know, the ones that listed the local school "stars"? There were John and Vicky, who were voted "most athletic." Then there were Liz and Barry in the latest chic fashions; they were voted—you guessed it—"best dressed." The guy with the electric smile? That's Scott. He made it as the one "most likely to succeed." It's questionable that he ever did, but his classmates thought he had a good chance. I never made that "dream-team" section of my yearbook, but I've looked at it and often wondered about the people listed there.

If the early Church had its own yearbook, it might have included a similar section. Peter probably would have been voted "most likely to succeed." After all, Jesus called him "blessed." Maybe John would have been named "most athletic" since he outran another disciple to the tomb on Resurrection morning. But I'm sure Paul the apostle would have had a place as well. He probably would have had the ignominious title "most likely *not* to convert to Christianity." That's what people thought about him.

This Jewish zealot was the last person anyone expected to have an encounter with Jesus. But he did. It was the conversion of the century. An event that would rock the world.

The encounter Saul of Tarsus had with Jesus of Nazareth is notable because it happened after Jesus rose from the dead and ascended into Heaven. Even after He left the earth, the resurrected Jesus was pursuing people in His desire to change their lives.

70

The Biography of an Unlikely Convert

Saul, from the ancient city of Tarsus in the province of Cilicia, was a religious terrorist. His blazing zeal drove him to protect his Jewish faith, which was being threatened by a new group claiming that a peasant from Galilee was the Messiah.

Saul's background was like that of no one else. He described himself this way: "Circumcised the eighth day, of the stock of Israel, of the tribe of Benjamin, a Hebrew of the Hebrews; concerning the law, a Pharisee; concerning zeal, persecuting the Church; concerning the righteousness which is in the law, blameless" (Philippians 3:5-6).

Religiously a Jew

Saul of Tarsus was a rising light in the intellectual and religious world of Judaism. As a Hellenized Jew of the Dispersion (those living outside Israel), he remained loyal to the God of his fathers while being raised in a pagan city. He was proud to be a Jew.

Saul's heritage was impressive. He was a "Hebrew of the Hebrews," a purebred. There were no mixed marriages in his family tree. Both his parents were Jewish through and through. Technically a person was considered to be a Jew even if only his or her mother was Jewish. But Saul's bloodlines were pure on both sides of his family.

His tribal roots were equally as impressive. Any Jew knew that Benjamin, whose name meant "the son of my right hand," was the patriarch Jacob's favorite son. The tribe of Benjamin was a small tribe numerically, but it was a spiritual giant among the other tribes of Israel. When the ten tribes revolted and broke away from the temple worship in Judah, only the tribe of Benjamin remained loyal. And when Israel needed a hero to save the Jews from Persian extinction, they found their man in Mordecai, a Benjamite. Saul was Jewish to the core!

Culturally a Greek

In many ways Saul was the consummate "man about town." He was cosmopolitan. Being from the Greek-speaking Roman province of Cilicia, he was versed in Greco-Roman culture. In this geographical bridge where Asia Minor kissed Syria, Saul spent his boyhood years. His education was well rounded.

His knowledge of his world made him at home among the religious elite as well as the garden-variety pagans.

Young Saul grew up in a bustling, vibrant environment. Tarsus was one of the oldest cities in the world, spanning six millennia. Along with its commercial and agricultural wealth, it boasted a great university and ranked with Athens (Greece) and Alexandria (Egypt) as one of the three top intellectual centers. The city's fine scholars were numerous.[1]

Talk about having an impressive résumé! Saul grew up at the crossroads of world influence and education. He had it all: Jewish birth and training, Greek cultural influence, and exposure to leading intellectual thought. And it showed. In the New Testament we find him quoting the Greek writers—*from memory*. In Athens he could discuss philosophy and religion with the leading scholars of the day (see Acts 17:22-31).

Nationally a Roman

Evidently many citizens from Tarsus enjoyed Roman citizenship, which was granted to them at the hands of Pompey, Julius Caesar, Anthony, and Augustus. Paul's ancestors were no doubt among them.[2]

Such citizenship brought certain rights and freedoms. Roman citizens could vote for judges and could even be elected to such positions. They could hold property in Roman communities and were exempted from certain methods of interrogation. Paul exerted his right as a Roman citizen as well as the right to appeal legal cases to the emperor (Acts 22:25-29; 25:11-12). This advantage was carefully upheld since the penalty for falsely claiming Roman citizenship was death. The unique blend of Jewish, Greek, and Roman influence made Saul able to relate well to all segments of his world.

Spiritually a Zealot

Like Nicodemus and Simon, Saul was a Pharisee, a member of the elite Jewish leadership. These enthusiasts spent a lot of energy guarding their tradition against corruption by other beliefs, including Christianity. The Pharisees' power to influence the masses was immense, and they used it to guard Israel from pagan pressure.[3] Jesus once remarked about their zeal to "travel land and sea to win one proselyte" (Matthew

23:15). As a Pharisee, Saul moved among influential people, and he used his clout to defend his Jewish faith.

Saul was schooled at the feet of one of Israel's most famous teachers, Gamaliel (Acts 22:3). Gamaliel was given the honor of being called "the beauty of the law" and had the unique title of *rabban*—one among only seven men who were given the title that indicated more authority than the title *rabbi*.[4] Gamaliel's grandfather, Hillel, was another celebrated Jewish teacher.

Into this heritage of spiritual leadership stepped young Saul of Tarsus, so full of spiritual zeal yet so empty of spiritual life. His days were spent memorizing whole sections of the Old Testament and drilling with Gamaliel in demanding question and answer sessions. Gamaliel was such a skilled teacher that when he died, the Talmud stated that the "glory of Law had ceased."[5] The great truths that Rabbi Saul drank in would largely lie dormant until one very dramatic experience unlocked them.

Defending the Cause

In his intense enthusiasm to protect Judaism against pagan Rome and the influence of Christianity, Saul turned to violence. "As for Saul, he made havoc of the church, entering every house, and dragging off men and women, committing them to prison" (Acts 8:3).

Saul had a hot head and a cold heart. Fueled by misconstrued loyalty, he unleashed his anger at the young Christian Church. In the Greek language, *havoc* refers to the kind of destruction that would be inflicted by a wild boar trampling a garden or an army sweeping through a city and devastating it. Like an untamed animal, Saul's unrestrained animosity toward Christians left its destructive marks on the Church. "Saul, still breathing threats and murder against the disciples of the Lord, went to the high priest and asked letters from him to the synagogues of Damascus, so that if he found any who were of the Way, whether men or women, he might bring them bound to Jerusalem" (Acts 9:1-2). Saul was clearly earning his place as the "most likely *not* to convert."

Like an athlete who expands his lungs to endure the race, Saul was filling his emotional lungs with the air of hatred and slaughter. Blinded by zeal and deafened by vengeance, this firebrand became the dominating personality of Christian persecution. Saul saw Christianity as a heretical cult that defamed the God of Israel by exalting a man called Jesus, and Saul measured his spiritual fervor by his hatred of Christians.

Surely if anyone was resistant to meeting with Jesus, it was Saul of Tarsus. But Saul had not reckoned with the persistence of a God who would lovingly pursue him even when he was trying to stamp out any mention of His name.

Showdown on the Damascus Highway

Saul thought he was on a mission from God. It turned out he was the mission! This militant persecutor was firmly in the sights of God's divine aim. How would God deal with this radical? *Radically!* God is never intimidated by obstinacy. God knew how to get his attention: "As he journeyed he came near Damascus, and suddenly a light shone around him from heaven. Then he fell to the ground, and heard a voice saying to him, 'Saul, Saul, why are you persecuting Me?'" (Acts 9:4).

The encounter was severe. God sought out Saul as surely as Saul was seeking out Christians in Damascus. A blinding light, greater than the sun's powerful rays, flashed around him in the middle of the day (Acts 26:13). An arresting voice spoke from Heaven, and Saul heard it in his soul.

Stunned by the moment, Saul then heard an even more stunning question, "Why are you persecuting Me?" (Acts 9:4). Saul at first had no idea who was doing the talking, but he must have had an uneasy hunch.

As if responding with a reflex, Saul questioned the voice, "Who are You, Lord?" (v. 5).

The answer fell on his soul like a mighty weight, "I am Jesus, whom you are persecuting" (v. 5). Saul was completely taken off guard. He never expected to hear that. Jesus? How is *that* possible? Saul didn't believe Jesus was even alive. He had heard that He had been crucified. But now, pinned to the ground, Saul heard Jesus speaking directly to him. And it seemed that Jesus was letting Saul know, in no uncertain terms, that He takes it personally when anyone comes after His people.

When God Prods the Heart

Like a skilled surgeon testing for sensitive nerves, God had been probing Saul's troubled soul. It was a process that this rabbi had been fighting, as indicated by Jesus' next statement: "It is hard for you to kick against the goads" (Acts 9:5). Saul understood those words. When beasts of burden failed to respond to simple commands, the farmer would stick the animal's hide with a goad—a rod with a pointed iron bit tied to the end. The goad gave the animal incentive. The phrase "kicking against the goads" came to mean resisting a push or pull. Jesus' statement indicates that Saul had been resisting some prodding going on inside his heart.

What the prodding was, is difficult to say. It could well have been a guilty conscience. Perhaps Saul was bothered by a past failure. Or maybe he was bothered by the gospel that he was trying to squelch. His route to Damascus may have brought him close enough to Samaria to hear of the fires of revival that had been ignited since Philip had preached there. People were turning to this rebel Messiah in droves. That very fact could have been like a piercing goad to his angry soul.

But something much deeper was probably eating away at Saul's conscience, something he had recently seen. The last thing he experienced in Jerusalem before heading on toward Damascus was the death of a follower of Christ, a man named Stephen. Rabbi Saul saw the whole episode and even gave his blessing to it. It was an incident he could never forget and an experience that would not let go of his soul.

As Stephen boldly preached to the high priest about Jesus Christ, Saul was there. When Stephen skillfully wove the history of Israel with messianic prophecy, Saul was there. As Stephen passionately gave his defense before a hardened audience, Saul was there. When the angry mob threw stones to silence Stephen, Saul was there. As Stephen in holy joy saw Heaven opened and Jesus standing to greet him, Saul was there. When the crowd of hate-filled spectators rushed to extinguish Stephen's last vision and words, Saul was there. And Saul was urging them to finish the deadly task (see Acts 6:8, 8:2).

Then Stephen did what Saul had seen no other person ever do: Stephen prayed for his persecutors. "And he fell to his knees, shouting, 'Lord, don't charge them with this sin!' And

75

with that, he died. Saul was one of the official witnesses at the killing of Stephen" (Acts 7:60, 8:1, NLT).

That scene had become indelibly etched on the walls of Saul's mind, and it would haunt him wherever he went. As he left Jerusalem, those memories followed. As he headed north to Damascus, that vision flashed across his mind. Stephen's gracious words, but especially his godly death, had lingering results. Those haunting incidents could well have been the goads that pierced the hide of Saul's conscience.

The assault of those memories, coupled with the guilt they produced, was breaking through the walls of Saul's hardened heart. Saul had never before seen a man who prayed like that as he bled to death. There seemed to be no malice in his heart. There was no animosity toward his executors. Rather than foul words of retaliation there flowed a prayer of pure forgiveness. It must have shaken Saul to his core. Finally, on that isolated piece of road, the goads of conviction penetrated, and Saul found it hard to fight.

An Adversary Becomes an Ally

In a blinding streak of light, the brilliant rabbi from Tarsus supernaturally met the resurrected Messiah from Nazareth. What remarkable love was shown in that encounter! Why would Jesus want to have anything to do with a person like Saul? He was antagonistic to Jesus and to everyone who followed Him.

But the very thing that we think would repel Jesus is what made Saul the target of His love: Saul was an enemy. Part of Jesus' life message was to "love your enemies" (Matthew 5:44; Luke 6:27, 35). He told His followers to do so, and He gave the ultimate demonstration of it on the cross. Now, in effect, Jesus again practiced what He once preached as He extended that love to this enemy. The one who hunted down Jesus' followers was being tracked down by the love of God.

When Saul had first heard the voice from Heaven, he wasn't quite sure who was speaking. After Jesus had identified Himself, Saul acknowledged Jesus as Lord—a radical confession for a man who loathed Christians. Then Saul asked an astounding question: "Lord, what do You want me to do?" (Acts 9:6). Not only did Saul recognize that he was in the presence of Jesus, but he was compelled to surrender his will. In that moment Saul opened his heart to the mercy of God. The dazzling light shone *on* him and blinded him, but the spiritual light dawned *inside* him and made him see! This enemy had been won over.

And what were the results of this encounter? The changes were sudden and radical. The hothead changed into a humble servant. He was willing to do whatever Jesus commanded. When He told Saul to go to Damascus and find a man who would give him further instructions, Saul complied immediately.

The one who hunted down Jesus' followers was being tracked down by the love of God.

Once Saul was inside the city of Damascus, he used his time to pray. Ananias was told to "inquire at the house of Judas for one called Saul of Tarsus, for behold, he is praying" (Acts 9:11). Why was that important to note? Saul had prayed since he was a child and had learned how to pray formally in his professional education. He was a "Hebrew of Hebrews." If anyone had a handle on prayer, it was Saul.

But this was different. This prayer was certainly more than rote and prescribed. Saul must have poured out his very soul. The knockdown experience shook him. Instead of kicking against the goads, he was moving in sync with his Master, communicating, worshiping, and asking for forgiveness for past misunderstanding. What an incredible change in this man! The mouth that once had breathed threats and murder was now breathing prayer and praise. The raging lion had been changed into a bleating lamb!

But no sooner did this bleating lamb recover from his supernatural ordeal than he became emboldened once again, this time to herald the message he had long fought against. And he didn't go unnoticed. How could he? The persecutor became the preacher! "All who heard him were amazed. 'Isn't this the same man who persecuted Jesus' followers with such devastation in Jerusalem?' they asked. 'And we understand that he came here to arrest them and take them in chains to the leading priests.' Saul's preaching became more and more powerful, and the Jews in Damascus couldn't refute his proofs that Jesus was indeed the Messiah" (Acts 9:21-22, NLT).

This enemy of the gospel had truly been won over by Jesus. Saul had been on his way to Damascus to imprison those who, although they attended the synagogues, believed in Jesus. Now he was in one of those very synagogues, preaching that very gospel. Saul was demonstrating what Jesus once had told another Pharisee named Simon: When a person has been forgiven much, he shows much love (see Luke 7:47).

The persecutor became the preacher!

What happened that day in Damascus was only the beginning. Saul of Tarsus would soon be known fondly by the Christian assemblies as Paul the great apostle. His love for the gospel that changed his own life would carry him throughout the Mediterranean world to the very heart of the Roman Empire. Three missionary trips would soon yield the beginnings of many churches, with thousands of conversions. Just as Jesus predicted, Saul of Tarsus was to become God's "chosen vessel" (Acts 9:15) to convey the love of God to the world at large—both to the Jews and the Gentiles. Paul's letters, which he sent to the new churches, were considered to be Scripture even while Paul was still living (2 Peter 3:16). The chief antagonist of the early Christians had become their chief protagonist.

The Church has been grateful for this encounter above all others. The Church still feels the results. Think of the impact that this man's life has had throughout the centuries. For the past two millennia, countless millions have read his New Testament letters. They have been translated into thousands of languages and dialects and distributed throughout the world. Great movements have been formed because of Paul's doctrinal positions.

When Saul met Jesus, the wretched rebel became the remarkable writer.

What the Road Teaches Other Travelers

Saul's road experience en route to Damascus speaks to us of how God still changes lives today. Three central truths emerge from the dramatic showdown on the Damascus road. These truths both encourage and challenge us.

1. No One Is beyond God's Reach

How often do you wonder about people whom we have dubbed "most likely not to convert"? How many do you know in your own social circles? Can you picture that brother, aunt, or friend whom you have written off in the past? Be honest—you may have even doubted that God could really penetrate the hardened soil of those hearts. They're beyond hope, beyond God's reach! You have shared the gospel with them. You have prayed for them daily. When you see them, you hope that this time they'll listen and respond. But then your hopes are dashed by their unbelief. You see no signs of life—no indications of a heart softening toward God.

Let the story of Saul's encounter with the Savior resurrect your faltering hopes. Jesus wants to meet with those people more than you will know. Just as He pursued Saul, He will pursue those whom you love.

God knows your earnest desires. God has heard your prayers. He sees your anguished efforts to help your loved ones to meet Him. And what's more, He can do something about it. And God is full of surprises. He loves going after the renegades. He specializes in restoring the lives of people we may not even bother to witness to. What's more, the very ones we think would never come may be closer than we think.

No one is beyond His grasp. No one is out of the reach of His influence. Let this promise bolster your hope: "He is also able to save to the uttermost those who come to God through Him, since He always lives to make intercession for them" (Hebrews 7:25).

It is said that the renowned Victorian preacher Charles Spurgeon loved to rephrase that wonderful verse and say that God is able to save to the "guttermost." In other words, God can reach even those who live in the gutter. He can reclaim even the most hardened and resistant person.

Ask Johnny Newton. As a young boy he learned Scripture from his godly mother, who wanted her son to be rooted in the truth of God's Word. But when she died suddenly when he was only seven years old, Newton was devastated. Unable to make any sense of this great tragedy, he joined the British navy and went off to sail the waterways of the world.

Away from the moral constraints of home, the young man's wild side began to take over. Seaman Newton ran away to Africa, not caring about the consequences. He indulged himself in a life of sin.

It is said that Newton could swear continuously for two full hours—without repeating himself once! Making questionable friendships, he soon found himself involved with Portuguese slave traders who were selling captured Africans to plantation owners in the New World. The selling of other human beings only served to harden his heart more. Whatever scriptural truths were in his heart were being eroded by a series of wrong choices.

Eventually Newton's coarse lifestyle forced him into becoming a slave to another. He was treated like an animal. No respect. No honor. He was even forced to pick up food with his mouth and was mercilessly beaten if he dared to touch it with his hands. From the godly environment of a Scripture-loving mother to the filthy deck of an ungodly slave ship, Newton had sunk to the depths. But he managed to escape his floating prison and take refuge on a nearby beach.

Emancipated, he decided to take a more responsible course of action. From the shore where he had been deposited, Newton signaled a passing ship and came aboard as part of the crew.

At the point of Newton's greatest rebellion, God met him.

Because he was such a skilled navigator, he soon became the ship's first mate. But his dark side was never too far away. One afternoon he urged the entire crew to get drunk while the captain was ashore. When the captain returned to his ship, he was furious. He struck John Newton with a powerful blow that sent him reeling off the ship and into the uncertain sea, where he almost drowned.

Hard to believe, isn't it? How can a tender boy grow up to become such a hardened man, with no regard for life, even his own? Beyond reach? A hopeless case? Impossible to save? One might be tempted to think so. Johnny Newton was a candidate for the title "most likely not to convert."

But the story doesn't end there. At the point of Newton's greatest rebellion, God met him. Newton was rescued from the sea, and while he was recovering, the Scripture verses he had learned as a young boy began to resurface. They became goads to the sailor's rebellious heart.

A week after returning to Britain, Newton cried out to God, his persistent pursuer. His burdened soul was made light by his close encounter with a forgiving God.

John Newton grew in faith and soon became a vibrant leader in the
Church of England and eventually chaplain to the British Parliament. Talk about change! Talk about taking an impossible case and reclaiming a soul! John Newton was never beyond God's reach.

Oh yes, and that same man, John Newton, went on to express his gratitude to God by giving us a song I think you'll recognize:

> *Amazing Grace! How sweet the sound that saved a wretch like me.*
> *I once was lost but now am found, was blind but now I see!*
> *'Twas grace that taught my heart to fear, and grace my fears relieved.*
> *How precious did that grace appear, the hour I first believed!*[6]

John Newton, like Saul of Tarsus, would have made the yearbook list as most likely not to convert. He was a hopeless case. Beyond reach. But that was before he met the God of the tough cases. We must remember that God can do anything— even get the attention of His enemies.

2. Some People Need Goads
Some people come to Christ without much effort. They don't have many questions. They just want relief from the burden of their sins immediately.

But not everyone is like that. Many people require time to let the message seep in or an event to get their attention. Nicodemus needed discussion with Jesus and time. Simon needed a heart-penetrating story. But Saul needed something more. He needed goads. Although he probably tried to deny them or cover them with zealous activity, the nerves of his heart were laid bare. Saul had to get into trouble with his own heart before he would ever get out of trouble with his God.

Everyone needs what Jesus came to offer, but not everyone knows his or her need. Jesus is willing to persuade men and women with whatever it takes, short of violating their free will. Jesus once said, "God blesses those who realize their need for him, for the Kingdom of Heaven is given to them" (Matthew 5:3, NLT). Many people change only after their hard hearts are exposed by goads.

I heard about a farmer who owned a stubborn mule. One afternoon the farmer was trying to get the mule to move from the stable to the field. The man shouted, tugged, and even kicked the critter, but it just wouldn't budge. The farmer's neighbor happened by, noticed the problem, and offered to help. "I can get that old mule to cooperate, you know."

"I doubt it," spouted the farmer, wiping the sweat from his brow. "But you can give it a try. It certainly can't hurt!"

So the helpful neighbor quietly walked over to the animal, picked up a hefty piece of wood that lay alongside the road, and gave the mule a sudden whack upside the head! When the neighbor took the reins, the dizzy beast immediately followed him out to the field.

"I don't get it," said the farmer. "How come he went with you? I yelled and tugged, but he didn't flinch one bit."

"Well, you see," replied his neighbor, "cooperation is all a matter of getting his attention!"

When God finally had gotten Saul's attention, he was ready to hear. It didn't take long once his conscience had been prodded. Some people are like that. They need to be prodded and pushed by the Holy Spirit before they'll respond.

A friend of mine prayed for his mother for years until the goads of personal remorse coupled with a frightening dream brought her to her knees to receive Jesus as Savior. God has His ways of getting to even the hardest of hearts.

And God may have to isolate a person before those goads make their full impact. A sudden tragedy or debilitating situation may be the only thing that will get some people's attention. When you pray for people, don't be surprised if you watch things get worse in their lives before they get better. Keep praying!

By the way, it's hard to watch someone going through this process, and it's harder still to be around those who are. Like Saul, those who are fighting the goads will often breathe out the most toxic words and attitudes. Those within firing range will get the brunt of such a lashing out. I feel especially sorry for the spouse of a person fighting God's divine goads. But be encouraged. There is light at the end of that tunnel.

If someone you know is fighting against the goads, take heart and pray for that person all the more earnestly. If you are the person kicking against the goads, know this: There is no pillow as soft as a clear conscience. Unless you run to meet Jesus, your situation will only get worse.

3. When We Hurt a Christian, We Hurt Jesus

Saul learned a startling lesson in his encounter with Jesus on the Damascus road. The first question the voice asked Saul was, "Why are you persecuting Me?" The question was not, "Why are you persecuting them?" No. Jesus personalized Saul's actions.

Saul was confused. How could he possibly be persecuting Jesus, whom he couldn't even see? Saul was about to learn that Jesus and His people are inseparably linked. When a Christian is persecuted, Christ feels it. When arrows are flung at God's followers, they're aimed at Him. Any blow struck on Earth is a blow felt in Heaven.

Although Saul did not fully comprehend this truth when he first heard it, it would become one of his great themes in his later writings. I believe that this encounter with Jesus had a direct impact on Paul's writings about the body of Christ (Romans 7:4; 1 Corinthians 10:16; 12:12-31; Ephesians 4:12). Paul drew a beautiful analogy of how the Church is like a human body. Jesus Christ is the head of the body (Ephesians 4:15), and we are its members (Romans 12:5; 1 Corinthians 12:20). As the head, Jesus gives the orders, and the message is conveyed to the various parts of the body. But the head also contains the brain, the core of the central nervous system.

When pain is felt at any point of the body, the brain knows about that pain and processes it.

If you have ever had the unfortunate experience of hitting your thumb with a hammer, you understand how this works. When the hammer hits your thumbnail, where does it hurt? Is the pain confined to the thumb itself? No! It shoots up your arm, radiates throughout the body, and rings the bell inside your head. That's how suffering works in the body of Christ too. When one person in the body suffers, so do the rest of us (1 Corinthians 12:26). Not only do the members suffer, but Christ, as the head, can feel the pain as well.

This truth is both challenging and encouraging. We must remember that when we hurt another Christian, we are hurting Jesus himself. That's sobering. But the truth is also comforting. When you are hurting, you can be assured that Jesus hurts with you.

The Effect of Meeting Jesus Is Unmistakable

Jesus meets each of just where we are. He met Saul in his rebelliousness. He met John the Baptist in his misunderstanding. He met Nicodemus in his questioning. He met the Samaritan woman in her spiritual thirst. He met Simon in his pride. He met the prostitute in her moral confusion.

And Jesus tailors his meeting to our individual need and circumstances. He surprised John the Baptist. He challenged Nicodemus' thinking. He went out of His way to meet the Samaritan woman. He told Simon a story. He forgave the prostitute. He blinded Saul. Each encounter differed.

But each encounter left an unmistakable change. Something was different after the experience. The people didn't glow in the dark. There was no airy sanctuary tone in their voices. They didn't suddenly sprout haloes. But each life was changed by the experience of the meeting.

When Saul was flattened by his encounter with Jesus, he asked the right question: "Lord, what do You want me to do?" (Acts 9:6). Then he went and did it.

The same should be true for you. When Jesus meets you—whether through your initiative or His persistence to pursue you—surrender yourself to Him. Allow Him to change you unmistakably.

— —

FOR REFLECTION AND DISCUSSION

1. Describe your life before your coming to Christ. Ask someone who knew you then to describe how open you were to following Jesus Christ. How did God get your attention? Was yours a slow progression toward God or a sudden transformation?

2. Do you know someone who has had a radical Damascus-road-type conversion? What similarities and differences does that person have with Saul's experience? Why do you suppose some people have such experiences (see Job 9:4)?

3. Is anyone close to you being "goaded by God" and fighting the conviction? Get others to join with you for consistent prayer for that person.

4. Who would you put on the top of your "most likely not to convert" list? Seriously consider contacting that person and sharing your beliefs and conversion experience over a meal.

5. What lasting changes in your personality and lifestyle can you identify after encountering Jesus (patience, willingness to forgive, refusal to hold grudges, boldness in standing for Him, etc.)?

6. In what contemporary settings is Jesus identifying and standing with those who are being persecuted for Him? How can you help respond as a member of the body of Christ?

part two

The Power of Jesus

The Power of His Touch

The Man No One Would Get Close To

*A*nd so it was, when Jesus had ended these sayings, that the people were astonished at His teaching, for He taught them as one having authority, and not as the scribes.

When He had come down from the mountain, great multitudes followed Him. And behold, a leper came and worshiped Him, saying, "Lord, if You are willing, You can make me clean."

Then Jesus put out His hand and touched him, saying, "I am willing; be cleansed." Immediately his leprosy was cleansed.

And Jesus said to him, "See that you tell no one; but go your way, show yourself to the priest, and offer the gift that Moses commanded, as a testimony to them" (Matthew 7:28, 8:4).

When I saw it again this week, my jaw dropped. It never gets old to see a shuttle launch from Florida's Cape Canaveral. What power! Imagine the staggering power that it takes to propel four and a half million pounds several hundred nautical miles into the air!

But what about God's power? What does it take to fling the planets into orbit or hang the curtain of stars across the sky? What kind of power is required to raise the dead or heal the crippling effects of a loathsome and debilitating disease? Divine power defies measurement and description. But it is *noticeable*.

And it is real.

Several New Testament passages reveal people who encountered both the person and the power of Jesus. When they did, they soared. When Jesus restored muscle tone to withered limbs, people were overcome with awe. When He restored sight, people stood in amazement. Such power! Such authority! Such love!

Jesus' power got people's attention. Like the visitors and residents around Cape Canaveral watching a liftoff, crowds of people took notice of Jesus' power encounters. In fact, the miracles involving Jesus' power gave proof to His person. He was the anticipated Messiah, and how He would handle power would demonstrate that. When John the Baptist's disciples wanted tangible proof that Jesus was the Christ, Jesus gave it to them. He said, "The blind see and the lame walk; the lepers are cleansed and the deaf hear; the dead are raised up" (Matthew 11:5).

But people saw even more than mended flesh and messianic proof. They observed a God who cared. They were watching the Creator step into their arena and show His concern for their ordinary lives.

Leprosy—The Disease of the Walking Dead

If anyone was in need of a powerful touch, it was the powerless Galilean leper who came seeking Jesus. Like others we have already noted, this man was not named in the account. We don't know anything about his background, his family, or his social life.

The only thing we do know about the man is that he was a leper. Just hearing the word leprosy made most people cringe or run for cover. It was truly an isolating disease.

Physical Manifestations

Because medical science was underdeveloped at that time, leprosy was regarded then much as AIDS is today. It was incurable, and it was often unbearable. It was the most feared plague of that age because of its communicability. New Testament scholar William Barclay graphically describes its progressive nature:

It might begin with little nodules which go on to ulcerate. The ulcers develop a foul discharge. The eyebrows fall out. The eyeballs become staring. The vocal cords become ulcerated, and the voice becomes hoarse. The breath wheezes. The hands and the feet also ulcerate. Slowly the sufferer becomes a mass of ulcerated growth. The average course of this kind of leprosy is nine years, and ends in mental decay, coma and, ultimately, death.

Leprosy might begin with a loss of sensation in parts of the body. The nerve trunks are affected; the muscles waste away. The tendons contract until the hands are like claws. There follows ulceration of the hands and feet. Then comes the progressive loss of fingers and toes, until in the end a whole hand or a whole foot may drop off. The duration of this kind of leprosy is anything from twenty to thirty years. It is a kind of terrible, progressive death in which a person dies by the inches.[1]

The disease was understandably feared and intensely loathed. Because it was highly contagious, God prescribed stringent regulations in order to control its spread (see Leviticus 13–14). If people suspected that they had the dread illness, they would go to a priest, who would examine their skin. If the priest thought they had leprosy, they were declared "unclean"—the death knell for their future.

When the disease progressed, it attacked the central nervous system and deadened nerve endings. While it was good that people couldn't feel any pain from the illness, it was not good that the pain signals, which serve to alert us to danger and thus preserve us, were also deadened. That left people very vulnerable to injury that people with pain sensors would avoid. Most of us have had the experience of having a shot of Novocaine at the dentist. While it's nice not to feel the pain, it's not good that, in the absence of pain sensors, we sometimes bite our numbed lip or cheek without knowing it.

The man who came to Jesus was in the advanced stages of leprosy. Luke, who was a physician, describes this same man as being "full of leprosy" (Luke 5:12). The bacteria had done their evil work to deaden the nerve cells so that this man was impervious to physical pain. He was, no doubt, terribly disfigured and discouraged. But this physical embarrassment would be only half of his terrible sentence. The social and relational rejection could crush the spirit.

Social Manifestations

The respected historian Josephus noted that lepers were treated like dead people. Like banished criminals they were completely estranged from society. They had to wear torn clothes, shave their heads, and cover their mouths with a cloth to prevent the spread of the disease. If people were approaching, lepers were required to shout the warning, "Unclean! Unclean!" Lepers could get no closer than six feet to anyone because of their defilement. Rejection and isolation became a way of life for the leper.

Imagine what that would mean if the leper was a family man. He wouldn't be able to live with his wife and children any longer. He would not be able to feel his wife's embrace or his children's cuddles. He was cut off from all warm touch.

He could observe normal society only from a distance. He was barred from social contact and public worship. He lived either in isolation or with other ailing ones. He became a man without a country, a man without a family. He suffered as a man without fellowship.

Lepers received public scorn and harsh treatment from the religious and social structure of the day. Paranoia about contracting leprosy was so great that one ancient rabbi derided, "When I see lepers, I throw stones at them lest they come near me."[2]

A Powerless Leper Meets the Prince of Life

Jesus was on His way down the hillside when the leper spotted Him. He had just delivered His Sermon on the Mount (see Matthew 5–7), and the crowds swarmed around Him.

The leper knew he was taking a risk approaching a crowd of people. If he became too conspicuous, he could ruin his chance to get close enough to Jesus. Maybe the leper was hoping that those in the crowd would be so preoccupied with Jesus that they wouldn't notice a cowering leper. At the right time he could maneuver his way in through the crowd long enough to get Jesus' attention. He would have to act fast—and talk fast. It might be his only chance. How would this leper command Jesus' attention fast enough so that the crowd would not beat him back with their shouts?

The man made his move. He came and immediately fell down before Jesus in the position of humble adoration (Mark 1:40; Luke 5:12).

It was the ultimate standoff—pain in the presence of God. How would Jesus react to an untouchable? What would He say to one who had lived in silent isolation for so long?

Life-Giving Touch

Jesus stopped for the man. He didn't brush him aside. He didn't berate him for not shouting out to warn the crowd. Jesus turned His full attention on the crumpled figure before Him.

Then the man spoke words as humble as the posture he assumed: "Lord, if You are willing, You can make me clean" (Matthew 8:2). It was a statement of pure confidence in Jesus' ability to heal. What was the source of his confidence? How did he know that Jesus had such power? He must have heard about Jesus and His miracles.

The issue was not Jesus' power but rather Jesus' purpose.

Note carefully what the man said to Jesus: "You can make me clean." He wasn't wrestling with whether or not healing was possible. He didn't need any convincing. The issue was not Jesus' *power* but rather Jesus' *purpose*. Was Jesus willing to heal him? Jesus had healed others, but the leper wasn't certain if God's divine purpose included his healing. He didn't assume that Jesus would heal him. Although the leper already knew the authority of Jesus' power, he surrendered to the authority of Jesus' will.

The man took a risk in throwing himself at Jesus' feet. Jesus also took a risk by stopping to meet this man. Jesus was "moved with compassion" (Mark 1:41). Scholars tell us that this is a strong word indicating that Jesus felt a physical reaction in the pit of His stomach. Jesus cared about the man. And because He cared, He acted.

A touch of healing. Then Jesus did something that made everyone gasp. He put out his hand to touch the man. Moses' law forbade touching a leper. Such an act would defile the touching person, not to mention place the person in danger of contagion.

Why would Jesus touch him? He had just given a message in which He flatly stated, "Whoever ... breaks one of the least of these commandments, and teaches men so, shall be called least in the kingdom of heaven" (Matthew 5:19). But this was different. There was no breaking of the law here. By the time Jesus touched this man, he was no longer a leper. The power was in Jesus' will and His word. The healing was instant. It was quicker than the human reflex of reaching out and touching. No law had been violated.

A touch of restoration. The touch also proved that this man was eligible to be included in the community once again. He was now as whole as anyone around. What shocking changes must have taken place before the eyes of onlookers as this distorted mass was transformed in that instant! We can only imagine how startling it was to see a deformed, shriveled, scaly, sore-covered man suddenly stand upright, with perfect arms and legs, with his face smooth and unscarred. Not only was the man's body restored but also his social standing.

A touch of caring. Jesus' touch was also a gesture that revealed something about Jesus. It showed that when Jesus is confronted with suffering, He is willing to get personally involved. His touch displayed deep affection. Jesus touched the one whom everyone, including His disciples, had deemed as an untouchable. Who knows how long this man had gone without human touch? How many nights had he lain awake longing for a handshake or an embrace—from anyone?

There wasn't a moment's hesitation with Jesus. He didn't flinch. No wincing before touching. There was simply and immediately a willing response that revealed one who cared. What a sight it must have been:

They were repulsed; Jesus was responsive.
They were shocked; Jesus was sympathetic.

They moved back; Jesus moved in.
They were horrified; Jesus was glorified!

When Obedience Becomes Difficult

The wonder of the moment was eclipsed by the weight of a command. "See that you tell no one; but go your way, show yourself to the priest, and offer the gift that Moses commanded, as a testimony to them" (Matthew 8:4).

Tell no one? How would that be possible? How could the man keep inside what was without doubt the most wonderful experience of his life?

Why would Jesus make such a demand? It wasn't that He didn't want the man ever to tell anyone about what happened. Rather Jesus wanted the man not to say anything yet. He was first to follow the scriptural requirements. He needed to have a temple priest examine him and declare that this was a bona fide healing miracle. Following this procedure would prove that Jesus had adhered to the Mosaic law. Also, if news of the healing reached the priests before they had a chance to examine the man, they would undoubtedly be a bit hesitant to declare this a miracle.

But this dramatic healing was too much to keep to oneself. The leper's enthusiastic joy over the miracle drove him to tell everyone he met! "But as the man went on his way, he spread the news, telling everyone what had happened to him. As a result, such crowds soon surrounded Jesus that He couldn't enter a town anywhere publicly. He had to stay out in the secluded places, and people from everywhere came to him there" (Mark 1:45, NLT).

What about You?

Are you caught in a hopeless situation, isolated by illness or guilt or pain? Do you also need to meet Jesus up close and receive His life-giving touch? Are you willing to risk everything and come to Jesus, throw yourself at His feet, and ask if He is willing to heal you too?

We can learn a lot about Jesus and ourselves by looking more closely at the two people in the story: Jesus, who is face-to-face with the human condition, and the man, who is face-to-face with the all-powerful God. Exploring these two perspectives will help us gain insight for our own suffering as well as for the suffering of others.

Face-to-Face with the Human Condition

Just as Jesus stepped close to the man and entered his suffering, He is willing to enter your life and touch your pain as well.

Jesus Cares about Your Pain

Ever since the Fall, suffering has been a part of the human condition. Every successive generation has felt its harsh embrace. Everyone suffers, even God's own precious children. As a pastor I see it all around me—both in the lives of people in our congregation as well as in my own life. But not everyone handles it the same way. Thinking about this one night, I decided I would keep track of some of the pain I see on a daily basis. So I made a list of the painful experiences of people I had contact with in that one week. Here's a sampling:

A Saturday evening phone call from the chaplain of a local hospital summoned me to the emergency room. Thirty minutes later I arrived to find a couple from our church holding in their arms the lifeless body of their three-day-old baby girl.

The next day we were informed that my wife's grandmother had died in the night from her long and tormenting battle with cancer.

The same week I dealt with a family in which one child had been molested and another abused.

I received a letter from missionaries I had just visited overseas. Nationals who were angry at the missionaries' preaching of the gospel were threatening their lives.

I counseled a couple who were going through a divorce after twenty years of marriage.

I counseled a young couple who had been living together but were not married to each other. During the counseling session the woman admitted that she was still married—to another man!

A close friend of ours was involved in a serious accident and was lying in the hospital in barely stable condition.

Distraught parents approached me after church about how to handle their daughter's predicament. She had been arrested that week in another state—for prostitution.

The presence of pain in our world challenges some people's ideas about God. But in this story we see Jesus walking in the midst of that world and dealing directly with pain. He didn't run away. He didn't gasp or hide His face. He looked firmly and directly into the eyes of a suffering man and ministered to his need.

And think of it. Jesus didn't try to avoid pain in His own life. He took on human flesh. He would suffer immensely the cruel torture of a Roman cross.

Jesus wanted this diseased man to understand that he was not cursed but loved—by God. Jesus' words "I am willing" were immediate, showing His eagerness to meet the man's need.

Your pain is no different. God sees the way your life's road has twisted and turned and where you are right now. He knows your pain, your anxieties, your depression, and your burdens. What's more He enters into them with you. Isaiah said of God: "In all their suffering he also suffered, and he personally rescued them. In his love and mercy he redeemed them. He lifted them up and carried them through all the years" (Isaiah 63:9, NLT). Just as Jesus promised never to leave or forsake His people, He will stand with you, caring for you in your pain (Matthew 28:20; Hebrews 13:5).

Jesus Sees Your Individual Need
Most often when Jesus preached or healed, He attracted a sizable crowd; sometimes thousands pressed around Him. Such was the case in this story: "Great multitudes followed Him" (Matthew 8:1). But I am impressed with how Jesus stops to notice and help one man whom everyone else would just as soon ignore.

Jesus saw beyond the crowd to an individual, to that person's individual need. We've seen Jesus' attention to the individual before. We've seen Him go out of His way to meet the Samaritan woman at the well.

This is true because Jesus had a single vision that impelled his philosophy of life. His purpose statement was simple: "The

97

Son of Man has come to seek and to save that which was lost" (Luke 19:10). Clear, concise, and full of comfort, isn't it? He was to be the Messiah of the lost and found. He would be about the business of locating individuals who had lost their way in life and direct them to the path of His eternal kingdom. He was the shepherd who left His flock of ninety-nine to find that one lost lamb (Matthew 18:12). So we are not surprised when this time He turns His attention away from the enthusiastic crowd and toward the leper. Unaffected by the throng, Jesus was motivated by this one whose heart was fixed on Him. Nothing gets Jesus' attention quicker than a heart full of worship.

We live a world filled with billions of people. Feelings of isolation and abandonment are becoming more common. Big cities filled with throngs of people destroy our sense of connectedness. People experience loneliness and depression as a result of being just another face in the crowd. But God knows who you are. You are not just another number to God. He knows your situation, your personal needs as an individual. What's more, He cares about you deeply.

God knows who you are. You are not just another number to God.

It helps to personalize your relationship to God. Paul the apostle did. He knew that Jesus died for the world and that everyone and anyone could experience new life. But he made that truth his own. To the Galatian Christians Paul wrote: "I was put to death on the cross with Christ, and I do not live anymore—it is Christ who lives in me. I still live in my body, but I live by faith in the Son of God who loved me and gave himself to save me" (Galatians 2:20, NCV, emphasis added).

Yes, Jesus Christ died for the sins of the whole world, but He also died for you personally. He knows more about you and what makes you tick than you do about yourself. The God who is aware of the billions of beating hearts worldwide is the God who also cares about you. Even in the midst of the crowds— when you drive on packed freeways and when you ride in overcrowded subways—Jesus sees you. Even though you may share an apartment building with thousands of others whose names you don't know and you may feel overwhelmed by the size of the city you live in, Jesus knows your name, and He knows your need. You're in His care.

God's Plan Includes Your Whole Person

Jesus came into the world to save people from their sins. That was the plan from the beginning (Matthew 1:21). Jesus came to bring salvation from sin to a world whose greatest need was forgiveness. But He did more.

The very fact that Jesus healed people's physical ailments indicates His concern for the whole person. Jesus poignantly demonstrated this when He reached out His hand to touch the leper. Like millions of God's servants who would follow in His footsteps to care for the sick and afflicted, Jesus knew the power of human touch.

In the excellent book *Fearfully and Wonderfully Made*, physician and author Paul Brand, along with Philip Yancey, reviews the importance of human touch:

> I think back on how Jesus acted while inhabiting a human body on Earth. He reached out his hand and touched the eyes of the blind, the skin of the person with leprosy, and the legs of the cripple. When a woman pressed against him in a crowd to tap into the healing energy she hoped was there, He felt the drain of that energy, stopping the noisy crowd and asking, "Who touched Me?" His touch transmitted power.
>
> I have sometimes wondered why Jesus so frequently touched the people He healed, many of whom must have been unattractive, obviously diseased, unsanitary, smelly. With His power He easily could have waved a magic wand. In fact a wand would have reached more people than a touch. He could have divided the crowd into affinity groups and organized His miracles—paralyzed people over there, feverish people here, people with leprosy there—raising His hands to heal each group efficiently, *en masse*. But He chose not to. Jesus' mission was not primarily a crusade against disease ... but a ministry to individual people, some of whom happened to have a disease. He wanted those people, one by one, to feel His love, warmth, and His

99

full identification with them. Jesus knew He could not readily demonstrate love to a crowd, for love usually involves touching.[3]

What a vital lesson for God's people to learn! In a world oozing with suffering, our theology must be coupled with compassion. It must include much more than just handing people a gospel tract. Making contact with hurting people, touching them with a hand that says "I care" will go a lot further than mere words. The right mix is creed and conduct. The best response is doctrine and duty. Hurting people need compassion. They are not going to find it on a television program or from a slick piece of direct mail from a megaministry. They must be touched by people, by the local church, if they are to encounter the power of the God who cares.

Hurting people need compassion.

A homeless woman visited a nearby church to request help. The response was an all too typical one. The pastor promised to pray for her but gave her nothing to help mend her condition. She later wrote this poem to express her view of a church that had refused to extend the touch of God to her.

I was hungry, and you formed a humanities group to discuss my hunger.
I was imprisoned, and you crept off quietly to your chapel and prayed for my release.
I was naked, and in your mind you debated the morality of my appearance.
I was sick, and you knelt and thanked God for your health.
I was homeless, and you preached to me of the spiritual shelter of the love of God.
I was lonely, and you left me alone to pray for me.
You seemed so holy, so close to God; but I am still very hungry—and lonely—and cold.[4]

Face-to-Face with the All-Powerful God

Not only was Jesus willing to step close and come face-to-face with suffering humanity, but we must be willing to meet with Him, to come face-to-face with His power and love.

Be Willing to Worship

Physical suffering creates an immense preoccupation. A person experiencing it finds it difficult to think about anything else. This leper displayed a different set of priorities in his approach to Jesus. His first move was not a request to alleviate his suffering; it was an act of worship. Both his posture and his words expressed his reverence. He acknowledged Jesus as *Lord*. This word is used more than six hundred times in the New Testament to indicate the recognition of Deity.

Amazing isn't it? A man with so much physical discomfort is *worshiping*. The one with so much emotional baggage from rejection is worshiping! Why? What ever would drive a person in that condition to praise God? Sure, he was hoping for a healing (which he did receive), but there's more. Even before he was healed, he worshiped. This was not an after-the-fact act. His adoration was not contingent on blessing; he worshiped before the blessing even came.

Worship is a response to who God is rather than what God does.

In a leper colony on the Caribbean island of Tobago, short-term mission volunteer Jack Hinton was leading music for a worship service. He asked the lepers to request their favorite songs. After several were played, he asked for one last song. Just then a woman whose back had been to the pulpit the whole time turned around. Hers was the most hideous face Hinton had ever seen. He was shocked. The woman's nose and ears were entirely gone. Her lips had almost rotted away.

But this woman lifted her hand—a hand that no longer had fingers— and asked, "Can we sing 'Count Your Many Blessings'?" It was too much for the young pastor. He quickly left the service, overcome with emotion. "Hey Jack," spouted another volunteer, "I guess you'll never be able to sing that song again, will you?" "Oh yes, I will," responded Hinton. "But I'll never sing it the same way again!"[5]

Worship is a response to who God is rather than what God does. He is worthy by His very nature. He is deserving of praise by His exalted position as God. The leper, either by observing Jesus or by hearing His messages, somehow knew that Jesus was deserving of worship. This bent and possibly deformed man was able to so delight in the presence of Christ that his praise overshadowed his own condition.

Don't let your personal pain ever diminish the need to give God His rightful place in your life. Don't allow the haunting questions regarding the problem of evil and suffering to rob God of worship and you of the joy it gives. A good model for approaching God is the one provided by this leper. Worship first, and then get around to the other items, including any requests.

Don't Separate God's Power from His Purpose

Jesus performed many powerful acts while He was on Earth. So many people in Israel were healed. But we are still left with the uncomfortable truth that not everyone was healed. The apostles were confronted by a crippled man who had been at the gate of the temple since he was a child (Acts 3). Yet Jesus had ministered throughout that temple area when He was in Jerusalem. Why then didn't Jesus heal the man? Why was he left in that condition until later?

The issue boils down to God's sovereign purposes, and the leper in this story understood that. His wasn't a demand for healing as much as it was a humble submission to Jesus' will. "If you are willing" were his opening remarks. He was bold in his approach but not brash. He didn't presume on the will of God. He came humbly, allowing Jesus to express His sovereignty. He didn't rant and rave to stake his claim in health. He was not like some, who insist, "It is not God's will for me to be sick, so God must heal me." No, rather, it was his choice to surrender to the Master's choice. The man's attitude suggests that if it had not been Jesus' will to heal him, he would take that as a divine verdict—and live with it.

I've been both shocked and amused to hear of some people who claim that Christians have the authority and the divine right to demand healing from God: "I claim it, I demand it, Lord. You must do it!" Where's the humility in that? Where's the sovereignty of God in that? God must do nothing unless He chooses to. I can still remember hearing one minister as he trotted across my television screen saying to his audience, "You don't know what power you have within you. You can make the world into anything you choose. Yes, whatever you want it to be." Really? I certainly hope not. I look around at a world that has done just that, and it's not a pretty picture! The leper's concern for his own healing was second only to his primary concern for God's glory. He had confidence in Jesus' power, but he had reverence for Jesus' will.

If you need a healing touch from God, be bold, like the leper. Approach Jesus. Tell Him your need. But also be humble, recognizing that Jesus is Lord. He is sovereign. He knows what is best. Submit yourself to His purposes, His will.

Evangelize with Discernment

Jesus plainly told the leper to be careful about how he told people about his healing. He was first to go to Jerusalem, show himself to the priests, and make the proper sacrifices. It was strange that Jesus told the man not to tell anyone until he had seen the priests, but this was not the only time Jesus told someone not to tell others about the miracle (see also Matthew 9:30; 12:16; 16:20; 17:9; and Mark 5:43).

We can understand the man's enthusiasm, which turned him into a walking advertisement for Jesus' power. Jesus knew that miracles can produce excitement, but people don't always connect the dots enough to let these miracles produce life-changing faith.

Excitement is understandable, yet Jesus' command brings up an important consideration. We must evangelize with discernment. Because this man told everyone he could find about what happened to him, Jesus' ministry became restricted by crowd frenzy so that He could no longer publicly enter a city. He was confined to the outlying, unpopulated areas (Mark 1:45).

Excitement without discernment can result in confinement of the very message we're trying to promote. The message requires wisdom from the messenger. We can sometimes overwhelm people with the Good News or share it in a way that will leave them unresponsive. We must be wise in our timing, consideration of the person's need, tone of voice, and the words we use.

An evangelist once came to a small town to hold a revival meeting. He was there for a few days and wanted to mail a letter. Leaving his hotel, he went in search of the post office.

Walking across the street, the preacher ran into a young boy selling newspapers, so he politely asked the boy for directions. The evangelist thanked the boy and then quickly said in a self-important tone, "Hey, you're a pretty smart fellow. Do you know who I am?" The evangelist straightened his frame and gave his best profile, thinking that the boy would recognize him as the famous evangelist.

"Nope, I don't," said the boy.

The minister, his voice growing louder, more sanctimonious, then explained that he was the man everyone in town was talking about and coming to see night after night in the revival tent. Then the preacher said, "If you come tonight, I'll show you the way to Heaven."

If we want to win some, we must be winsome!

"No thank you, sir," the courteous boy replied. "I don't think I could take your word for it. You don't even know the way to the post office!"[6]

The boy's response illustrates why a lot of people don't listen to some Christians. No one is interested in taking direction from someone who would make them uncomfortable to be around—for all eternity! If we want to win some, we must be winsome!

What a marvelous combination we have in this story: a hurting world and a helping Savior! His words were fresh, and He astonished the crowds with His authority. His works were merciful, and He astonished the crowds with His compassionate individuality. An unidentified outcast became a recipient of pure grace in a wonderful instant. The God of restoration touched an isolated man and made him into an enthusiastic evangelist.

You may feel (for whatever reason) like an outcast. Maybe it was your parents' divorce that left you lonely and afraid. Perhaps you've always been considered by some to be socially awkward, and you are afraid to risk deeper relationships. It could be that your appearance or personality tends to push you out of popular places. All of those experiences are painful.

Let Jesus enter into your painful place. Be assured that He cares for you individually. Allow Him to care for you personally. The best place to start is to pause—right now—and worship

Him. You'll find that the most elevating place you could ever be while in your pain is in bowed adoration before God.

— —

FOR REFLECTION AND DISCUSSION

1. As a basis for a meditation, go on a mental journey with me: You are living in the Milky Way, one of billions of galaxies that make up the universe. The Milky Way contains several billion stars and measures roughly 70,000 light-years in diameter. The sun, our nearest star, is 93 million miles away, and the next nearest neighbor star, Alpha Centauri, is 25 trillion miles away. The sun is 860,000 miles in diameter, large enough to fit 1.2 million planets the size of Earth inside it. Earth moves through space at 45,000 mph and is home to about six billion people at present. Of all those creatures, God knows your name, your problems, and your pain. He wants you to experience His comfort. Read over Psalm 8 and pray the truths found there into your life this week.

2. Describe a time when someone embraced you or touched you in a healing way. How can healthy human touch communicate God's love?

3. If your life is particularly difficult at the moment, how can you worship God in the midst of the pain? What can you do to tell Jesus that you submit to His sovereign will?

4. We live in a culture that thrives on creature comfort and sees pain not only as a major inconvenience but also as something to be avoided at all costs. How have you seen God use suffering in good ways?

5. How can God use your life to minister healing to hurting people? Consider getting involved in the following: supporting a Christian relief organization that helps rebuild torn nations or cities; visiting people in a cancer ward or hospice unit; going with a church group to a soup kitchen, homeless shelter, or prison.

SEVEN

The Power of His Word

A Desperate Father and His Dying Son

So Jesus came again to Cana of Galilee where He had made the water wine. And there was a certain nobleman whose son was sick at Capernaum. When he heard that Jesus had come out of Judea into Galilee, he went to Him and implored Him to come down and heal his son, for he was at the point of death. Then Jesus said to him, "Unless you people see signs and wonders, you will by no means believe."

The nobleman said to Him, "Sir, come down before my child dies!"

Jesus said to him, "Go your way; your son lives." So the man believed the word that Jesus spoke to him, and he went his way. And as he was now going down, his servants met him and told him, saying, "Your son lives!"

Then he inquired of them the hour when he got better. And they said to him, "Yesterday at the seventh hour the fever left him." So the father knew that it was at the same hour in which Jesus said to him, "Your son lives." And he himself believed, and his whole household (John 4:46-53).

W hen I was a kid, I was always skinny. More precisely, I was a rail. I knew I could never make it on the school football team, and trying out for wrestling would be a joke. I could have chosen to involve myself in golf or long-distance running, which were more better suited to my body type, but the truth is, I wanted to be a superhero. My older brothers were celebrated football heroes in their schools. Why couldn't I be more like them? I tried to bulk up by eating more at meals, but it didn't work for me. I even went so far as to drink cartons of pure cream just to gain extra weight. But it just seemed I was consigned to a lanky frame.

I'm still lanky, but I occasionally put in time at the gym to build my muscles. I try not to take it too seriously. And maybe that's the problem. Maybe I'm not serious enough. Looking around at others, some of whom look like people straight out of Greek mythology, I know that these people have been committed to the long and painful process of muscle development. It didn't happen for them in a week, a month, or even a single year. They've logged in the hours of pain and sweat, and it shows. They know that building muscles requires development.

The story of the nobleman is the story of a man whose faith muscles would be stretched and developed through his unusual encounter with Jesus.

A Government Official on an Unofficial Mission

We don't know a great deal about the man from the passage, but historical records give us some clues. The Greek word for "nobleman" is *basilikos*, from which we get our English word *basilica*. While the word is usually used to describe a medieval church, it also was associated with the court of a king or ruler. Thus, the term *nobleman* literally means "one who belongs to a king."

Most biblical scholars believe that this man was a person of high standing, perhaps a courtier or king's officer in the ruling court of Herod Antipas, one of the governing authorities of Israel at the time. This Herod, a tetrarch, ruled one quarter of Israel—the Galilee region. Given the nobleman's title and association with the Herodian dynasty, we know that he in some way helped the court in governing the region of ancient Galilee. He was in society's upper crust.

The heart of the story isn't so much that this was a royal representative as much as he was a desperate dad. His son, on his deathbed, was in the Galilean town of Capernaum. The nobleman probably didn't live there; he most likely lived in the western area of the Lake of Galilee in the town of Tiberius, which Herod appropriated as his own royal town.[1] Almost certainly the man had taken his son by boat from Tiberius to Capernaum, expecting to find Jesus there since He had made Capernaum His base of operations early on (Matthew 9:1; Mark 2:1).

But Jesus was not in Capernaum when the nobleman arrived. When he entered the city, he learned that Jesus had gone to Cana, a village to the southwest. By this time the man's son was too sick to travel any farther. Leaving the boy in Capernaum, the official set out in desperation toward Cana, a twenty-five mile trek by foot!

This man sought out Jesus because he had nowhere else to go. His personal situation seemed hopeless. His son was barely clinging to life, and like any devoted dad, he was bent on seeing his son cured—by whatever means.

The passage suggests that the nobleman's faith was not fully developed yet. He obviously had heard enough about Jesus to have come to Him, but he was not a believer at this point. His faith in Jesus at this point was perhaps merely shallow and frantic.

But it was a start, and the man's faith would soon have an opportunity to grow. Like a skillful coach, Jesus would take this man through his paces and begin to tone his spiritual muscles.

A Desperate Father Gets a Faith-Lift

Arriving in Cana after his long, fatiguing journey and still filled with adrenaline, the government official went straight to Jesus. When he found Him, he "implored Him to come down and heal his son, for he was at the point of death" (John 4:47). There's a lot of tension built into those words. Despair drips from his plea. It must have been a wrenching experience to have his child hover between life and death.

It's at this point that the faith-building exercise begins. There are three distinct stages in the building of this nobleman's faith. As each stage unfolds, Jesus offers him a new challenge. Like a trainer who adds an extra weight in his trainee's routine to bulk up the muscles, Jesus will increase the pressure until the man's faith is well toned. The gain will be well worth the pain.

Stage One: Faith in a Power

What drove the man to Jesus? The nobleman did not come to Jesus because He had a proven track record of healing people. This was still too early in His ministry for that. Although Jesus had turned water into wine at a wedding party in Cana (John 2:1-11), this man knew nothing of Jesus' power to heal the human body.

In his desperation, the official probably came to Jesus on a hunch that He could somehow "work His magic" on his son. This man's faith is not in Jesus personally; it is in Jesus' reputation of being a miracle worker. The man had no commitment to the person of Christ or to the spreading of His message. He had simply heard that the same Jesus who had once worked wonders in Cana was back in that town. *Maybe He's here for a repeat performance, the official may have reasoned. Perhaps this time rather than turning water into wine, Jesus would transform sickness into health!* When the man came to Jesus, he had a most primitive faith—faith in a power.

Jesus sensed this. His first words to the man are, "Unless you people see signs and wonders, you will by no means believe" (John 4:48). Those were sharp words; they sound almost too abrupt for the Jesus we're familiar with in the New Testament. But it was a statement meant both for the crowd gathered around as well as for the nobleman himself.

For the crowd it was a rebuke. Jesus knew that many of the people of Cana who had gathered around this sick boy's father had come just to see the "fireworks." They wanted to see some mighty display of power before they would believe. He had turned water into wine. What would He do this time? The rebuke was meant to stop such spiritual thrill seeking.

For the man the statement was both a reprimand and an enticement for him to press further. It was designed to work the flabby muscles of this nobleman's faith. With an arrow of tender rebuke, Jesus took the nobleman's weak, primitive faith and drew it out to a stronger expression.

Stage Two: Faith in a Promise

The man wasn't slowed by Jesus' challenge. Remember he was desperate. As Jesus throws more weight on the bench press, this man lifts it. He constrained Jesus further. "The nobleman said to Him, 'Sir, come down before my child dies!'" (John 4:49). He wouldn't let go. He wouldn't be turned away. He had come this far believing something could happen, and he wouldn't just leave after hearing a reproof about the proper motivation of faith! So he pleads more. "Please come and fix my boy." It's already starting to work. The man with the desperate faith in a higher power is now face-to-face with Jesus, the man with power to spare.

The nobleman was seeking Jesus, but Jesus was also seeking him. Jesus knew the shape this inconsolable man was in. He was aware that his son was near death. He knew his faith was weak. Jesus also knew that there was something greater than physical life and temporary healing. Jesus wanted

The nobleman was seeking Jesus, but Jesus was also seeking him.

this official to know about deeper spiritual realities. Soon he would. What a picture—a father with a dying son in the presence of the Son sent to die by His Father. Jesus had the situation sovereignly, securely in control.

Jesus responded to the man's plea with another abrupt statement: "Go your way; your son lives" (v. 50). A command and a promise. A beautiful promise indeed, but it wasn't what the man expected—or asked. Yes, this father wanted nothing else than to have his son cured. But he wanted Jesus to "come down" with him to Capernaum and perform this deed.

There was daring challenge in Jesus' voice as he ordered the man to go to his son. Why did Jesus send the man away? Why didn't He walk with the man to Capernaum? Jesus would have had a wonderful opportunity to talk with this man about spiritual things as they traveled together. Jesus could have spoken with the crowd along the way. He could have arrived at the house, healed the boy, and used it as an opportunity to teach many things to many people.

But He didn't.

Why not? I believe that Jesus wanted to strengthen the man's faith in a way that would forever benefit his spiritual life. Thus, He threw more weight on the trainee. "No, I won't come. That's too easy. You go. You'll find your son healed."

Jesus gave the man nothing more than words. Jesus simply, calmly spoke a promise. But what a promise it was! Could it be true? Would the man act on it? That would certainly be a truer expression of faith than just a cry for help.

Jesus understood what made this government official tick. As a royal courtier, this man had authority and power. Jesus knew the man was used to being in control. He was used to giving commands to other people and having them obeyed. He knew how to get a job done. But on this occasion this powerful man had to submit to someone else's power, to someone else's command.

Imagine for a minute what might have happened if Jesus had done what the official had asked. What if He had promptly stopped all of His activity to follow the man twenty-five miles to Capernaum and perform a healing service? Rather than build the man's faith, that action might have squelched it. The royal official might have concluded that Jesus was just another resource that he could control, another person who would follow his command. Oh, the official certainly would have been excited for a while after the healing. His response would have been emotional, but eventually he might have concluded that Jesus had healed his son simply because He had followed the nobleman's instructions, like anyone else. That would only have increased the man's faith in himself.

Jesus wasn't about to let that happen. This very important and powerful man stood helpless and dependent. It's where he needed to be. He had been used to giving commands most of his career. Now he's been given one. "Go your way!" Would he submit? Would he rise to the next level of faith? Would the combination command-promise be enough for him to act on?

The man responded to the challenge: "So the man believed the word that Jesus spoke to him, and he went his way" (v. 50).

Notice the change. He believed what Jesus spoke. He trusted His word. The promise was enough. This wasn't the same kind of faith the man started with. He hadn't even met Jesus before this. He had come because he believed there was a *power* at work in Him. To him that power was inexplicable but essential for his need. Now it's different. This time the man believed the *promise* that Jesus gave him and was willing to obey His command.

Jesus gave the man nothing concrete. He didn't write a prescription for the latest drug. He didn't give the man a sign. But He gave him a promise and a command.

Without having anything to hold on to except Jesus' promise, the man believed. He turned on his heels and left. Deep down inside, he knew his son was better. His muscles of faith were being toned.

Stage Three: Faith in a Person
Already the man who had come to Jesus with primitive faith was leaving with a more substantial kind. And now, coming closer to his son's sickbed in Capernaum, he was about to get another "faith-lift." The journey would have taken about five or six hours. Imagine what was going through the father's mind as he walked. Finally he was close enough for the townspeople of Capernaum to notice his arrival. When his servants heard that he was back in town, they rushed to him to break the astonishing news: "Your son lives!" (John 4:51).

How the father's heart must have raced to hear his servants' words, which echoed Jesus' promise. He made the connection immediately. "Then he inquired of them the hour when he got better. And they said to him, 'Yesterday at the seventh hour the fever left him.' So the father knew that it was at the same hour in which Jesus said to him, 'Your son lives'" (v. 52-53).

There was no doubt about it—the child was alive and very well. The father knew how it happened. And he knew that it happened at exactly the same time that Jesus told him to go home to the cured boy.

The servants had seen the whole episode. They were in the room when the child stirred. They were there when the boy sat up in bed. They felt his forehead and knew the life-threatening fever was gone. And they noted the time of day it occurred. But they had no clue that while they were seeing that little boy get better, their boss was twenty-five miles away believing the promises of Jesus.

Once the royal officer put it all together and understood the sequence of events in this perfectly timed scenario, his faith completed its journey. He ascended to the highest plane of personal faith. This was markedly different from the first two stages. He started with faith in a power. Jesus put him through the spiritual paces to bring him to faith in His spoken promise. Finally he reached the pinnacle—faith in the person of Jesus Christ. "And he himself believed" (v. 53).

The man pieced all the elements together. His faith had been challenged by rebuke, and he persevered. His faith was then challenged by a command, and he acted on it with a stronger faith. Now, realizing what had just occurred and that Jesus had healed his son by just the power of His word, he believed in the fullest sense of the word. But the story of his blossoming faith didn't end there. It was contagious. "And he himself believed, and his whole household" (v. 53).

Others joined this officer in his faith. This dad obviously couldn't keep his joy to himself. We can visualize him enthusiastically recounting the details of his visit with Jesus. His whole family and perhaps even his servants listened and joined him.

This encounter was about more than healing a boy. It was about more than building the faith of a powerful man. This encounter with Jesus resulted in an entire family's—a family connected to the court of Herod—coming to faith in Jesus Christ.

What a beautiful journey the man made. He encountered Jesus and His power to heal. He was face-to-face with Jesus and His word. His shallow faith grew to full surrender to the person of Jesus Christ. The nobleman who served an earthly king now also believed and served the King of kings.

Tips for a Faith-Building Workout

Jesus may be meeting you in a similar way. Maybe you have come to Him, believing somewhat vaguely in His power and asking Him to do certain things. He may have refused to do what you ask and instead commands you to do something else. You feel the pain and the disappointment that He doesn't act the way you expect Him to act, but he asks you to believe His promises.

Like the nobleman, you have a choice. You can allow Jesus to challenge your faith and help you grow, or you can walk away. The choice is yours.

But if you choose to allow Jesus to develop your faith, be prepared for a workout.

Tip #1: Don't Be Afraid of the Pain

You've heard the saying, "No pain, no gain!" In any workout, pain is part of the package. Look at the faces of those who consistently develop their muscles at the gym. Their grimaces reveal the truth. But pain can be our ally in several significant ways.

First, pain awakens our deepest need. We can imagine that the face of the nobleman was painted with anguish. The pain of his son's illness awakened his need. Eventually the pain drove him to find Jesus.

Many people see God as only a last resort. During the normal course of their lives, spiritual things hardly ever cross their minds. They live for the here and now. The hereafter can wait. Most people focus on enjoying life, getting some personal satisfaction, and having their fair share of nice things. That is until the bottom drops out! When something unexpected comes along to upset the status quo, those same people often blame God or run to Him.

God sometimes allows pain in our lives so that we are forced to seek Him. That was the case with the nobleman. His son's illness was in retrospect a blessing. It displaced him from his spiritual oblivion and drove him to Jesus. After encountering Jesus, the man gained not only what he came for—his son's healing—but also what he didn't know he needed—a well-developed faith that led to eternal life for himself and his entire household.

I'm not suggesting that because God uses adversity to bring us to himself that you should expect a truckload of bad things to come your way. But it helps us to remember that God is in control of life's events, and He will sometimes use even the painful events to get our attention so that He can build our faith muscles.

You may find that He will come to you through an illness, a loss, a time of unemployment, or a disappointment. Don't be afraid of these painful circumstances. God can use them to help you grow. As you are confronted with the very thing you fear, you will discover that He'll meet you there and draw you close. David knew that and came to the place of faith where he admitted in prayer, "in faithfulness You have afflicted me" (Psalms 119:75).

One day while sifting through my e-mail, I found this great piece that a friend sent. As I read it, I could immediately relate. Along the same lines of the nobleman's ordeal, it unveils how often God may have to get our attention.

About ten years ago, a young and very successful executive named Josh was traveling down a Chicago neighborhood street. He was going a bit too fast in his sleek, black, twelve-cylinder Jaguar XKE, which was only two months old.

He was watching for kids darting out from between parked cars, and he slowed down. Suddenly he saw something come at him. Whump! A brick sailed through the air and smashed into the Jag's shiny black side door.

Screech! Brakes slammed. Gears ground into reverse, and tires madly spun the Jaguar back to the spot from where the brick had been thrown. Josh jumped out of the car, grabbed the kid, and pushed him up against the parked car. He shouted at the kid, "What was all that about, and who are you?" Building up a head of steam, he went on. "That's my new Jag. That brick you threw is gonna cost you a lot of money. Why did you throw it?"

"Please, mister, please ... I'm sorry! I didn't know what else to do!" pleaded the youngster. "I threw the brick because no one else would stop!" Tears were dripping down the boy's chin as he pointed around the car. "It's my brother, mister," he said. "He rolled off the curb and fell out of his wheelchair, and I can't lift him up." Sobbing, the boy asked the executive, "Would you please help me get him back into his wheelchair? He's hurt, and he's too heavy for me."

Moved beyond words, the young executive tried desperately to swallow the rapidly swelling lump in his throat. Straining, he lifted the boy's brother back into the wheelchair and took out his handkerchief and wiped the scrapes and cuts, checking to see that everything was going to be all right. He then watched the younger brother push the wheelchair down the sidewalk toward their home.

It was a long walk back to the sleek, black, shining, twelve-cylinder Jaguar XKE—a long and slow walk.

Josh never did fix the side door of his Jaguar. He kept the dent to remind him not to go through life so fast that someone has to throw a brick at him to get his attention.

I've dealt with my share of bricks, have you? Each time one comes flying my way, I am somehow reminded that behind each one is the sovereign hand of a loving God, who is trying to make sure I don't stay a bantamweight when it comes to my faith. He wants to make sure that my faith grows. That's a comfort to me. I hope it is to you too.

Second, pain challenges our personal faith. When our status quo is upset, we immediately ask soul-searching questions about what we believe. Pain challenges our view of God. How will we process these questions?

Very often, even for those of us who have been following Jesus for some time, we lose the ability to see clearly. We allow our faith to degenerate from a vibrant one to a distant one.

Suffering can drive us to refocus. Pain awakens us, and we are challenged to see things differently, to trust God in new ways and in a new context.

Alan Redpath knew that from personal experience. The British-born preacher once pastored the Moody Memorial Church in Chicago as well as Charlotte Chapel in Edinburgh, Scotland. His ministry was a bright star in the evangelical sky. But his life changed on September 5, 1964, during a family gathering. Retiring to his study to prepare for a wedding that afternoon, he lost control of his pen while writing. A cerebral hemorrhage rendered him unable to talk, and his right side was paralyzed. He was beginning a long and slow journey. One he had not made before.

Spiritual despair set in. Questions of all sorts erupted in Redpath's mind and lingered for days. During those long days and nights he had time to think about his life and examine the progress he had been making on his spiritual journey. He tells the story this way:

> Then, as I looked back over the corridor of memory at the past twenty-five years of ministry in London, Chicago, and Edinburgh, it seemed a pattern had been developing in my life, which I had imagined was spiritual: namely (to quote a chorus), to "work like any slave for God's own Son." I had never had a regular day off a week, never had time for my family or my children, for I was always too busy in Christian work for that. Sinful man that I am, I had imagined that it was all so spiritual! The Lord showed me that I was putting work before worship. The busyness of a barren life had taken its toll, and my priorities had become all wrong, even my quiet time and my Bible had become less disciplined than in former years, and this had all built up tremendous pressure in the ministry which God had given me.
>
> Furthermore, I saw that I had become so proud of being orthodox in doctrine—a sound, conservative evangelical. But alas, not nearly so concerned about my obedience to the doctrine which I preached. How desperately easy it is to demand a greater measure of obedience from a congregation than one is prepared to give in one's own life. How humiliating to make such a discovery! Yet, further still, I realized that I had become much more concerned with the knowledge of truth than the knowledge of God; much more interested in turning to my Bible to find neat outlines for sermons than to seek for food for my own soul. Paul's great ambition was "that I may know Him" (Phil. 3:10), not "that I may know truth." The Lord Jesus had become a much more theoretical and doctrinal Christ than a saving, experimental Christ day by day in my life.[2]

I must sadly admit my own failure in this. There have been times when I approached God as if He were some celestial vending machine dispensing what I thought I needed at the time. I wanted to experience the higher power rather than the

118

power of the Most High. In my mind I was, after all, the center of the universe. Everything revolved around me, and I wanted God to bless me! My life during those times was simply out of focus. Pain helps to clarify the purpose for our existence.

Tip #2: Focus Your Faith on Specific Promises
Generic faith is powerless. The nobleman came to Jesus because he believed there was power to be found in Him. But it wasn't until he placed his trust in Jesus' promise that he discovered power.

It's fashionable today to worship a nondescript god. It's vogue to strip Deity of any personality and ascribe generic power to a vague, genderless, and nameless being. Multitudes flock to worship at the altars of the supernatural and the paranormal. It's not really God whom many people trust but rather the "god concept."

Unfortunately, many people who willingly admit to a higher power care only to experience the *force* without caring about the *source*. Their motives are purely pragmatic and self-serving: they have a need, and they want to have it met. The approach is simple: "I have a problem. Give me whatever it takes to fix it!" In their quest for answers, they may try any and everything.

Individuals are not the only ones who try this shotgun approach to faith. I once saw a faith statement produced by a congregation that identified itself as a church:

> We affirm the inseparable oneness of God and ourselves, the realization of which comes through spiritual intuition. The implications are that we can reproduce the divine perfection in our body, emotions, and all of our external affairs. We affirm that God is within us and we are one with God and we love one another. We affirm that our mental states carry forward into manifestation and become our experience through the creative law of cause and effect....

As I read the information about the church, I learned that they offered everything from Raja Yoga workshops to self-discovery meditation classes. While this group believe in

119

the idea of a higher power, they seem primarily interested in controlling their own lives rather than in knowing and loving God. This is the approach of primitive faith; it's the groping of those who seek but who have not yet found. It is the faith of the child who instinctively knows there is someone or something out there and hopes one day to discover it. It is the belief of the agnostic who acknowledges some cosmic "superessence" but isn't sure just what it is yet.

While generic faith is powerless, specific faith is powerful. When the nobleman implored Jesus to heal his son, Jesus gave him a specific command attached to a specific promise: "Go your way; your son lives." The man believed in a specific way, and the results were powerful. When we trust in specific commands of Scripture, which are God's revealed will, the muscles of our faith strengthen.

"Seeing is believing" says the old American proverb, but Jesus shows that we must believe first and then we will see His powerful work. The nobleman was challenged to believe without seeing, and he did by grabbing hold of Jesus' words as if they were his life preserver.

The late scholar William Barclay said of faith: "It is of the very essence of faith that we should believe that what Jesus says is true. So often we have a kind of vague, wistful longing that the promises of Jesus should be true. The only way to enter into them is to believe in them with the clutching intensity of a drowning man."[3] This official's faith was more than wistful; it was immovable, and it was powerful.

But learning to trust isn't easy. It wasn't easy for the nobleman to turn around and travel for another six hours just because he was told everything would be all right. It seems absurd. Indeed it would be if the one making the promise were just a mere man. But because the nobleman sensed that Jesus had the authority and was therefore trustworthy, the man left.

He was learning to lean on Jesus. He was learning what telephone repair people are taught when they're trained to climb telephone poles. The climbers are outfitted with two pieces of special equipment: spiked shoes, which allow them to get a firm footing on the pole, and a harness, which wraps around both their body and the pole. Learning to use the harness is the hard part. In order for it to give support, climbers must learn to lean back, placing their full body weight outward against the belt.

It's as difficult as it sounds. It goes against the grain of the climbers to lean away from the pole as they climb. Their natural tendency is to lean forward and hang on to what they can see. But that's a mistake. If the workers lean forward into the pole, there isn't sufficient tension to keep them in place.

Eventually, climbers learn that the safest recourse is to lean back into the harness, trusting the tension to hold them. By learning to go against their instincts, the repairpersons learn to climb the poles successfully.

The nobleman learned quickly. He leaned completely on the promise of Jesus Christ even though everything inside him must have been screaming, "This is crazy." When he did, his primitive faith was strengthened. He went from the "lightweight" kind of faith to the "lean-back" kind. The willingness to trust Jesus' spoken word proved it. With each step he took back to Capernaum, he was "bulking up" his spiritual physique.

Sometimes we feel as if we are suspended high on a telephone pole, and we need to get down. It feels scary to lean back and trust in God's promises. But when we lean toward the pole instead, we start to slide down. After a few painful slips we're faced with the inevitable—trust the harness; lean back hard on it. When we place our weight properly on the harness of God's specific promises, we find that we can move to safety.

Dwight L. Moody, evangelist of the nineteenth century, once remarked, "I prayed for faith and thought that some day faith would come down and strike me like lightning. But faith did not seem to come. One day I read in the tenth chapter of Romans, 'Faith cometh by hearing, and hearing by the Word of God.' I had up to this time closed my Bible and prayed for faith. I now opened my Bible and began to study, and faith has been growing ever since."[4]

How can your faith become specific? What are some specific promises God may be asking you to believe in your situation? Is He asking you to trust that He will be with you, no matter what (see Deuteronomy 31:6, 8)? Is He asking you to believe that He is in control, even though things in your life seem very out of control (see Genesis 45:5-8; 50:20; Romans 8:28)? Is He challenging you to trust that He will take care of your enemies (see Psalm 94:1; Romans 12:19; Hebrews 10:30)? Is He reminding you to entrust your children's future—rocky as it seems—to Him (see Proverbs 22:6; Luke 11:15-24; Ephesians 6:4)? Has He been prompting you to stop worrying so much about the future that He promised to unfold (see Matthew 6:25-34)? Learn to make such promises your own. Lean hard into them. They will keep you from sliding down the splintery pole of uncertainty.

Tip #3: Allow God to Use Your Spiritual Muscles
The spiritual muscles that you will develop each time you lean hard on God's promises will pay off. Not only will you learn to trust God personally with the deepest matters of your life, but others will learn to trust Him too. Faith is contagious. When the nobleman believed, the members of his household were affected, and they also believed. The nobleman's spiritual muscles became instruments for God to touch others.

My friend Ross Rhodes from Charlotte, North Carolina, tells the heartwarming story of his visit to Bosnia one Christmas. He was there helping to distribute shoe boxes that had been packed by American families. Each family had packed boxes with pencils, crayons, a book, a toy—things children anywhere in the world would like.

Ross thought he was in Bosnia to give something to needy children; and he was. But God also wanted to strengthen his spiritual muscles, as well as the muscles of other people who would witness one scene.

While Ross and others were distributing the gifts in a refugee ward of a Bosnian hospital, he came to a boy who had suffered the effects of an explosion and was now blind. Ross was feeling some anxiety for the boy. What would a blind child do with a book or a pencil? The contents of the box might be worthless to him. The experience was sure to be anticlimactic to say the least.

Ross inched his way to the bed and saw the look of anticipation on the boy's face. With a box in his hand, a lump in his throat, and a prayer in his heart, Ross gave the box to the boy and was ready to explain that the people who packed the gift at least had good intentions.

Ross was stunned by what he saw when the boy opened the box. There on top was a Sony Walkman, complete with headphones, batteries, and cassette tapes of praise music. The gift could not have been better planned or better timed. A blind boy in Bosnia got the gift that met his unique needs—a gift that ministered to his ears rather than his eyes!

God's timing is impeccable. Ross could have picked up any number of gifts from any one of the many piles in the room that day. But he didn't. He chose the right one at the right time—one that was packed months before by someone in another part of the world. Perhaps that family prayed, "Oh, Lord, show us what we can put in that box that will be a blessing to the right person at the right time." They would have no way of knowing in advance who would receive the gift. Months later it would be unloaded by volunteers in another country and given to just the right boy at just the right time in his life. And that boy's faith in God would get an extra special boost! So would Ross's. So would everyone else's in that room that day.

The faith that grows inside of you as you experience God's faithfulness will give you spiritual bulk. As you tell others about it, as others see and hear God's work through you, you become the needed instrument to bolster their *faith* in God. Your influence may be, like the nobleman's, confined to only your household. You may not reach the whole world like the Apostle Paul or an entire region like the Samaritan woman. That isn't the issue though. As you face the trials and the pressures of life and learn the lessons of leaning hard on God's character and promises, your faith will blossom, and others will see its beauty and be changed.

FOR REFLECTION AND DISCUSSION

1. Think of an episode of suffering you have experienced. Describe how suffering has awakened your need to depend on God; driven you toward a greater submission to God's will; produced a greater compassion toward others; and made you more like Jesus.

2. Think of someone who lives in the bantamweight class of "faith in a power." What is that person's level of confidence and assurance in life? Does that person seem to have solid answers for the future? Why is seeking the force without knowing the source dangerous?

3. Look up the following passages, and write in your own words the place of faith in your life.

Deuteronomy 1:31-32
Psalm 119:66
Matthew 6:30
Matthew 9:28-29
Mark 9:23-24
John 14:1
Acts 14:9-10
Romans 10:17
1 Corinthians 2:5
Galatians 2:16

4. In what ways is God challenging your faith? How are you responding? What specific promises can you cling to as you face this challenge?

5. What three Scripture promises have you seen fulfilled in your life? How has your faith developed when they were?

6. What is the difference between "faith in faith" and "faith in God"? What different results does each kind of faith produce?

7. Have you ever seen powerful faith in action? Whose was it? How did it affect you and anyone else who watched it being exercised?

8. How is God using your spiritual muscles to touch other people? Are you willing to let Him tone your muscles even more?

EIGHT

The Power of His Love

God's Love Invades the IRS

As Jesus passed on from there, He saw a man named Matthew sitting at the tax office. And He said to him, "Follow Me." So he arose and followed Him.

Now it happened, as Jesus sat at the table in the house, that behold, many tax collectors and sinners came and sat down with Him and His disciples. And when the Pharisees saw it, they said to His disciples, "Why does your Teacher eat with tax collectors and sinners?"

When Jesus heard that, He said to them, "Those who are well have no need of a physician, but those who are sick. But go and learn what this means: 'I desire mercy and not sacrifice.' For I did not come to call the righteous, but sinners, to repentance" (Matthew 9:9-13).

Virginia's eyes radiated with hope. She stood next to the one person she had always wanted to marry. And it was finally happening. Love was powerful as this young couple exchanged marriage vows. Soft melodies enhanced a picture-perfect ceremony that had been rehearsed for days, planned for months, and anticipated for years. I was the officiating pastor at this magnificent service. Mark and Virginia first met in seventh grade and never dated anyone else. Now they were being joined for life. What are the odds?

Mark was raised in a home where Christ reigned supreme and biblical values were not compromised. Since the day he was born, his parents prayed for just the right girl to marry their only son—a young woman strongly rooted in the faith.

However, Virginia came from a home where intellectual freedom reigned and religion was scorned. It would have seemed that Mark and Virginia were completely incompatible. But they were getting married. Mark and his parents remember the day when Virginia admitted that intellectual freedom wasn't enough and they had led her in a prayer to receive Jesus Christ. What are the odds?

Odds don't matter in real life. Success comes from seeing past the practical and into the potential. I looked at this twenty something couple and wondered about the potential yet to come. What would they do with their lives? What turns in life's road would they take together? What would their love accomplish? They had always seen the potential of their life together. God had always known that potential and was now weaving their lives into a unit. As I pondered that moment, I kept thinking, *Love sees the potential.*

Mark placed on Virginia's finger the ring dotted with tiny diamonds. Those diamonds represented the potential of this young couple. Behind the resplendent glory of those jewels is a long and hard development. After ages of formation, they were uncovered in some South African mine as unimpressive, dull, roughly shaped rocks. The beauty was revealed by a master craftsman who was skilled and experienced enough to see their potential. He took the raw material and made them sparkle.

Jesus' approach to the man named Matthew was like that of the skilled craftsman. Jesus saw Matthew's potential, and He loved him. He knew what the power of His love could accomplish.

Apostle With an Identity Crisis

The account of Jesus' interaction with Matthew is first found in the Gospel that bears his name. It is, in part, his autobiography. But Matthew wasn't always sympathetic to the gospel message or to Jesus. The day that Jesus came to Matthew's place of business was for him a new beginning.

The passage gives us his conversion story in his own words. Although it is a brief account, it still gives us a good picture of who Matthew was, what he did, and what became of him.

He introduces himself as "a man named Matthew sitting at the tax office." Later he lists himself among the apostles as "Matthew the tax collector" (Matthew 10:3). Everyone knew him by his name and his occupation. It's interesting to note that two other Gospel writers, Mark and Luke, introduce Matthew by another name: "Levi the son of Alphaeus" (Mark 2:14; Luke 5:27). Since his father's name is also mentioned, we can infer that Levi was Matthew's original name and that it was changed at some point later in his life.

Levi was an especially Jewish name, one that pointed back to the tribe of Levi, the third son of the patriarch Jacob and his wife Leah (Genesis 29:34). It's safe to conclude that Matthew was raised in a Jewish home and was probably named after the head of his own tribe. Naming children in this way was a common practice, but here it reveals an uncommon occurrence. Since the tribe of Levi was designated by God as the priestly tribe, the last thing anyone would have expected would be for this Levite to become a tax collector. Talk about an identity crisis! It could mean that Matthew was at one time destined to serve in the temple as a priest. But he certainly was no priest when Jesus met him. Rather, he was on the opposite end of the occupational spectrum. Being a tax collector was considered light-years away from serving as a priest!

Job Description of a Traitor

Matthew, though Jewish and a resident of Israel's commonwealth, worked as part of the Roman government's equivalent to our Internal Revenue Service. Tax collectors have never been popular in any society during any age, least of all during Matthew's era. Few people understand how stigmatizing this line of work was at the time. Other Jews would have detested him. He was considered to be a traitor because of his alliance with the Roman tax system.

The Jews hated the Romans, who had forcefully entered the Holy Land and imposed a despotic rule, oppressing the people. To be a Jew working for the Romans was nothing less than traitorous. As a tax collector for the Romans, Matthew was taking money from his own people to line the pockets of their enemies.

The Romans taxed virtually everything. How else could they fund all those monuments, roads, and temples? First, there was the poll tax. Every male from age fourteen to sixty-five and every female from age twelve to sixty-five paid it. This was a tax simply for the privilege of living and breathing "Roman air." Then there was the ground tax, which placed a tariff on crop growers. One tenth of all the grain as well as one fifth of all wine was to go to the Romans. Beyond these were taxes according to occupations. If you were a local fisherman, guess what? You paid a *fish tax*. You would be taxed according to the amount of your catch. If you transported goods, you would have to pay a *cart tax* that charged you for each wheel that spun on your cart. Then there were levies for roads, bridges, harbors, and imports. On top of these each citizen paid a flat 10 percent income tax. It appeared as if the Romans sat up nights figuring out ways to get more money to fund their empire.

To make matters worse, tax-collecting businesses were issued through a system of tax farming, which granted the businesses, similar to modern franchises, to those who could qualify, usually the highest bidder. Tax collectors were ironically required to pay a tax to Rome, but they could keep the rest of the money they collected. It's easy to see how such a system could become abused, and it was. Collectors often became greedy, oppressing the poor and extorting them in an attempt to get more money for themselves. The rich could often bribe these collectors to evade paying their dues, while the middle class and poor strained under the financial burden.

For these reasons, tax collectors were hated and shunned. Although many of these revenue officers were Jewish, they were barred from many synagogue services because they were considered unclean, like non-kosher animals.[1]

What a picture—a man who was possibly groomed for the Jewish ministry now barred from the Jewish synagogue. Having forsaken the heritage of his forefathers, Matthew was considered an outcast by his contemporaries.

A Change in the Wind

At some point the man's name was changed from Levi to Matthew. We aren't told when or by whom, but we can make a fairly educated and even scriptural guess. It was in all probability Jesus who changed his name. He did it with others. He changed Simon's name to Peter, which means stone (Mark 3:16). He gave James and John the nickname "Sons of Thunder," a humorous jab at their attempt to burn a Samaritan village by invoking fire from Heaven (Mark 3:17; Luke 9:54). It wouldn't be out of character for Jesus to have changed the man's name from Levi to Matthew.

Why? It must have been Jesus' way of demonstrating His ability to see potential. The name Matthew is a significant one. It means "a gift of God." A gift of God? This tax collector? This traitor? That's not how the citizens of Galilee saw him. That's not how the Jewish taxpayers viewed him. They probably had their own names for this turncoat, but no one saw him as a gift, especially a gift sent by God.

Then why would Jesus give him such a promising name? It wasn't because of what he was at the time. It certainly didn't reflect what he did for a living. It must have been a prophetic title—an indication of what he could become. Jesus could look at this tax collector and envision what he could be with a little work and love. The odds didn't matter. The Master Craftsman could see the potential.

I Surrender All!

The account of the meeting between Jesus and Matthew is noteworthy for its sheer economy of words. It is short and straightforward: Jesus saw, Jesus spoke, and Matthew surrendered.

Jesus said two words: "Follow me." It is the shortest evangelistic sermon on record!

The response was equally as amazing: "So he arose and followed him" (Matthew 9:9). I like the way *The Living Bible* renders Mark's account of this story: "And Levi jumped to his feet and went along" (Mark 2:14). No lag time. No internal battle. No sweet anthem to soften the emotions for the altar call. Just a simple command and a simple response.

Each encounter Jesus had with people was unique from all the others. With some he lingered in conversation. He scaled the barrier of callousness with the woman of Samaria. He questioned the leper who came to Him at Galilee. He spent the evening with Nicodemus and talked the theology of the new birth. He blinded Saul of Tarsus to get his attention. But with Matthew, Jesus was straightforward and abrupt, yet inviting.

It's not difficult to imagine the dynamic of this scene. Without question Matthew had already heard of Jesus. Since Jesus' headquarters was at Capernaum, where Matthew worked, he no doubt overheard conversations about Jesus, possibly even overheard some of Jesus' sermons. He may have seen cured cripples walking to the tax booth to pay their dues. Matthew's pump was primed. He was ready.

But he must have been surprised when Jesus asked him to come and follow Him. They were both so different from each other. The people loved Jesus; they hated Matthew. They thought Jesus was the salt of the Earth; they thought Matthew was the scum of the Earth. Jesus freely gave His time, His words, and His love to anyone who wanted it; Matthew took anything he could from anyone he met. Jesus healed people physically and emotionally; Matthew crippled people financially and emotionally. Jesus was the Messiah; Matthew was a menace. These two could not be further apart.

Jesus was the Messiah; Matthew was a menace.

Yet Jesus walked up and gave the invitation: "Follow me." It seemed unprecedented that Jesus would ask a man like Matthew to join His staff of disciples. If others heard the invitation, they must have been shocked.

Jesus may have engaged Matthew in conversation, although none is recorded. In fact, there is no record that Matthew said anything at all to Jesus in this interaction. When Jesus walked toward the tax booth, He "saw" the man and then spoke. Those eyes that saw things and people so differently than anyone else saw Matthew the man, Matthew the tax man, and gave an executive order. Matthew was decisive: He heard the call and responded immediately. He was ready for the change. Maybe he'd been thinking hard about his life and future. Maybe his soul had felt so empty even though his wallet had been full. Whatever the circumstances that day, Matthew followed Jesus.

Luke gives us more information about Matthew's choice to obey and follow Jesus. "So Levi got up, left everything, and followed him" (Luke 5:28, NLT). When Matthew got up from his desk that day, his tax booth would forever be in his rearview mirror. He knew he was severing the cord with Rome forever. Following Jesus meant forsaking his livelihood. He was saying good-bye to the stuff that had brought him comfort and security. But the next few years with Jesus and even beyond would be the adventure of a lifetime.

We can safely assume that soon after Matthew's landmark conversion, the news would have hit the Galilean grapevine. If they had had a local newspaper, the headlines probably would have read: "Tax Collector Gets Religion! Quits Job for the Ministry!"

The gossip mill in Capernaum was undoubtedly rife with the news of this infamous money collector's radical conversion. We can just imagine what the banter was:

"Hey, did you hear? That tax guy, you know, Matthew, is following that religious leader."

"You mean the one who's been ripping us off all these years?"

"Yeah! They say he just up and left. They say he left everything—money, papers—everything!"

"He probably got into some trouble and is fleeing the country. Rome doesn't take well to disloyal collectors, you know."

"If I were that Jesus fellow, I'd think twice about letting him tag along. Matthew's probably scheming some way to con Jesus and His followers out of their money."

The Life of the Party

Matthew made his life-altering choice to follow Jesus. Then he made another choice; he arranged a huge feast at his own house and invited a few old friends—tax collectors and perhaps neighbors—and his new friend, Jesus. I love Matthew's style. He must have known how skeptical people would be of his spiritual maneuvers. Their suspicions were understandable. He had been considered their enemy for as long as they could remember. How could he now reach out to them and invite them over for dinner?

Luke writes about the occasion: "Then Levi gave Him a great feast in his own house. And there were a great number of tax collectors and others who sat down with them" (Luke 5:29).

Matthew brought together quite a group of people. First there was a group of his tax-collector buddies. Then there were the "others." (Matthew's own account refers to them as "sinners." Funny that he made a distinction between his profession and sinners. Probably no one else would have. Actually, the word *sinner* was a technical religious term referring to anyone who did not submit to the Mosaic law.) Besides these there were Pharisees and scribes—leaders of the religious community. And, of course, there were Jesus and His disciples. Jesus was there right in the middle of it all, and He was literally the life of the party.

Imagine what it looked like. People who might have poked their heads in the courtyard of Matthew's house that night would have been shocked at what they saw. It wasn't a religious gathering. To the unsuspecting and uninitiated, it didn't look good. There in the middle of the room, surrounded by lowlife, was Jesus. He sat with them, sharing food and conversation. It was a great opportunity to reach out, but it still didn't look good. What kind of Messiah would hang out with people like these? It just wasn't *sacred*. It didn't seem proper. But then again, Jesus was never one to worry about the shallow judgment of outward appearances. He could see into the heart, and He could also see the potential.

Self-Righteousness Collides with Mercy

The diverse group made the feast all the more interesting. Although the passage doesn't say it, I suspect that the religious leaders may not have been invited guests. I imagine them on the outside looking in, perhaps observing from a surrounding courtyard. They maybe wouldn't dare enter a tax collector's house, but they would get close enough to condemn anyone who did.

The presence of Pharisees around the compound was almost a sure sign there would be trouble. And there was. Pharisees were guardians of the ancient traditions. They were not trained to see potential in others, unless it was to see potential problems with people who did not keep the laws.

They were not happy that Jesus was playing it loose and eating with this group. And so they spoke up, but not to Jesus. He seemed to be too caught up in the action. The Pharisees targeted Jesus' disciples: "When the Pharisees saw it, they said to His disciples, 'Why does your Teacher eat with tax collectors and sinners?' " (Matthew 9:11).

Wherever the Pharisees were when they spoke, Jesus overheard it. He knew exactly what they were saying and why. He knew that those Pharisees considered His actions to be taboo. He was quite aware that Jews considered eating with someone as one of the most intimate forms of fellowship possible. So when the Pharisees saw Jesus eating with tax collectors and sinners—becoming one with them in the intimacy of a shared meal—they questioned His behavior. The Pharisees reasoned, "These people are sick! Look at them! They revel in their sinfulness!"

Then the conversation suddenly became public. Jesus challenged the thinking of these finger-pointers by meeting them at the level of their own reasoning. He countered their self-righteous criticism with an observation: "Healthy people don't need a doctor—sick people do" (Matthew 9:12, NLT). He agreed that He was indeed in the company of people who were sickened with sin. "You're right, they are sick," Jesus in effect was saying, "and sick people need a doctor, not just a diagnosis!"

That's why He had come. Like a gracious doctor, Jesus was simply making a house call! The Pharisees were spiritual quacks. They were good only at tossing out diagnoses; they did not offer a cure. They loved to point a finger at people and tell them what was wrong with them, but they didn't lift a finger to help their spiritual need.

Then Jesus pressed the Pharisees further by quoting the Scriptures: "But go and learn what this means: 'I desire mercy and not sacrifice.' For I did not come to call the righteous, but sinners, to repentance" (v. 13). That quote was lifted right out of the familiar story of Hosea the prophet. Hosea was married to an unfaithful wife, who went back to her old ways of prostitution, leaving her husband to mourn her adultery.

He showed her mercy by receiving her back with forgiveness. The prophet's example then became an object lesson to the nation of Israel of God's merciful love. It would be the power of God's love and acceptance that would be the nation's cure. And it was God's love that needed to be shown that day to those "tax collectors and sinners."

Jesus demonstrated that love and its effects were profound. The lesson of God's love as displayed by Jesus' mercy toward the undeserving and the outcasts was the lesson the Pharisees sorely needed to learn.

Love—The Most Powerful Force in the World

The God who prefers mercy to sacrifice is a God of love. Jesus said to one of His disciples, "He who has seen Me has seen the Father" (John 14:9). To see Jesus in action is to view the very heart of God, for Jesus was God in the flesh. The snapshot of Jesus with the New Testament's most infamous tax agent is a picture of divine love interacting with common humanity. Matthew experienced it, responded to it, basked in it, and spread it around.

The same Jesus who met Matthew comes to you. He sees your potential. He extends to you His mercy. He loves you. And that love will have an impact on your life in a variety of ways.

Love Sees More

Love sees a person honestly. Jesus "saw" a man named Matthew (Matthew 9:9). He saw him at his workplace collecting money for Rome and for himself. But it was more than mere observation. Jesus knew what Matthew was like. He knew his past. He knew his corruption. He knew his reputation. Jesus didn't have a naïve view of the man. Jesus knew Matthew completely yet loved him readily. He knew the thoughts of the Pharisees, yet He loved them too.

> *Jesus knew Matthew completely yet loved him readily.*

God sees clearly into your life as well. He knows everything about you—your past failures as well as your present doubts.

134

His love for you keeps you fully in view. Paul spoke of this quality of love in his famous description to the Corinthian Church: "Love suffers long and is kind; love ... bears all things" (1 Corinthians 13:4, 7). This kind of love presupposes a complete knowledge of one's faults and shortcomings; it anticipates the need to bear with the failures of another.

Jesus saw Matthew for who he was. He sees you for who you are. He knows how you felt this morning and what you did twenty years ago. His love for you isn't because of how you act or think or feel; He loves you in spite of all these things. His love is based on His character, not yours.

Love sees a person's potential. Jesus saw much more than what Matthew was personally and professionally. Jesus knew what Matthew would become. That's why He named him Matthew, the gift of God. Jesus was seeing into the future, and He knew the potential that was there. As the ultimate Craftsman, He doesn't look for perfection already displayed. He takes the rough and raw materials to hammer out His expression. One look at Jesus' team of disciples would prove that! Forget all those pictures you've seen with symmetrical, perfect halos painted around their heads.

His love is based on His character, not yours.

The guys on Jesus' list would have been on most other people's blacklist. But that's His style. The reason is pretty obvious. Once God gets done reworking them thoroughly, they'll shine. And when they do, God's glory goes up several notches. Paul the apostle put it this way: "God has chosen the foolish things of the world to put to shame the wise, and God has chosen the weak things of the world to put to shame the things which are mighty; and the base things of the world and the things which are despised God has chosen, and the things which are not, to bring to nothing the things that are, that no flesh should glory in His presence" (1 Corinthians 1:27-29).

Paul knew that craftsmen's skills and abilities become all the more apparent when they can make a masterpiece out of meager stuff. Jesus interacted with Matthew the tax collector with the same philosophy. He could see the potential in this man so dirtied by years of selfishness. He knew that He could cut and refine this life into a powerful instrument to reflect His glory, and He did.

We are still grateful today for Jesus' encounter with Matthew. Were it not for this encounter, we would not be reading the Gospel of Matthew! His writings were circulated to convince the Jewish people that Jesus was their Messiah. The writings have since become an inspiration to millions for the last two thousand years. Think of it. All that Matthew was by birth and upbringing would be used to further God's Kingdom.

One interesting feature of Matthew's writings is his frequent use of messianic prophecy. He was fond of saying things like, "That it might be fulfilled by the prophet who said...." All of that religious schooling paid off in the end. The Scripture planted in his heart as a young child would blossom and fill the Earth with fruit! No one who knew Matthew could ever have known that, except one. Besides that, according to the historian Irenaeus, Matthew went on to preach the gospel among his Jewish neighbors and then traveled to other countries such as Ethiopia, Macedonia, Syria, and Persia.[3]

It's all because God sees potential. The odds don't matter. They didn't matter with Matthew, and they don't matter with you.

Andrew Carnegie knew about potential. He came to America from Scotland as a small boy and began working at a variety of jobs, eventually ending up as the largest steel manufacturer in America. At one time he had forty-three millionaires working for him. A reporter asked Carnegie how he had managed to hire forty-three millionaires. His response was astonishing: "Those men were not millionaires when they started. They became millionaires as a result!" The next question to Carnegie was predictable: "How did you develop these men to become so valuable to you that you have paid them this much money?" Carnegie replied, "Men are developed the same way gold is mined. When gold is mined, several tons of dirt must be moved to get an ounce of gold; but one doesn't go into the mine looking for dirt—one goes in looking for the gold."[4]

I'm certain that most career specialists would have advised Jesus against choosing a person like Matthew. He was too much of a risk! He could ruin Jesus' whole ministry. If the religious elite in Jerusalem were to get wind that Jesus had a tax collector on his team, the movement could fizzle out rapidly. Why take the chance? Load up the team of disciples with obvious winners, not tax collectors!

But Jesus didn't take a risk with Matthew. He saw beyond the obvious into the potential. He wasn't trying to dig up dirt but gold. The Master Craftsman knew that with Matthew it would just be a matter of time.

Centuries ago a huge marble block was cut out of the stone quarries in the hills of Italy and sent to Florence. It was to be inspected by the great sculptors for their work. When it arrived in Florence, the sculptor Donatello studied the stone but rejected it because of a flaw that ran through the core. Sculptor after sculptor inspected the imperfect marble block, only to reject it. Until one artist walked around it and said, "I'll take it."

"It's of no value!" insisted a observer.

"It's valuable to me," insisted the artisan. "There is an angel imprisoned within, and I must set it free!" That artist was able to see past the flaw to the potential work of art. In 1504 in Florence, Italy, that artist—Michelangelo—unveiled *David*, one of the most superb and famous sculptures in the world. What are the odds?

Every single one of us has flaws. A close examination reveals an endless supply of them. God looks at us and sees beyond the flaws to the potential of a beautiful man or woman. Matthew's contemporaries saw a flawed and corrupt tax collector. They saw a crook who wanted to take advantage of everyone. They focused on the cracks. But Jesus saw a flawed individual who, with some chiseling and sanding, would become "a gift" to humanity.

God sees you as a gift too. Your life is not a mistake. When He looks at you, God sees the finished product, not just the present condition. He knows not only what you are but also what you will become.

Love Produces More

Love produces swift obedience. Matthew's dramatic decision to leave his past and follow Jesus was all part of the crisis that Jesus' love produced. It seems as if this tax collector had been yearning for such a call. It appears that there was a process already going on inside him, preparing him for Jesus' command to follow Him. Matthew moved immediately. Nothing quite like it is recorded in Scripture. The simple command "Follow me" was enough for the man with the empty soul to get it filled up without any delay.

God's love can produce obedience more quickly than any set of rules. Stipulations and regulations can produce external compliance, but genuine love generates genuine submission. Where legalism fails, love prevails. There was good reason that the common people of the day were drawn

Where legalism fails, love prevails.

to Jesus and repelled by the traditional religious systems of the day (Mark 12:37). People, even the worst kind of people, felt strangely comfortable around Jesus. Maybe they knew deep inside that Jesus' love and forgiveness were exactly what they needed. His manner and His message seemed so appealing to them. It was the unmistakable appeal of divine love.

Our world is skeptical these days of supposed "conversions." Even with all the programs in place to help prisoners, drug addicts, and alcoholics, we get suspicious whenever someone claims to be suddenly changed. Nothing that is lasting, we reason, can happen so abruptly.

But Matthew's encounter with Jesus vividly demonstrates that it is possible to change and do so radically and immediately and permanently. That's not to say that Matthew never struggled with his choice after this. It's not to say that he didn't have second thoughts when things got tough. But he did change. He did get up and leave everything. He did follow Jesus immediately. And Matthew did become God's gift to many others.

Love produces similar action. Matthew responded to Jesus' love by loving others. He went out and duplicated the process that Jesus established—calling sinners. He reasoned, "If Jesus could love the likes of me, He can help some of my friends." So, in an act that conveyed inclusive love, Matthew had a dinner party and invited his friends. It may not seem like an impressive thing to do, but it turned out to be great evangelism. His friends had the chance to see and hear Jesus personally.

Matthew's style of evangelism was based on friendships he had made. His method is worth noting: He became friends with Jesus. He also had become friends with unbelievers from his past. Then he simply introduced his friends to each other! That's effective evangelism because it's relational evangelism. It's based on love and friendship. It's informal, less intimidating than large-scale events, and let's face it, everyone loves to eat—including Jesus! Matthew knew that unbelievers would more readily respond to an invitation to a home than one to a church.

Jesus' and Matthew's approach to people speaks poignantly to our own methods of outreach and evangelism. We all want people to encounter the living Jesus. But we are uncertain as to how to go about the task. More often than not we have some daunting expectations for unbelievers. We want them to climb some pretty high walls that we have erected in our evangelical kingdoms. One is the wall of *turf*. We insist they come over onto our turf if they want to hear truth. "We've cornered the market when it comes to truth," we insist, "so you had better come to our church on Sunday morning at ten, or you can just forget about hearing any!"

Jesus taught his followers another way, a more effective way. He modeled it here, and he taught it again by precept just before he ascended into Heaven. He said, "Go into all the world and preach the gospel to every creature" (Mark 16:15). The King James Version puts it a bit more formally: "Go ye." Why is it that we have reversed it? The message we've conveyed is "Come ye"! Come to our churches. Come to our meetings. Come to our turf. Jesus came to Matthew's turf, and Matthew in turn invited people to the informal turf of his home. It had been a hangout that tax collectors and "sinners" were familiar with.

Another wall we evangelicals sometimes erect is the wall of *programs*. We want things to be in just the right order to capture people's attention. There's nothing inherently wrong with organization; in fact, it can serve people's needs up to a point. But I wonder what that feast would have been like if some modern ecclesiastical tacticians were running the show.

Perhaps Peter would have given a warm welcome followed by an opening prayer. Then the group would have sung a chorus and listened to some brief announcements given by Andrew or John. Jesus would be introduced as the featured speaker after a lengthy list of credentials given to impress the crowd. After the sermon, Matthew could give his personal testimony and brief account of what happened at the tax booth when Jesus called him. It could be two or three minutes, just long enough to keep the crowd on the edge of their seats.

None of that occurred, of course. It was much plainer than that. Jesus was simply *with them*. He was sitting among the crowd, mingling, engaging in conversation, and sharing truth in a very uncomplicated and uncluttered manner. Matthew had erected no walls for the guests to climb over first. Jesus came to them on their turf and at their level without compromising any values of truth or morality. Not everyone was thrilled with the night. And it will be risky business if we operate this way in our evangelism. But it's worth it—*if* you can see the potential.

Don't misunderstand. Large-scale crusades and outreach events that give opportunity for Christians to invite their unsaved neighbors and friends can be highly effective as well as inspiring to those who attend. The lost can be reached, and the church can be renewed. The events can give unparalleled opportunity for many churches in a community to work together.

But it's not the only way. Consider what Matthew did as a model for bringing people to Jesus: (1) make friends with Jesus; (2) make friends with unbelievers; (3) introduce your friends to each other!

George MacLeod wrote a great poem that I think challenges every church and every church leader in this area of evangelistic style.

> *I simply argue that the cross be raised again*
> *at the center of the marketplace*
> *as well as on the steeple of the church.*
> *I am recovering the claim that*
> *Jesus was not crucified in a cathedral*
> *between two candles:*

But on a cross between two thieves;
on a town garbage heap;
At a crossroads of politics so cosmopolitan
that they had to write His title
in Hebrew and in Latin and in Greek …
And at the kind of place where cynics talk smut,
and thieves curse and soldiers gamble.
Because that is where He died,
and that is what He died about.
And that is where churchmen should be,
and what churchmen should be about.[5]

Love Embraces More

Love embraces the spiritually sick. The Pharisees who came to observe at Matthew's house that night were separatists. The very name Pharisee means "separated ones." These self-righteous ones could spot a sinner anytime, anywhere. That is, they could spot certain kinds of sinners. One thing was for certain—they kept a safe distance from such sick people. They, of course, needed the Doctor's touch as much as the "sinners" at the meal did, but they were blind to it.

These religious quacks could only partially diagnose. They had neither the ability nor the desire to cure. Their hardened hearts had no room for mercy. Their narrow religious vision kept them from embracing anyone else.

But Jesus loved people, and He extended mercy to them. His mercy allowed Him to see more potential in the tax collector than anyone else did. He saw more in the party crowd than anyone else could see. And when He saw people in spiritual need, He mercifully embraced them in order to cure that need.

We often fall into the same trap that the Pharisees did. We are uncomfortable being with "sinners." We insulate ourselves in our churches and cut ourselves off from the very people who need to experience God's merciful love. Sometimes I think Christians need to "get out more." We can become so ingrown and myopic simply because we surround ourselves with people like us. It's fairly easy to sever the nerve of compassion toward unbelievers simply because we're not around them long enough to observe their pain. Ask God to help you see people differently, through eyes of love and mercy. Ask Him to fill you with divine love—the kind that would extend mercy.

We displease God when we get so caught up in the outward trappings of our Christian experience that we fail to extend mercy to a hurting world. God speaks very sharply to the Old Testament people who were too busy "doing" religion:

> *"The multitude of your sacrifices—what are they to me?" says the Lord. "I have more than enough of burnt offerings, of rams and the fat of fattened animals; I have no pleasure in the blood of bulls and lambs and goats. When you come to appear before me, who has asked this of you, this trampling of my courts? Stop bringing meaningless offerings! Your incense is detestable to me. New Moons, Sabbaths and convocations—I cannot bear your evil assemblies. Your New Moon festivals and your appointed feasts my soul hates. They have become a burden to me; I am weary of bearing them" (Isaiah 1:11-14, NIV).*

Then God tells them what the real problem was. He thought their prayers, feasts, and religious ceremonies were a sham, not because of what they did, but because of what they *didn't* do. They failed to show compassion to those who really needed it: "Learn to do right! Seek justice, encourage the oppressed. Defend the cause of the fatherless, plead the case of the widow" (Isaiah 1:17, NIV).

Love embraces the sincerely repentant. Jesus plainly stated His mission at Matthew's house: "For I did not come to call the righteous, but sinners, to repentance" (Matthew 9:13). As a result of meeting Jesus, Matthew repented; he made a full about-face from his life of sin to follow Jesus.

Every so often the media carry a story about a notorious criminal who has committed heinous acts and then has a religious experience while in prison, sometimes while awaiting the death penalty. Some of these conversions are no doubt legitimate. But as soon as the news hits the wire, it provokes a flurry of negative opinions: "That guy can't expect to be forgiven that easily after what he's done." "That's not fair!" "Where's the justice in that?" Granted, it seems quite convenient to suddenly become religious while awaiting the death penalty, but if there is sincere sorrow and genuine repentance, God will grant forgiveness.

For those who know they are terminally ill in the spiritual sense and have no thread of hope that they could ever be cured on their own, repentance is their only option. When that occurs, God in His great love will embrace the person—and so should we. We ought to be quick to demonstrate acceptance to anyone who demonstrates a heart of sorrow and a desire to change. To do otherwise would be to sit in the camp of the Pharisees.

A billboard on a Canadian highway declared, "The wicked will go to Hell and live there forever." Not the best approach, is it? Would that attract you to Christ? While it's true that there is eternal punishment awaiting those who reject Jesus Christ, if we fail to offer the cure and receive those who take it, we are no better than the spiritual quacks who chided Jesus that evening at Matthew's home. In the 1960s and 1970s heavy-handed religious legalism and stiff formalism caused some people to parade the streets of our country with placards that read Jesus, Yes; Christianity, No! How sad that they saw a distinction between the two. Christians can too often be known only for what they are against rather than what they are for!

When Jesus said that He had not come to call the righteous to repentance, He was referring to those who saw themselves as righteous. Self-righteous people have no awareness of their need. They don't know they need salvation. And because they are not willing to admit their need, they do not seek the cure—repentance that leads to a relationship with Jesus.

But when they do admit their need, things change.

A friend of mine was recently diagnosed with a very aggressive form of cancer. As soon as he discovered that he was terminally ill, he altered his life radically. He contacted specialists in other states. He is intensely exploring alternate treatments. He is doing anything and everything to find a cure. Why? Because he knows he is facing a death sentence unless he finds the right treatment soon.

Conversion results when a person accepts both the death sentence and the gift of life. God's love is powerful, and it will embrace everyone. But not everyone is open to God's love.

If you have not admitted your need and come to Jesus for the cure, do so today. His love awaits you. He sees who you are. He is willing to embrace you. He will forgive you. And He will ask you to follow Him into a purposeful life of service.

― ―

FOR REFLECTION AND DISCUSSION

1. Think of two or three popular love songs. What is the thrust of the lyrics of these songs? What are the differences between their message and the kind of love that Jesus showed to Matthew and the others at Matthew's house?

2. Can you name any good reasons why Jesus should have picked you to be a part of His discipleship team? What would you list as your advantages? What would be your disadvantages?

3. Name some people whom God is using in the extension of His Kingdom. Were they always as devoted as they are now? Do you think that these people are nearly perfect, or do they have flaws? Why do you suppose God uses imperfect people?

4. Read 1 Corinthians 1:26-29. Insert your name in the appropriate places and commit it to memory. For example, if I were doing this exercise, the verses would look like this: "For you see your calling, brethren, that not many wise according to the flesh, not many mighty, not many noble, are called. But God has chosen the foolish things of the world [like Skip] to put to shame the wise, and God has chosen the weak things of the world [like Skip] to put to shame the things which are mighty; and the base things of the world and the things which are despised [like Skip is to some people] God has chosen, and the things which are not, to bring to nothing the things that are, that no flesh should glory in His presence."

5. How would you describe your friendship with Jesus: formal yet respectable, distant but aware of Him, close and

intimate? Which of these would attract someone to become a Christian?

6. Consider implementing this strategy in evangelism: (1) make friends with Jesus; (2) make friends with unbelievers; (3) introduce your friends to each other.

NINE

The Power of His Forgiveness

Jesus Reveals His Priorities

*A*nd again He entered Capernaum after some days, and it was heard that He was in the house. Immediately many gathered together, so that there was no longer room to receive them, not even near the door. And He preached the word to them. Then they came to Him, bringing a paralytic who was carried by four men. And when they could not come near Him because of the crowd, they uncovered the roof where He was. So when they had broken through, they let down the bed on which the paralytic was lying.

When Jesus saw their faith, He said to the paralytic, "Son, your sins are forgiven you."

And some of the scribes were sitting there and reasoning in their hearts, "Why does this Man speak blasphemies like this? Who can forgive sins but God alone?"

But immediately, when Jesus perceived in His spirit that they reasoned thus within themselves, He said to them, "Why do you reason about these things in your hearts? Which is easier, to say to the paralytic, 'Your sins are forgiven you,' or to say, 'Arise, take up your bed and walk'? But that you may know that the Son of Man has power on earth to forgive sins"—He said to the paralytic, "I say to you, arise, take up your bed, and go to your house." Immediately he arose, took up the bed, and went out in the presence of them all, so that all were amazed and glorified God, saying, "We never saw anything like this!" (Mark 2:1-12) .

A friend handed me this piece of tongue-in-cheek humor that pokes fun at the prevalent but serious fact that we are a needy culture:

> "Hello. Welcome to the psychiatric hot line.
>
> "If you are obsessive-compulsive, please press 1 repeatedly.
>
> "If you are codependent, please ask someone to press 2.
>
> "If you have multiple personalities, please press 3, 4, 5, and 6.
>
> "If you are paranoid-delusional, we know who you are and what you want. Just stay on the line so we can trace the call.
>
> "If you are schizophrenic, listen carefully, and a little voice will tell you which number to press.
>
> "If you are manic-depressive, it doesn't matter which number you press. No one will answer."

We are a society that is coming to grips with its neediness. We are ready to admit that we need help. In this "kinder and gentler" era of ours, we are told to acknowledge and own up to personal failures and foibles. Gone is the social stigma of behavioral issues that we once were taught to keep hush-hush.

But we still have a problem—it is a problem of priorities. Which need is most important? How can we place the essential issues over the less vital ones unless we can identify them as such?

The old adage "The main thing is to keep the main thing the main thing" is true. So often that's where we fail. Blaise Pascal was right, "The last thing one knows is what to put first."[1]

Jesus was good at that. He always seemed to move His life carefully around a set of fixed spiritual priorities. He was on a definite time schedule as He went on His way to the Cross to pay for the sins of the world. In every situation he was able to master all the personal elements in order to keep focused on the main concern at hand. In every encounter that Jesus had with people, we find that He knew His priorities.

148

An incident in the shoreline town of Capernaum emphasizes this. Some friends brought to Jesus a paralyzed man whose need was obvious. Or was it? The friends saw the physical need; Jesus saw beyond this need to a deeper soul need. Jesus knew what to put first.

The Preacher Is Back in Town

The Jewish town of Capernaum, nestled on the northwestern slope of the Sea of Galilee, had become Jesus' residence. It was His launching pad for ministry and was therefore a hub of activity. He had already performed many stunning signs in the local synagogue as well as in private residences (Mark 1:21-31). He had cured leprosy, driven demons away, and healed the sick. Crowd reaction was reaching such fever pitch that it was difficult for Jesus to go out in public. People literally were coming to Jesus "from every direction" (Mark 1:45).

Jesus had been away for a while, and when He returned, He may have lived in Peter's home. In fact, He may have been there when this incident occurred. The townspeople streamed to Jesus, and soon the house was packed to capacity. They spilled out of the doorway, and some peeked through the window. Others just waited outside. They wanted to see Him. They wanted to hear Him. And this day they would do both. The crowd that pressed tightly in and around that village home would see and hear things they would never forget. So would one very needy and helpless man.

While most of the people who came to hear Jesus were from Capernaum, others were not; scribes and Pharisees came from every town in the local area of Galilee and from as far south as Judea and Jerusalem (Luke 5:17). As Jesus began to speak, the din of the crowd lessened. All eyes were fixed on Him, while people outside strained to catch every word.

Horizontal and Helpless

Somewhere nearby four men grabbed the corners of their paralyzed friend's cot and made their way toward the packed house where Jesus was speaking. We don't know much about the man except that he was obviously helpless. He couldn't move much at all. His body, a withered mass, had to be carried.

He may have even been a quadriplegic, his life having been spent in the horizontal position.

In any society, being a cripple carries a certain stigma. For many who suffer from paralysis, it's embarrassing to go out to public places. Life was more difficult in ancient cultures, which didn't have the modern conveniences of wheelchairs or special moving equipment. Unless the paralytics were surrounded by a loving family unit, they often faced neglect and rejection.

In ancient Israel, this stigma was even more pronounced because the Jews associated any outward handicap with personal sin. They believed that personal suffering was the result of personal transgression. One rabbi even said, "No sick person is cured of his sickness until all of his sins have been forgiven."[2] Others believed physical maladies were the result of someone else's sin.[3]

One of the more common beliefs held in that day was that paralysis was the result of venereal disease. In such a case there would have been a direct cause-and-effect relationship between sin and suffering. Perhaps the people believed that this paralytic was now paying the high price of an immoral lifestyle.[4] Whether or not that was actually the case here, this paralytic still bore the societal stigma that he was a sinful man who was paying for his misdeeds. He must have felt uncomfortable being hauled around like this in public. What a spectacle he was as his four friends bounced down the road toward the home where Jesus was teaching.

Rooftop Love

The friends' determination to get their paralyzed friend to Jesus was immediately challenged by logistics. The crowd was thick and would not budge. How would they be able to carry a stretcher and get close enough to Jesus through this throng? "Excuse me! Sick man coming through!" they may have shouted. It was of no avail. Everyone had his or her own issues to deal with. It was obviously a case of first come first served. At this point, these four men may have been tempted to say to each other, "It's just not God's will. Let's turn around and go home. If God were in this, He would have made a way." Not these guys! They had their own priorities and would not be dissuaded. Their love made them consider an alternative.

Noticing the staircase running up the side of the house, one of the fellows probably offered, "I've got an idea. Follow me." And they climbed the stairway, hoisting their friend's cot onto the roof.

The flat rooftops of homes in Israel were more than a covering. They were the equivalent to a modern patio or porch where the family could retreat to enjoy the cool of the evening. In summer months many people slept up on the roof to enjoy the breeze. But on this day these four Galileans would create a stir.

You've got to admire these four men. They loved their handicapped friend so much that getting him to Jesus was worth an unconventional approach. They had heard and seen Jesus around Galilee. They had heard about the leper who was cleansed and the tormented people who were now sane. Knowing that their sick friend could never get to Jesus without their help, they were determined to get involved. They would do whatever it took. Yes, it was risky. Yes, it would be difficult because of the huge crowd. Yes, it was a dangerous mission fraught with the possibility of misunderstanding and ridicule. But holy determination mixed with creative love pushed them forward. They were fixed on their mission to get help for the friend they loved. The rooftop was the only option left.

Heads Up!

The paralytic's encounter with Jesus began with a disturbance. The moment was dramatic, jolting, and suspenseful. The room was already uncomfortable as the bodies were pressed together to accommodate as many as possible. The sweaty skin-against-skin atmosphere was made even more uneasy by the presence of religious leaders who were already suspicious of Jesus' getting all the attention. But everyone listened carefully to His words, until they were interrupted.

You can imagine the scene. Suddenly, shuffling footsteps were heard on the roof. The coarse sound of pounding and digging turned everyone's head upward. As they looked, a shower of debris rained down onto the guests. Jesus stopped His message. Those in the crowd inside rubbed their eyes. The Pharisees jumped up to brush the twigs and dirt from their fine, pressed robes. Some were frightened, while others were outraged at this messy and rude display. As daylight streamed into the room from the hole in the roof, someone shouted, "What's going on? What are you doing up there?" Confusion and annoyance replaced the crowd's attention to Jesus' sermon.

The four men worked without a response. Making the opening large enough, they knelt down and lowered their embarrassed friend through the hole and down into the midst of the room. "Our friend needs help; he needs to see Jesus. Sorry for the inconvenience." The ropes were lowered until finally the paralyzed man, once separated by a crowd, was face-to-face, eye-to-eye with Jesus. The Preacher and the paralytic, the needy son of Capernaum and the noble Son of God have met.

Jesus didn't flinch at the interruption. He didn't swell with anger at the fact that His sermon had been sidetracked. He may have liked it. He saw this interruption as an opportunity to make a dramatic point. Perhaps He had been preaching about God's love and mercy for everyone. That was, after all, a common theme in His teaching. Maybe He had spoken to them of the power of forgiveness to those in need of it.

As Jesus looked down at the helpless man lying on the crude stretcher, He spoke three separate statements. What He said shocked everyone in the room as well as the four peering through the hole in the roof.

Looking at each of the statements will give us insight not only into the man but especially into Jesus. Jesus didn't do what the four friends expected Him to do because He knew how to put first things first.

Words That Changed Everything

The paralyzed man was no doubt fearful and embarrassed when he landed on the floor in front of Jesus. He had just been let down through a hole in a stranger's roof into the middle of a gathering to which he was uninvited. Given the thinking of the day, everyone probably stared at him, wondering what sin he had committed to end up in such desperate shape. Seeing Jesus and knowing he had just disrupted the meeting, the man anxiously wondered how Jesus would react. What would He say? Would He be put off, or, worse yet, would He be angry?

Tender words. Jesus' first words were soothing: "Son, be of good cheer" (Matthew 9:2). Jesus' gracious words immediately set the man at ease. "Be of good cheer" or better yet, "Take courage, son." It was meant to imply that this helpless man had absolutely nothing to worry about. "Banish your fears. You are welcomed here!" Although the paralytic may have been neglected and shunned by his culture, he was with Jesus now. With tender dignity Jesus opened the man's heart and readied him for the next statement.

Forgiving words. Jesus' next words were startling: "Your sins are forgiven you." No one was expecting that. Maybe, "How long have you been paralyzed?" or, "What would you like Me to do for you?" But forgiveness? What a letdown! What an anticlimax! The four sweaty friends on the roof looked at each other puzzled. They had just carried their friend through town, to the top of a house, and in through a hole to get help. Jesus didn't even pay attention to their friend's need: paralysis. All Jesus could say was "Your sins are forgiven."

What was the crippled man thinking? He was paralyzed. Why would Jesus talk about a spiritual issue? Why did He bring up the forgiveness of sins?

It was a matter of priorities. Jesus had determined that this man's priority need was not what everyone else thought it was: to walk again. Although that was a concern to Jesus, it wasn't His first concern. Forgiveness was. Why? Sin ruins everything eternal. Temporary health is meaningless if an eternal disease eats away at a person.

It's significant that Jesus spoke of the paralytic's "sins," plural. Jesus must have known that the man was suffering inwardly as well as outwardly. His outward condition was but a reflection of how he felt inside. One demonstrated the other. His paralytic condition was a parable of his spiritual condition. He was totally dependent on others for getting around; he was also totally dependent on another for spiritual health. Jesus' gracious words indicate that this man was sensing his spiritual inadequacy in Jesus' presence. All of his shortcomings, failures, every wrong thought, all were forgiven. Jesus knew that the man's greatest need was not outward. Jesus' priority was the man's internal condition.

This was the first instance in the New Testament record that Jesus declared a person to be forgiven. There would be others, but this was the first, and it created quite a stir! The proud scribes and their counterparts, the Pharisees, were steaming. As they stroked their beards, they exchanged furious looks. To them this was no less than blasphemy since the only one who can forgive sin is God himself. They were right, of course. Only God can grant forgiveness because He is the one who is sinned against. It was as if Jesus were making a clear demonstration of His divinity. And the religious leaders heard the message loudly and clearly.

For a moment Jesus turned His attention from the paralytic to the religious leaders. Jesus, in a disarming demonstration of Deity, "perceived in His spirit" exactly what they had been thinking. (See Mark 2:8-9.) He knew fully what their looks meant. He could read every signal going on in their religious brains at that moment. So He asked, "Why do you reason about these things in your hearts? Which is easier, to say to the paralytic, 'Your sins are forgiven you,' or to say, 'Arise, take up your bed and walk'?"

Good question—which is easier? Neither one was possible for the scribes and Pharisees; both were possible for Jesus. He was about to demonstrate that healing is a visible work while forgiveness is invisible. Only God can heal a person miraculously and instantly, and only God can forgive sins.

Healing words. Turning back to the paralytic, Jesus spoke the third statement that He wanted the religious leaders to understand. He wanted to demonstrate to them that He had power both to forgive and to heal. "I say to you, arise, take up your bed, and go to your house" (Mark 2:11). A hush descended on the crowd. As they watched, they marveled. The reaction was immediate. As the onlookers sat in utter amazement and the spiritual leaders frowned in utter contempt, the man moved.

The body that had known no feeling or muscle tone for so many years straightened and stood erect. He was perfectly healed!

I think there was a lot more emotion in this scene than is indicated by the words "he arose, took up the bed, and went out in the presence of them all" (Mark 2:12). I can't see the paralytic just quietly rolling up his mat and saying, "Hey, thanks a lot, Jesus. I'll see you next Saturday in synagogue." I'm sure he was jumping, skipping, and shouting for joy, "I can walk! I can really walk! I'm cured! Oh, happy day!" Applause probably erupted as the four friends scrambled down and hugged their friend. Tears flowed freely as joy grew intensely.

The crowd seemed to be affected as well: "All were amazed and glorified God, saying, 'We never saw anything like this!' " (v. 12). Interesting that the response of the crowd was focused only on the outward. Their emotion was a reaction to the physical healing that they witnessed. They said nothing about what was Jesus' priority—forgiveness. No mention by these dazzled onlookers of the fact that the most important miracle of all had just occurred—a man's sins had been absolved by the only one who could grant forgiveness.

When the man walked away, he carried more than his bed; he carried a forgiven heart.

When the man walked away, he carried more than his bed; he carried a forgiven heart. No more guilt, no more anguished soul. And while the limbs that were healed that day would one day die and wither in a dusty grave, he himself would live forever. His life was eternally changed because he was forgiven.

A Short List of Basic Priorities

Someone once said, "Life is like a coin. You are free to spend it any way you wish, but you can only spend it once!" That's precisely why we need to live according to a set of principles and choose our priorities carefully. The paralytic's encounter with Jesus illustrates this. Jesus stuck to His priorities, and so should we. We ought always to assess and prioritize our lives.

We can do this in a variety of ways, and we need to consider many things when we do. But two main things stand out in this story: our vertical relationship with God and our horizontal relationship with other people.

A Vertical Priority—A Clean Slate

The first thing Jesus did for the man wasn't to heal him but to forgive him. Yes, he needed to be healed in order to stand and walk in this life; but he needed to be forgiven in order to live in the next life. One was only a temporal benefit; the other was both a temporal and an eternal benefit.

A cathedral in Italy admits people though three entrances, each next to the other and each having an inscription over the portal. Over the left entrance is written the words, "All that pleases is but for a moment." Over the right entrance is inscribed, "All that troubles is but for a moment." In the center, between those two, is the larger main entrance over which is one sublime simple statement: "Nothing is important except that which is eternal!" That is why the word of forgiveness was given to the paralyzed man. It was his greatest need. But not everyone saw it that way.

Forgiveness isn't always a priority. Many people don't regard forgiveness as an essential. Jesus did, but the four men who carried the poor fellow and dropped him through the roof didn't. They must have felt slighted when they first heard the words to their friend, "Son, your sins are forgiven you" (Mark 2:5). They hadn't come for a sermon or a pep talk about sins being forgiven. They came to see the man healed.

And what about the crowd? What were they so excited about? They responded enthusiastically to the spectacular display of power of the physical healing, yet they completely ignored the most significant thing—a forgiven heart.

We often overlook the reality that forgiveness is one of our greatest needs; it's not a bonus. That's why Jesus brought it up first in this encounter. He must have seen deep inside the paralyzed man's life and was able to read his heart and touch his conscience.

Anyone who has ever counseled others understands that forgiveness is a paramount issue. Many of us struggle with guilt from our past. Painful memories can stay with us for years, creating an increasing sense of shame. Society tries hard to minimize the importance of forgiveness, but deep inside we yearn to be free. Sin has left its stain on the human soul.

Some years ago in Spain a father and his teenage son had become estranged. As a result of one disagreement, the boy ran away from home. His father realized his mistake and began a journey to search for his rebellious son. Finally, in a last desperate effort to locate his son, the man put an ad in the Madrid newspaper: "Dear Paco, meet me in front of the newspaper office at noon. All is forgiven. I love you. Your father." At noon on the day after the ad was run, eight hundred Pacos showed up in front of the newspaper office. Each one was seeking forgiveness and love from his father![5]

Deep inside we all long to have the slate wiped clean. We want to know that all is forgiven.

What about you? How's your slate? Have you let the need for forgiveness get overshadowed by the busyness of everyday life? It ought not to be that way. Forgiveness is central to the gospel, and it should be central to you. Remember that God specializes in clean slates.

When you experience God's deep forgiveness for yourself, be willing to offer that same hope to others. Make God's forgiving love a hallmark of your interactions with other people.

Forgiveness can be difficult to face. It must have been embarrassing for the cripple to be brought out in public as he was. He was already in a helpless condition. But to face a crowd that included such judgmental leaders like the scribes and Pharisees was emotionally difficult. Knowing that many people considered his paralysis to be a result of his sin made the encounter even more awkward for the man. Then hearing the words "You are forgiven" exposed him all the more.

To embrace forgiveness is to acknowledge transgression. It requires an admission of guilt. We must be willing to see the grim reality of our sin. That is not an easy task, and it requires courage. I remember the first time a trusted friend told me that I needed to ask God's forgiveness just as he had. He was both forthright and assuring at the same time that God would receive me but that I must acknowledge my need and confess my sin. I was angry. What right did my friend have to tell me, a church-going man, that I needed to take his spiritual counsel? He wasn't any better than I was. The truth was, I was afraid. I was scared to face up to the truth because if I did, I knew that things must change. But my friend was right, and

God gave me the courage to admit my sin to Him and receive the comfort of His forgiveness.

Being exposed is the first step to being healed.

That wasn't the only time I needed to honestly face the need for forgiveness. In fact, asking for forgiveness has become a lifestyle. Since we are sinful creatures both by nature and by choice, we have an ongoing need to seek forgiveness from both God and other people. It seems that the hardest words to articulate to anyone are still "I'm sorry," "I was wrong," and "Please forgive me!" I have often needed God's courage to seek forgiveness from my wife, my son, as well as a host of other close friends and associates. But I have found that liberation always follows this kind of humility. Being exposed is the first step to being healed.

Let me encourage you to practice admitting your sin. Yes, you read it right—practice it! You'll have to because admitting you're wrong doesn't come naturally. But it can bring health to your relationships with both God and people. It won't be easy, but it's a priority you can't afford to live without. And since forgiveness isn't just a onetime event, you'll need God-given courage. Pray for that in every relationship that you have.

Forgiveness is often controversial. The scribes and the Pharisees in the biblical story didn't like Jesus' talk about forgiveness. They ignored both the man in need and the need of man. In a display of self-righteous elitism they didn't believe

Although performance is a necessary requirement for productive living, it is not God's requirement for acceptance.

Jesus was who He claimed to be—God. However, their spiritual feathers were ruffled for another reason. In their minds Jesus had done an unjust thing. In their theological system people had to prove that they *deserved* forgiveness. The paralytic had done nothing to deserve forgiveness. He hadn't gone to the synagogue to make atonement for his wrongdoing. He hadn't offered sacrifice at the temple. The spiritual leaders had no clue that God forgives on the basis of grace, not merit.

Most of us struggle with the idea of grace. As children we learned that merit ruled our lives in the classroom. But although performance is a necessary requirement for productive living, it is not God's requirement for acceptance. His method is to declare the penitent sinner forgiven and justified *first* and then work on behavioral change. He takes us the way we are—crippled by sin and exposed.

But forgiveness is not without controversy. Philip Yancey insightfully reminds us, "Jesus never met a disease He could not cure, a birth defect He could not reverse, a demon He could not exorcise. But He did meet skeptics He could not convince and sinners He could not convert. Forgiveness of sins requires an act of will on the receiver's part, and some who heard Jesus' strongest words about grace and forgiveness turned away unrepentant."[6] Don't let pride keep you away from being refreshed in the fountain of God's forgiveness.

A Horizontal Priority—A Well-Connected Life
How fortunate this helpless man was to have a network of four helpers. It would have been easy for him to have become bitter and isolated. He could have erected walls of emotional protection to keep out pain caused by vulnerability. I've met many people like this, including some who are handicapped like the man in the story. Mother Teresa of Calcutta once noted that the most serious disease is not leprosy or cancer but rather the feeling of being uncared for and unwanted, of being deserted and alone.

The man needed his four friends to carry him to Jesus. We also need the help of a network of other people to carry us through rough times in life. God wants us to be well connected. He declared, "It is not good that man should be alone" (Genesis 2:18). We were never designed to be an island standing alone in the sea of independence. We need to be interdependent; it's the way God wired us.

Yet many people live without a supportive network of friends. In an article about men's need for friendship, Patrick Morley noted:

Few men today have close friends. During the career-building years, men have little time for friendships, and

159

usually their families meet most of their relationship needs. Adult friendships are the most difficult to start and to maintain. Many men develop a certain level of fellowship with other men they work with, but what they often don't realize is that when it comes down to real relationships, they have a "friendship deficit." Men desire the approval of others, but the fear of rejection often keeps them from initiating a deeper relationship. Vulnerability is the price of friendship.... Friendship requires a big investment of time and trust.[7]

Someone has said that most men could get six pallbearers for their funeral but hardly anyone to "carry their stretcher" through life. Think about your friendships. Do you have friends who would help you carry your stretcher? Are you willing to carry someone else's stretcher?

What kinds of friends would be good stretcher bearers? Look for people who are Christ-centered, persistent, and creative.

Cultivate Christ-centered friendships. The four men in the biblical story had one single passion—to get their friend to Jesus. Their priority in the relationship was very admirable. At any cost, at any inconvenience, this man must meet Jesus. It was his only hope, and they knew it.

Happy is the person who has the kind of network this cripple had. Friends like that make life's hardships bearable. Without these four men the man would not have experienced forgiveness, healing, or hope.

When you choose friends—and by the way, you do choose them, they don't just *happen*—look for people who are focused on Christ. Add to your network people who are devoted to spiritual matters and devoted to finding God's solution. In times of need they will be like an anchor to keep you from sinking. When you're unsure, they will provide stability. When you are hurting, they will help you to see the Healer. When you seem out of God's reach, they will lower you into His presence.

In the Old Testament, Jonathan did this for his friend David. During one of David's most difficult and painful periods, during which King Saul was trying to assassinate him, he hid

160

in the wilderness. But his loyal friend Jonathan—Saul's son—found him and helped him to refocus his thoughts. Jonathan was able to lift his friend to new spiritual heights. "Jonathan went to find David and encouraged him to stay strong in his faith in God" (1 Samuel 23:16, NLT). David was a seasoned believer, but his trust in God was wearing thin. His spiritual edge was getting dulled. And Jonathan's friendship sharpened it.

Don't wait for this to "just happen" in your life. Find men and women who will hold you up when you feel you are breaking down. Find friends who will sharpen your spiritual edge.

Then be willing to *become* that kind of friend to others, both believers and unbelievers. Emotional pain can draw people to spiritual things, or it can drive them to desperation. Help draw your friends to Christ. Your friendships are crucial in times of pain. And if your friends get angry at God or wrestle with doubts, don't be surprised. Instead, patiently and tenderly help them regain their spiritual footing.

Cultivate persistent friendships. True friends don't give up easily. They aren't quickly dissuaded from helping. It takes a lot to slow them down.

The steady commitment of friends can be the one thing that sustains us in a crisis.

The four friends in our story displayed "rooftop love." They loved their paralyzed friend so much that they wouldn't let a little thing like walls and a roof stand in the way of getting healing for their friend. These guys were persistent. They weren't about to let a crowd slow them down. Determination drove them.

Happy is the person who has such connections! A British newspaper once ran a contest offering a reward for the best definition of a friend. Several entries were submitted, but the winning one was "A true friend is one who comes in when the rest of the world goes out." Do you know anyone like that? Are you like that?

I thank God for the persistent friends I've had. I can think of many, but one stands out. Paul has been a mentor to me as well as a consistent source of refreshing encouragement. When my early Christian life was rocky and I was having trouble at home, Paul was there to give me counsel. When I wanted to "try out" for the ministry and needed a place to start, Paul was there to give me a chance by letting me take his Sunday-night Bible study. When my brother was killed on his motorcycle and I was emotionally scrambled, Paul was there. When I first moved to a new town to begin a fledgling church and needed encouragement, Paul was there; he called me and visited us to show support. When my father died of congestive heart failure and I felt alone, Paul was there at the funeral, sitting in the church, giving me comfort. I preached at my dad's funeral, and it was difficult. Paul's presence made it all the easier.

Good friends refuse to be shocked by our condition and are driven to help us. Keith Miller and Bruce Larson make some interesting observations about this kind of friendship.

> The neighborhood bar is possibly the best counterfeit there is to the fellowship Christ wants to give his Church. The bar is an imitation dispensing liquor instead of grace, escape rather than reality, but it is permissive, it is accepting and it is an inclusive fellowship. It is unshockable. It is democratic. You can tell people secrets, and they usually don't tell others or even want to. The bar flourishes not because most people are alcoholics but because God has put into the human heart the desire to know and be known, to love and be loved. And so many people seek a counterfeit at the price of a few beers. With all my heart, I believe that Christ wants His Church to be unshockable, a fellowship where people can come in and say, "I'm sunk, I'm beat, I've had it." Alcoholics Anonymous has this quality—our churches too often miss it.[8]

Don't let yourself miss this priority. Determine to be the kind of believer who latches onto those who hurt and refuses to be shocked by their condition. Jesus isn't shocked, so why should we be? Remember, He's all about fixing broken lives, not expecting perfect ones!

Cultivate creative friendships. When the four friends got the man to the house where Jesus was teaching, they faced several significant obstacles. But they weren't deterred. They did some creative thinking and came up with a great plan. They couldn't get inside the house because the crowd was so dense. Forget about asking people to move aside; they knew all about human nature. They also knew that the front door wasn't the only way to get inside that room. Seeing the staircase on the side of the house, they decided to try access from the roof. Was it risky? Of course! Was it breaking decorum? Certainly! Was it embarrassing? Not to them. Their determination drove them to a creative expression of their friendship.

Dawson Trotman, former president of the Navigators, died under unusual circumstances. He was an expert swimmer, but he drowned in Schroon Lake, New York. When a boat Trotman was on began to sink, he dove into the lake to rescue people who could not swim. First he rescued a little girl. He then dove again to recover another person, and then another. When he went back for yet another person, he did not resurface. Rescuers found his body a few hours later. When *Time* magazine ran an article on Trotman's life, the article bore his name and this caption beneath it: "Dawson Trotman: Always Holding Somebody Up." If the paralytic's friends had an article written about them, the caption might have read, "Four Creative Friends—Always Lowering Somebody Down."

Creative friendships look for solutions that most people never think of. What solutions do your friends need? Is one of your friends discouraged? How can you use your creativity to get your friend's attention and focus it on Jesus? Ask God to help you discover new ways to reach out. Let your friend know that your friendship is a priority and that, if need be, you'll even be there to pull a few tiles off a roof!

The paralyzed man encountered Jesus with a little help from his friends. He left with a forgiven heart and a restored body. And he walked away with four friends who helped it all happen. God uses people to introduce their friends to Jesus. What kind of friends do you have? What kind of friend are you?

FOR REFLECTION AND DISCUSSION

1. Make a list of your priorities (specific relationships, activities, interests, commitments, responsibilities). Then in the blank at the right of each priority, indicate how many hours a week you spend on each of these priorities. Example:

Priority	*Hours*
Spouse	15
_____	_____
_____	_____
_____	_____
_____	_____
_____	_____
_____	_____
_____	_____
_____	_____
_____	_____
_____	_____

2. If your top priorities were forgiveness and friendship (vertical and horizontal), how might your list change? Would you have different priorities? Would you spend a different amount of time on each priority?

3. In what ways have you felt helpless in your life (perhaps a physical condition or an emotional distress)? Did you feel embarrassed by it? Did you have friends who encouraged you and relieved the burden? During that episode, what did you consider to be most important?

4. Look at the following list of people and think about those to whom you find it hardest to admit you were wrong. Rate them in order, with 1 being hardest and 8 being easiest:

___ Spouse
___ Parents
___ Children
___ Co-workers
___ Friends
___ Minister
___ Coach
___ Boss

In what specific ways can you cultivate forgiveness in these relationships?

5. Which of the following describe you as a friend?

___ Aloof and uncommitted
___ Self-serving
___ Self-sacrificing
___ Loving but sporadic
___ Persistent and creative
___ Christ-centered and edifying

Now, if you're feeling especially accountable, ask a friend to take these descriptions and grade your friendship.

6. Think of a friend whom you would like to bring to Jesus. This could be either a non-Christian friend who has been resistant or a Christian friend who is struggling with God. How can you be a Christ-centered, persistent, and creative friend to this person?

7. Write a letter to someone who has been a true friend and helped carry you when you were feeling helpless. Express gratitude that that person never gave up. Ask God to make you that kind of friend to another.

TEN

The Power of His Mercy

Stepping into the World of Pain

After this there was a feast of the Jews, and Jesus went up to Jerusalem. Now there is in Jerusalem by the Sheep Gate a pool, which is called in Hebrew, Bethesda, having five porches. In these lay a great multitude of sick people, blind, lame, paralyzed, waiting for the moving of the water. For an angel went down at a certain time into the pool and stirred up the water; then whoever stepped in first, after the stirring of the water, was made well of whatever disease he had. Now a certain man was there who had an infirmity thirty-eight years. When Jesus saw him lying there, and knew that he already had been in that condition a long time, He said to him, "Do you want to be made well?"

The sick man answered Him, "Sir, I have no man to put me into the pool when the water is stirred up; but while I am coming, another steps down before me."

Jesus said to him, "Rise, take up your bed and walk." And immediately the man was made well, took up his bed, and walked.

And that day was the Sabbath. The Jews therefore said to him who was cured, "It is the Sabbath; it is not lawful for you to carry your bed...."

For this reason the Jews persecuted Jesus, and sought to kill Him, because He had done these things on the Sabbath. But Jesus answered them, "My Father has been working until now, and I have been working." (John 5:1-10, 16-17)

The phrase is etched into my memory bank: "God helps those who help themselves." It sounded right, I guess. Some people even said it came right out of the Bible. Then I started reading the Bible for myself, and I made a discovery; I found that neither the phrase nor the idea was there. The fact is, the God of the Bible more often helps those who are helpless, those who are downtrodden, those who have been passed by. "He delights in mercy" (Micah 7:18).

God's mercy is such a distinguishing mark of His approach to us that the word *mercy* is used almost three hundred times in Scripture. God's mercy is an ever-flowing stream that spills out to thirsty lives, saturating the soul and transforming a person permanently. Mercy leaves its mark. People who are touched by God's mercy want to touch others with it.

Sometime after a Christian woman's husband had been brutally murdered, she decided to visit the killer in prison. It was a bold step and one that stunned everyone who knew the situation. More than that, it stunned the prisoner. Why would she come? Was this a morbid display of grief and loss? Was she studying the man in order to plan her revenge? Neither! She had come to extend mercy. She came to forgive. And she came back many times. On one particular visit the prisoner broke down. With a Bible in his hand, the killer began to explain that God had been changing him. The woman's visits had caused him to reflect and think about God in a whole new way. Thrilled to see such spiritual progress, the bereaved widow made an even bolder step. She decided to take some of the insurance money she had received from her husband's death and help her new Christian brother in prison! Life had been taken away, but a new one was just beginning. The power of mercy!

House of Mercy or House of Misery?

As Jesus wound His way through the streets of Jerusalem for the annual Feast of Tabernacles, He went straight to a place that, strangely enough, had been given the name *Bethesda*, which meant the "House of Mercy." But it was hardly that. It was more like a house of misery, a prison with inmates who were chained behind bars of loneliness from long-standing infirmities.

Bethesda was the large, deeply cut pool in Jerusalem. It was neither a resort nor a hospital but a crowded gathering spot for people with a variety of ills. In reality it wasn't a place in which anyone got any better. It amounted to a huge outdoor waiting room, where the masses of sick people clung to each other in the fellowship of misery. Like a Third World infirmary, this place housed people who were passing their time at a snail's pace. Their chief activity was inactivity. They were waiting for something less than credible—for water to move in a mysterious manner.

This five-sided pool had been a sort of superstitious Mecca for healing. It appears that intermittent springs once fed the pool, causing the surface of it to bubble up. People believed that an angel came and stirred up the water and that the first person to touch the water would be healed.

The Gospel of John introduces us to the sick man who met Jesus that day. John doesn't tell us his name. Perhaps it was because John wanted us to know that the man didn't stand out from the rest of the huddling people at the pool. He blended in. Most people would never have noticed him, but Jesus did. Jesus saw him and stopped to talk with him.

We don't know exactly why the man was at the pool. Because he needed someone to put him in the pool, we can guess that he had some sort of paralyzing illness (John 5:7). But we do know that he had been debilitated for thirty-eight years. For almost four decades he was alienated, seeing life through the lens of hopelessness. It was an entire lifetime for many people in those days.

The man must have watched that pool eagerly—at least at first—so desperate to reach it when the waters bubbled. He would have given anything to have the cure people said would come to the first person who would get into the pool. He perhaps had screamed to passersby on more than one occasion to help him reach the pool. He probably wiggled his pathetic paralyzed body toward the water, frantically trying to secure the desired results.

Those results never came. Maybe his friends had come to visit him in the beginning, but they probably tired of the lack of change and gave up. Years passed slowly but steadily. And so the helpless man's world was confined to the tiny space occupied by his mat on the pavement stones that surrounded the complex. He no longer struggled to reach the water in the pool called the House of Mercy. The name was nice, but it meant nothing to this guy—until the day when a visitor arrived and singled him out of the crowd.

The Incapable Meets the All-Powerful

Jesus had come to the Holy City for one of Israel's three great feasts, the Feast of Tabernacles. It was a spiritual festival that commemorated God's merciful provision for the nation while they migrated through the desert to the Promised Land. God had cared for them in a place that had few natural resources. Those ancient refugees were unable to find adequate food and water in that barren wilderness. That's where God came in. What Israel could not do for themselves, God did for them. Although the people bitterly complained to God, He extended His mercy to them in their helplessness.

Jesus came to Jerusalem during the Feast that memorialized such mercy. It was a case of "like Father, like Son." Jesus sought out this helpless man to mercifully give him what he could not provide for himself.

Jesus was alone when He walked to Bethesda. He looked over the mass of human tragedy; then He spotted the man. As the omniscient Son of God looked at the man, He knew how long he had lived like that, and He knew why.

But the man didn't know who Jesus was. This is suggested in the fact that he made no demands on Jesus for healing when he saw Him. The passage tells us that when the man was questioned by the authorities later in the day, he indicated that he did not "know who it was" who had healed him (John 5:13). He had been so isolated, so cut off from current news, that he had not heard about Jesus' miracle-working power.

When the man heard Jesus approach him, he looked up. Then Jesus asked him an unusual question: "Do you want to be made well?" (v. 6). What kind of a question is that? Can you imagine asking someone who has been ill for almost an entire lifetime if he wanted to be well? Imagine the people within earshot of this encounter. They would have immediately bristled, thinking, *How cruel to ask such a thing.*

Why *would* Jesus ask such a question? He wasn't being cruel; He was being deliberate. He was holding up a mirror to this fellow's condition, forcing him to face the hopelessness of it and to focus all his attention on it. This man, along with everyone else gathered there, was waiting to be healed. It hadn't worked. He was still unchanged, still in a pitiful state. Any hope for getting better had pretty much vanished by now. No angel ever showed up to heal *him*; no person came to help him in. There was no improvement for all the years he had waited. Solomon was right: "Hope deferred makes the heart sick" (Proverbs 13:12). This man, now sick of heart, had despaired of ever getting better. His hopes had given way to frustration. The question was simply meant to force him to think of his condition. "Do you want to be healed, or would the return of hope be too painful to bear?"

With the command came the capability.

The sick man was polite but frank: "Sir, I have no man to put me into the pool when the water is stirred up; but while I am coming, another steps down before me" (John 5:7). He didn't really answer the question. Instead he offered an excuse why he wasn't better. His excuse was twofold: He didn't have a helper, and other people moved quicker than he could. In his mind, his situation was impossible.

But things were about to change.

Then, with calm authority, Jesus commanded, "Rise, take up your bed and walk" (v. 8). Again, anyone watching this scene and hearing not only Jesus' question but also His command would be furious. How insensitive and downright malicious to tell a handicapped person to perform an impossible task! What cruel humor to taunt a cripple by telling him to get up off the ground!

But Jesus' command wasn't a taunt; it was a passport. With the command came the capability. Jesus' words were the man's ticket to health. What had been humanly impossible in the past because of impotence was now possible because of omnipotence. The man got up and walked. For the first time in thirty-eight years he walked! What a sight! The stunned onlookers watched as this man meandered away from the pool that was once his only home.

What a compassionate episode this was! Going to Jerusalem's place of misery was the Man of Mercy, who followed in His Father's footsteps. He provided what no one else could or would. The man didn't know who Jesus was. He exhibited absolutely no faith in Him whatsoever. Jesus healed other people in response to some confession or expression of faith. Not here. This was pure mercy! The miracle came first; the faith followed later.

What Could Be Worse?

Jesus made three separate statements to this man. The first was a question about the man's desire for healing; the second was a command to walk. The third was a warning. The warning came after the healing, in a second encounter the man had with Jesus. Some time elapsed between the healing and the second meeting. The newly healed resident of Jerusalem was walking around the city in the joy of a newfound freedom. When Jesus sought him out again, He found him in the temple. The man was probably responding to his healing by worshiping. Perhaps he even brought the appropriate offering to the temple priests. The mercy he had received deserved the fitting expression of thanksgiving.

As Jesus encountered the man the second time, He issued a reminder mixed with a word of caution: "See, you have been made well. Sin no more, lest a worse thing come upon you" (John 5:14). Some biblical scholars suggest that this man's illness had been the result of some sinful behavior, although that is not the case with all illness. It could be that Jesus had singled him out to make this point clear. Sin no more.

Lest a worse thing come upon you. But what could possibly be worse than the situation he had been in? He had lived a tragic existence for thirty-eight long years.

Jesus' comment indicates that He is concerned not only with the man's physical healing but also with his spiritual healing. Jesus' mercy extends to the man's body as well as his soul.

Sin no more, Jesus insisted. He wasn't demanding a future untainted by imperfection. He wasn't suggesting that this man could walk through the rest of his life without failure. Jesus was probably addressing the temptations that this man would face. If indeed the man's illness had been related to sin in his life, Jesus was warning him not to go back to that sin. To do so would bring "a worse thing." Simply put, thirty-eight years as an invalid was nothing in comparison to an eternity in hell. Jesus' point was sobering: Sin has consequences that are far worse than any physical and temporary malady.

Mercy Has Consequences

Because Jesus healed the man on the Sabbath day, His act of mercy didn't go over very well with the unmerciful caretakers of Jewish law. The man had picked up his bedroll and carried it away with him, as Jesus had commanded. And that's where all the trouble began. The Sabbath was the day when people were to *rest*, not *roam*. By carrying his mat, the man was violating a Jewish law. No one was allowed to work on the Sabbath, and carrying a "burden" was considered to be work. According to tradition, anything that weighed as much as two dried figs was considered to be a burden.[1] Carrying the mat was clearly "over the line."

God is always restless in the presence of human misery and can't take a day off.

It was more than coincidence that Jesus healed him on the Sabbath. He knew the system. He was aware that those traditions had become more important to the religious leaders than the original scriptural regulations. And He acted in perfect accord with His Father when He extended mercy to a man who needed it. When harassed by the religious leaders about the healing act that resulted in "work," Jesus replied, "My Father never stops working, so why should I?" (John 5:17, NLT).

Jesus deliberately healed this man on the Sabbath. He knowingly told the man to carry his mat. He had violated the Sabbath before in Galilee, inside the Capernaum synagogue (see Mark 3:1-6). He once gleaned grain from the fields on a Sabbath and taught that "the Sabbath was made for man," not the other way around (see Mark 2:23-28). Why did He do it that way? Was He just stirring up trouble? No. He was making the point that God is always restless in the presence of human misery and can't take a day off. At the pool named after mercy and on the feast day when everyone remembers God's merciful provision, Jesus was extending mercy.

How amazing that these leaders were not happy about what they were seeing! They were blinded to the obvious. Here was a cripple now able to walk. This was hardly an everyday occurrence. How ironic that they were blinded by their own supposedly merciful Sabbath law! The Sabbath itself was a day of rest and reflection. It should have reminded them of God's mercy to their people in the past. But for some it had become a stumbling block. It rendered them harsh and merciless. Instead of feeling joy that a suffering man had been set free, they displayed the typical self-righteous emotion of supercilious anger. These were the enemies of mercy.

But something else occurred, and it was far more serious than a rabbinical skirmish. Because Jesus performed an act of healing on this "holy day" and was already suspect by the Jewish authorities, He put himself at risk: "For this reason the Jews persecuted Jesus, and sought to kill Him, because He had done these things on the Sabbath" (John 5:16). But when Jesus said He was just continuing the family business of showing mercy to people, it put the leaders over the edge. Their anger knew no limits. Jesus must be stopped! "Therefore the Jews sought all the more to kill Him, because He not only broke the Sabbath, but also said that God was His Father, making Himself equal with God" (v. 18). This momentous healing on the Sabbath placed Jesus on a collision course that would result in His crucifixion. Such a merciful action would ironically invite a merciless retribution!

What Mercy Looks Like in Us and on Us

Jesus, as the unique Son of God, demonstrated His Father's compassion. People could see into God's heart while they watched Jesus operate on Earth. When Jesus stopped to look over a crowd, it was God studying human need. When Jesus touched a sick person, it was God reaching out to alleviate pain. When Jesus wept, it was God caring about the condition of His fallen creation. When Jesus taught and preached, it was God wanting people to know the freeing power of truth.

Mercy is part of God's nature. He introduced himself to Israel saying, "I am the Lord, the merciful and gracious God"

(Exodus 34:6, NLT). The psalmist agreed and wrote from personal experience with God: "The Lord is merciful and gracious; he is slow to get angry and full of unfailing love" (Psalm 103:8, NLT). Paul called God "rich in mercy, because of His great love with which He loved us" (Ephesians 2:4).

God's mercy extends to you. It is a soft cushion for your weary heart, a place to find relief from your faults, failures, and sin. "God's right hand is full of righteousness" (Psalm 48:10), but since we all fall immeasurably short of His righteousness, His left hand must be full of mercy. If you fall from God's right hand, He will catch you with His left hand! Jesus' actions at the Pool of Bethesda and Jerusalem's temple reveal the power of God's merciful hand. His words and works put sinews and flesh to the bare bones and sometimes nebulous concept of mercy.

Mercy Is a Response to Misery

Jesus' words to the religious leaders were particularly revealing: "My Father has been working until now, and I have been working" (John 5:17). Jesus indicated that the Godhead is restless in the face of human misery. Jesus demonstrated that repeatedly. Jesus cared enough to go and face human tragedy head-on. He didn't turn away from the stench and the sights of suffering. No stained-glass barrier protected Him from the reality of pain.

It seems God has always had a soft spot for the underprivileged, the underdog, and the unfortunate. Throughout Scripture God shows himself to be sensitive to the human condition. Whether it was an Old Testament law requiring Israel to leave the gleanings of their harvest for the poor or a New Testament miracle of healing, the message is the same—God cares. He cares enough to act. He cared enough to enter our world from Heaven and be born into poverty. He cared enough to touch a leper, find a forgotten man at a misnamed pool, and weep at the grave of a dear friend.

God's right hand is full of righteousness, but His left hand must be full of mercy.

Your misery matters to God too. He is not passive when you suffer. His empathetic concern shines through in passages like Isaiah's prophecy: "In all their distress he too was distressed" (Isaiah 63:9, NIV). When the people of Israel were suffering at the hand of Pharaoh in Egypt, God said, "I have surely seen the oppression of My people who are in Egypt, and have heard their cry because of their taskmasters, for I know their sorrows" (Exodus 3:7). God didn't stop there. He delivered His people. And Jesus came to the man at Bethesda to invade his space and set him free.

God wants to be a part of your pain. In the very least He will promise you that He will be with you and that the experience will shape your life for the best (Romans 8:28). He may also deliver you from the experience and even heal you. But a word of caution here: Jesus did not heal everyone at the pool that day. For the purpose of His mission, Jesus selected one out of the crowd. Jesus did heal him, but the man waited for thirty-eight years for that touch! Pain has its place in God's strategy, but know that He is restless when you hurt.

God not only responds to you in mercy, but He also wants you to extend that same mercy to others. We are God's body, His presence on Earth. We can touch lives in His name and extend mercy for His sake. He expects us to do that. One of Jesus' solutions for this suffering world is to send us out into it. We can fight pain and suffering and help to alleviate it. It's not an option but a mandate. John, who wrote this Gospel account, also wrote: "But if anyone has enough money to live well and sees a brother or sister in need and refuses to help—how can God's love be in that person? Dear children, let us stop just saying we love each other; let us really show it by our actions" (1 John 3:17-18, NLT). Through "mercy ministries" (shelters, relief agencies, food pantries, medical missions, etc.) we demonstrate to the world that God cares.

I have often spoken to self-proclaimed atheists who wonder why God (if there is one) would allow the horrible atrocities we see daily. How could a loving God allow a world to suffer? I understand the question. Pain is all around us, and it is no respecter of persons. But when was the last time the United Atheists Society built an orphanage or a hospital for AIDS patients in Africa or for war victims in Eastern Europe? Most "mercy ministries" we hear about are sponsored by Christian groups who are compelled to help heal the world's wounds because of Christ's example and mandate. St. John Chrysostom was right: "Mercy imitates God and disappoints Satan."[2]

Mercy Isn't Something We Deserve

The man at the pool wasn't worthy of what Jesus did. He did not deserve Jesus' mercy. When God gives us what we deserve, He is expressing His *justice*; when He gives us good things that we don't deserve (or doesn't give us bad things that we *do* deserve), He is expressing His *mercy*. God is both just and merciful—a difficult combination. How can God do it? How does God balance both? Through the act of substitution. The Cross of Christ enabled God to treat Jesus as if He had committed every sin committed by every person. The Father punished the Son on the Cross as if He had lived our lives. Why? He did this so He could treat us as if we live Jesus' life. That's substitution. That's how God can be both just (punishing sin) and yet merciful (not giving us the punishment we deserve). The man at Bethesda was treated on the basis of mercy. Jesus was on Earth to take the penalty of humanity's sin and was giving a preview of coming attractions.

So, what elicits God's mercy? As we concluded earlier, mercy is God's response to misery. When we are helpless and hopeless, God reaches out in mercy to us.

Helplessness. The man at the pool protested that he couldn't help himself into the water, and he couldn't find anyone else to help him. He was utterly without help. He was, in fact, a perfect candidate for the power of mercy to be shown. Rather than help those who can help themselves, God helped a helpless man. When everything else fails, when friends or loved ones aren't around to give us what we need, when the cries for help seem to bounce against the heavens, God's mercy steps in.

When the Prussian King Frederick II was inspecting a Berlin prison, he noticed that the prisoners begged to be released. One by one they cited their innocence, protesting that they had been treated unfairly by the system and didn't deserve their sentence. But one prisoner remained silent, not joining in the refrain. He caught the king's eye.

Frederick turned to address him: "I suppose you're innocent too and shouldn't be here!"

"No, your Majesty. I am here for armed robbery, and I deserve my punishment."

Amused and refreshed by the honesty of this prisoner, Frederick summoned the jail keeper. "Release this man at once before he corrupts all these fine and innocent people here!" The man was promptly released.

He didn't deserve it. He was at that point helpless—chained by the consequences of his own misbehavior.[3]

God extends His mercy in much the same way. Maybe you feel that you've been abandoned and all outside help has vanished. You've tried by self-improvement techniques to better your situation, but they didn't work. Then you are a perfect candidate for Jesus' merciful touch.

Hopelessness. Helplessness and hopelessness are not the same thing. When the helplessness lingers so long that no thread of optimism remains—that's hopelessness. Years passed for the man at Bethesda— thirty-eight of them crawled by. He was convinced that things would never get any better for him. It was in that condition that Jesus approached him. The man didn't deserve to be healed, and he did not exhibit any faith to warrant a response from Jesus. He didn't even know who Jesus was.

I deal with people all the time who struggle with long-standing habits they've wrestled with, some for many years. I've also watched these desperate ones regain hope as God in His mercy intervenes. I've watched drug users be restored to their families and broken marriages glued back together. One "impossible" case that stands out was a Christian woman who was married to an unbelieving husband and whose marriage was on the rocks. Kathy loved Vincent and held on to hope until it seemed there was none left. Their relationship deteriorated over time. It finally reached the meltdown stage when he fathered a child with another woman while still married to Kathy. Afterward he filed for divorce. Kathy, willing to forgive, hoped for reconciliation, but the divorce went through. Then, seemingly out of the blue, Vincent called Kathy, begging for her forgiveness. He asked God to forgive him and restore the marriage. Months later I officiated at the ceremony of their second marriage to each other. It was a hopeless relationship until Jesus showed up!

Mercy Involves Vulnerability

Think of the risks Jesus took that day at Bethesda. First, speaking to the man in the manner in which He did could easily have been misunderstood. Jesus pressed the man, getting him to face his dilemma honestly. But it was risky business. C. S. Lewis noted that "the hardness of God is kinder than the softness of men, and his compulsion is our liberation."[4] Jesus' pressure could easily have been taken as cruelty. Second, the healing itself brought Jesus into confrontation with the established protectors of the Sabbath law. He elicited the anger and hatred of the religious leaders simply by acting mercifully.

In one sense, God still takes risks today. We don't think about it much, but it's true. Just take a quick look around at some of us whom He has chosen to be His children. Throughout history many Christians—representatives of the Kingdom of God—by word and action, have given God a bad reputation. Let's face it—we're far from perfect. We're watched carefully every time we blunder, and we're judged for it by outsiders. Their judgment may not be fair, but it's a fact nonetheless. How many people have walked away from God simply on the basis of how His children act? That's part of the risk God runs in accepting any of us into His family. We all have the potential to give His family a bad name. One wonders how many prodigals have been kept out of the Kingdom of God by those of us on the inside. Yet, God still risks it. To Him there is joy in forgiving the unworthy and unlovely. Aren't you glad?

I sometimes travel to remote places in the world to help support relief workers who give their time to alleviate pain and help heal the world's sores. So many are involved in showing mercy to people who are like the Bethesda crowd. Those who do it always risk something. They become vulnerable to hostility, misunderstanding, and discomfort. I think of Dr. Eleanor Soltau, an American doctor who went to live in the Middle East after graduating from medical school. She lived and served in a Jordanian sanatorium, treating Bedouin patients who were suffering from tuberculosis. While serving out her years of retirement, she was burned to death in an accident on the hospital premises. Eleanor lived and died showing mercy.

Dr. Jurisic Josip from Bosnia is another model of mercy. He was the only neurosurgeon in a hospital of six hundred beds. Many of the patients needed emergency surgery due to war injuries. Dr. Josip often found himself operating while bombs were exploding around him. When the electrical supply was hit, he operated by flashlight. A friend of mine, a surgeon who operated with Dr. Josip, tells of the time when a young patient died because someone forgot to put fuel into the generator that powered the respirator. Dr. Josip feared for my friend's life because my friend's name was written on the log as the surgeon who operated. Knowing the fanaticism of the region and that the young man's friends would blame the surgeon, Dr. Josip decided to take the ultimate risk. He erased the name of that surgeon and replaced it with his own! The willingness to lay down his life for another was not only merciful but it also reflected Jesus, who risked so much because He knew the power of mercy.

Yes, showing mercy is risky business. It was for Jesus. It was for Eleanor and Jurisic. It will be for you as well. But ask anyone who has lived mercifully if it was worth it. Is the sacrifice worth it? You know the answer. If the results are that people are able to walk and lives are transformed by such humble power, then temporary discomfort is well worth the outcome.

Mercy Involves Responsibility

Mercy can't be forced on someone. Jesus didn't walk up to the man and say, "You're going to be healed, whether you like it or not." Although the man was helpless, he was not unable to respond. So Jesus asked, "Do you want to be made well?" (John 5:6). The excuses the man offered revealed his hopelessness, but he still yearned for health. Jesus didn't force it, but He made the man face the responsibility of his desire.

Jesus also expected the man to cooperate. "Take up your bed and walk," He commanded (v. 8). With the instruction came the power to fulfill it, but it still required a level of responsibility. The man may have thought briefly, *What? I can't walk. That's the problem. Don't you think that if I could walk,*

I would have done it years ago? But then he discovered the power of mercy. "Immediately the man was made well" (v. 9).

God never forces His mercy on us. It must be received. We must cooperate. Although God is "not willing that any should perish" (2 Peter 3:9), we still see people all around us perishing in the sea of stubbornness.

What about you? Do you really want to change? Do you really want to walk where He wants you to walk? Will you cooperate with Him? When He gives you a command to do something, maybe to go into an area of spiritual service, what is your response? When He gives you a command to love someone whom you find difficult or beyond love, will you say, "I can't"? Take a bold step. *Just do it!* Instead of sitting there, get up and say, "Lord, by your strength, I will do what you ask."

Mercy Fosters Accountability

Jesus told the man, "Sin no more lest a worse thing come upon you" (John 5:14). The disease had robbed the man of the best years of his life, but sin could rob him of eternity. When Jesus told the man not to sin, He didn't suggest he could make it through life without sinning. Jesus was talking about lifestyle. The man's body had changed instantly, and now the rest of his life must follow. When God's mercy touches us, we do not have the right to ignore it and persist in sinful behavior. Instead, we should be grateful. Mercy should have an elevating effect on us. Encounters with God's mercy should give us a new perspective of both the temporal as well as the eternal.

A dear woman in our church had been praying for her wayward son. She came to church one night worried that he was running with the wrong crowd. She suspected that trouble was imminent, and she was right. That night her son was with some buddies, and he was accidentally shot in the face with a handgun. Her worst fears were coming true. When she arrived at the hospital, she was told the wonderful news that the bullet would leave no lasting damage. If it had traveled a few millimeters laterally in either direction, it would have either killed her son or paralyzed him.

Two weeks later that young man stood in line at church to tell me his story and to let me know what he had learned.

He knew it was by God's mercy that he was still living, and he knew that God had a purpose for him to fulfill. He wanted to get serious with God and was now determined to become an obedient disciple. I grabbed his hands, and we prayed together. The young man had realized a new level of accountability from his painful but merciful experience.

How often does God try to get through to us? How often do we forget that were it not for His mercies, we would be consumed? (See Lamentations 3:22.) A friend sent me this fictional but poignant letter illustrating how God's merciful reminders surround us daily and how we can take them for granted.

My Dearest One,

I had to write to tell you how much I love and care for you. Yesterday, I saw you walking and laughing with your friends. I hoped that soon you'd want Me to walk along with you too, so I painted you a sunset to close your day and whispered a cool breeze to refresh you. I waited. You never called. I just kept on loving you.

As I watched you fall asleep last night, I wanted to touch you. I spilled moonlight onto your face—trickling down your cheeks as so many tears have. You didn't even think of Me; I wanted so much to comfort you.

The next day I exploded a brilliant sunrise into glorious morning for you. But you woke up late and rushed off to work. You didn't even notice. My sky became cloudy, and My tears were the rain.

I love you, oh, if only you'd listen. I really love you. I try to say it in the quiet of the green meadow and in the blue sky. The wind whispers My love throughout the treetops and spills it into the vibrant colors of all the flowers. I shout it to you in the thunder of the great waterfalls and compose love songs for birds to sing for you. I warm you with the clothing of My sunshine and perfume the air with nature's sweet scent. My love for you is deeper than any ocean and greater than any need in your heart. If you'd only realize how I care.

My Dad sends His love. I want you to meet Him— He cares too. Fathers are just that way. So, please, call on Me soon. No matter how long it takes, I'll wait—because I love you.

Your Friend, Jesus

— —

FOR REFLECTION AND DISCUSSION

1. Think of an episode when you were miserable. What things did you do to alleviate your condition? Did anything that you tried on your own help? What was it? Are the results lasting ones?

2. Look up Matthew 5:7 and 2 Corinthians 1:3-4. Rewrite the verses in your own words. How does God's mercy transform us into agents of His mercy?

3. Have you ever been "burned" while trying to do the right thing and extending mercy to someone who needed it? Describe the experience. Did it make you hardened to any future risk? Did this "backfiring" effect prevent Jesus from any further merciful ventures (see John 5:18-21)?

4. Find a person or family who is regarded as helpless or hopeless. Organize a team to serve this person or persons. Suggestions:

Take meals to the person, or invite him or her to your home for a meal.

Do yard work and minor repairs around the person's house.

Clean the inside of the person's home, and then thank him or her for allowing you to come and do it.

Visit the person, taking along musical instruments and other vocalists to sing songs to the person as an encouragement.

5. Think of the significant ways that Jesus has shown mercy to you. Using those experiences as themes, write Jesus a letter of love and appreciation for His mercy.

part three

The Glory of Jesus

ELEVEN

Restoration Glory

Defector from the Kingdom of Darkness

They sailed to the region of the Gerasenes, which is across the lake from Galilee. When Jesus stepped ashore, he was met by a demon-possessed man from the town. For a long time this man had not worn clothes or lived in a house, but had lived in the tombs. When he saw Jesus, he cried out and fell at his feet, shouting at the top of his voice, "What do you want with me, Jesus, Son of the Most High God? I beg you, don't torture me!" For Jesus had commanded the evil spirit to come out of the man. Many times it had seized him, and though he was chained hand and foot and kept under guard, he had broken his chains and had been driven by the demon into solitary places.

Jesus asked him, "What is your name?"

"Legion," he replied, because many demons had gone into him. And they begged him repeatedly not to order them to go into the Abyss.

A large herd of pigs was feeding there on the hillside. The demons begged Jesus to let them go into them, and he gave them permission. When the demons came out of the man, they went into the pigs, and the herd rushed down the steep bank into the lake and was drowned.

When those tending the pigs saw what had happened, they ran off and reported this in the town and countryside, and the people went out to see what had happened. When they came to Jesus, they found the man from whom the demons had gone out, sitting at Jesus' feet, dressed and in his right mind; and they were afraid. Those who had seen it told the people how the demon-possessed man had been cured. Then all the people of the region of the Gerasenes asked Jesus to leave them, because they were overcome with fear. So he got into the boat and left.

The man from whom the demons had gone out begged to go with him, but Jesus sent him away, saying, "Return home and tell how much God has done for you." So the man went away and told all over town how much Jesus had done for him (Luke 8:26-39, NIV).

B efore I became a Christian, I dabbled in the occult. At first I was merely fascinated by my friends' involvement in tarot cards, séances, and aural readings. But the fascination soon led to experimentation. After reading several books on the unconventional practices of autohypnosis and astral projection, I decided to delve in. I found myself "traveling" the cosmos with my soul and documenting the experiences and sights I had seen. I even astral projected into the home of a skeptical friend and then described it to her the following week in *graphic detail*—the layout of her furniture, the color of her curtains, and what she was doing while I "visited" her. I had tapped into something far greater than myself, and it was addictive.

Once while on a student trip to Mexico, a friend and I decided to try spirit writing. He explained to me that I needed only to sit quietly with my pencil in my hand and loosely hold it over a single sheet of paper. He encouraged me to "open myself up" to the spirit world and even invoke the spirits to take control of me and reveal my past life experiences. My experimental nature was fueled by the possibilities of such a visit, so I breathed slowly and deliberately. Soon I became aware that there was another force in the room. Suddenly my arm began to move quite apart from my own control. I wrote letters and sentences that I later read as messages from departed spirits. I thought, *It worked!* This was the beginning of a whole new episode of spirituality for me.

Then the thought struck me one day, while considering my strong religious upbringing, that if there really is a God, why was I messing around with all this stuff? I found that if there was this much power on the *wrong side*, the dark side of the spiritual fence, then there must be greater power for living on the *right side*. It was there that my real quest for the things of God began. I had been on the wrong side and wanted to find out the truth. I was ready to "defect"! And defect I did. Although I dabbled for some time in the spiritual underworld, my curiosity moved from the past life experiences to my future life. I wanted to make sure that eternal things were in order. My decision to follow Christ included my decision to renounce any occult activity. I discovered that Jesus had the power to break the hold of Satan on my life.

The Man Everyone in Town Avoided

Jesus traveled to the other side of the Sea of Galilee one morning with his disciples and encountered a man who was definitely on the wrong side spiritually. The previous night Jesus had calmed a great storm on the tumultuous lake. He was now about to face a worse storm inside a tormented man.

The man whom Jesus was going to meet was possessed by demons, and as a result he was tormented, self-destructive, repulsive, and isolated. Jesus intended not only to touch this man but also his family and an entire region that wanted nothing to do with Him.

He was tormented. The man had been tormented by demons for quite some time (Luke 8:27). Perhaps progressively he had lost control of his life, but he was now under the control of forces much greater than himself. Those foul beings had "driven" him away from everything he once knew and everyone he once loved. He had become so dangerous that he needed not only to be guarded but also to be bound with chains and shackles, as if he were a vicious animal (v. 29). This tormented soul cried out day and night, howling from his miserable condition (Mark 5:5).

Attempts to restrain the man were unsuccessful. Exhibiting superhuman strength, he broke the fetters as if they were toys. To have that kind of physical power trapped in a normal human body was devastating. No doubt the man had severe and perhaps permanent damage to his flesh and even to the bones of his wrists, possibly resulting in deep scarring and deformity. His body was probably full of bloody cuts and infected scars.

He was self-destructive. Although the Gospels do not give the man's name, both Mark and Luke record the name of the demons that lived inside the man. When Jesus asked the spirits

189

to identify themselves, they said their name was "Legion," indicating that a whole hellish host was controlling his life. (A Roman legion was a band of six thousand armed soldiers, often accompanied by over a hundred horsemen as well.)

These diabolical entities inhabited and held control over the man's entire being, including his motor functions. The foul spirits would regularly seize him (Luke 8:29). Such violent fits were out of his control, humanly speaking; the spirits that possessed him forcefully compelled him to move. This was pure and severe demon possession.

Besides the man's sudden fits of frenzy, observers could see physical evidence of his self-destructive behavior. The Gospel of Mark mentions that he cut himself with stones (Mark 5:5). With something that resembled a masochistic form of insanity, the possessed man appeared to act suicidal at times.

He was repulsive. Completely naked and covered with sores, this man was a repulsive sight. Scars and scabs covered his body. Skin ulcerations reopened wounds that had become infected. If people saw him, they naturally gasped and turned away from him. Matthew, who also relates the story, tells us this man was "exceedingly fierce, so that no one could pass that way" (Matthew 8:28). He was wild, untamable, and certainly unapproachable. His savage mannerisms probably repelled everyone in the region.

He was isolated. It seems that this man had once lived in the nearby town (Luke 8:27), functioning in reasonable normalcy, living with a family (v. 39). Those were things of the past. His home now was in the tombs among the nearby hills on the eastern side of the Sea of Galilee. His only company were the corpses of the departed townspeople. For the Jews, any contact with the dead resulted in ceremonial defilement and required ritual cleansing to restore one back to worship. But worship was the last thing these demons wanted to do—at least until this very unusual encounter.

A Collision of Two Kingdoms

The encounter Jesus had with this man could better be described as a head-on collision. Two spiritual kingdoms clashed in this encounter: the kingdom of darkness and the kingdom of light. When Jesus arrived on the scene, the man approached Him.

190

What did the disciples think when they saw the man? What was their first reaction? They were no doubt shocked by the naked, scarred, and howling creature. It was a highly charged and emotional encounter. It was also an extremely ironic one because the demons recognized the Son of God.

Adoration. When the demon-possessed man saw Jesus, he did something unusual. He rushed toward Him, fell down at His feet, and cried out: "Why are you bothering me, Jesus, Son of the Most High God? Please, I beg you, don't torture me!" (Luke 8:28, NLT). It may have seemed that the man was mocking Jesus, but Mark's account of the same incident states that the man "ran and worshiped Him" (Mark 5:6). As if compelled by a power greater than the demons, the man fell to the ground and worshiped Jesus. The demons inside the man confessed to Jesus' absolute authority as the Son of the Most High God. Even these satanic beings acknowledged that they were under submission to the Son of God.

Liberation. Jesus' purpose was to set free this victim of hellish terror. The liberating moment came as Jesus "commanded the unclean spirit to come out of the man" (Luke 8:29). With absolute authority and without any fanfare, Jesus spoke His powerful words: "Come out of the man, unclean spirit!" (Mark 5:8). It was a display of glorious sovereignty. Jesus, as always, was the master of the situation. It is obvious that there was no great struggle here. Because of who Jesus was, the devils were not only compelled to bow down and worship Him but also forced to leave the tormented victim. They knew very well the chain of command, and they knew that they must obey.

Negotiation. In response to Jesus' command for them to leave the man, the demons came up with a contingency plan. They resorted to begging, wanting to be driven into a nearby pig herd rather than to be consigned to the abyss (Luke 8:31). These evil spirits were apparently afraid of torment. They understood that there was an appointed time for their judgment and punishment to eternal condemnation, but this wasn't the appointed time. Although they were busy tormenting God's creation, they themselves wanted no part of divine punishment.

Destruction. Without any struggle whatsoever, the evil spirits responded to Jesus' command. Demonic spirits are powerful entities that could even match wits and strength with obedient angels such as the archangel Michael (Daniel 10:13). But there was no hesitation and no battle here. These demons submitted to the Son of God. As soon as the demons entered the pigs, the herd rushed down the precipitous hillside and was destroyed in the lake below. And the torment caused by years of demon possession in one man's life was forever destroyed.

Chasing Away the Glory

Word traveled fast in this rural community. Local residents curiously poured out to investigate what they had heard about the man whom they had avoided at all costs. When they arrived at the scene, they saw the man completely changed. He was no longer wild and tormented. He wore clothes and sat calmly. He was mentally stable. His countenance was bright, and his eyes were alert and grateful. This man had "switched sides." He had *defected* from the kingdom of darkness to the kingdom of light through Jesus' glorious power.

While the man was incredibly grateful for what Jesus had done, the crowd was not. They were afraid. They were not relieved to see one of their own restored. They were not awed by Jesus' power and authority. No. They were full of fear. So they begged Jesus to leave their area.

They were keenly aware that something supernatural had occurred; they just didn't know what it was exactly. And they didn't want to find out. It must have something to do with God's power and glory. The miracle was undeniable: There, sitting in front of them, sat the man they had once chased away. He was perfectly cured. They all knew it.

What made them afraid? We don't know for sure. Maybe they were distrustful of what Jesus would do with His power. Maybe they were angry with Him because they had lost a valuable herd of pigs when the possessed creatures had plunged to their death. Maybe the people were more interested in their source of income than in the man's source of freedom.

Rather than offer a unified anthem of praise, the crowd solidified in a unified attitude of pessimism. Rather than being grateful that a menace had been healed, they were fearful that another menace had healed him. They didn't urge Jesus to remain a few more hours while they brought their sick friends. They didn't ask Jesus about who He was and what His mission was. They just plain wanted Him gone.

The liberated man responded differently of course. He knew better. He didn't want Jesus to go; He wanted to make worshiping Jesus his preoccupation. He begged Jesus to let him stay with Him. Who could blame him? He had just been sprung from the worst prison a human being could ever know. He had just experienced the glory of restoration. Now he begged for continued fellowship with the only one stronger than the spirits who had once inhabited his tormented body.

Surprisingly Jesus denied the man's request. "Go home," Jesus replied in so many words. It sounds strange to our ears. This man could have been an asset to Jesus. He could have given his testimony in every village where they went. He could have made a powerful impact on people as he showed them the scars where the shackles had torn his wrists and the stones had cut him. Why not allow him to join the team of roving disciples?

Jesus clearly instructed the delivered man to go back home. Restored and set free, the man had a commission to fulfill. He was to go back to the house he hadn't been in for so many years and tell what happened to him that day. His family probably had dismissed him long ago. They may have been stunned to see him coming up the road that afternoon. In obedience and with a grateful heart, the man delivered from demons delivered his message. He went to his own home, to his town, and to nine other towns in the surrounding area (see Mark 5:20). In each of these places he told as many as he could that he had defected from the kingdom of darkness and now lived in the glorious kingdom of light.

What a sad day it was as the disciples and their Lord got back into their boat and went back home. When they left, the "glory had departed," just as it did in ancient Israel, when the ark of God was removed (see 1 Samuel 4:21). The people had chased away the glory.

Glorious Revelations for Future Followers

Modern society doesn't take well to the idea of a personal devil. They may admit that an evil force exists, but they reject the idea that Satan is a personal malevolent being as a primitive and naïve notion. Satan doesn't mind; an enemy is never more dangerous than when he is dismissed as trivial. But a quick look around at our world leads us to conclude that something more is going on than meets the eye. Indeed! Something is going on.

> Men don't believe in the devil now as their fathers used to do.
> They've opened wide their broadest creeds and let his majesty through.
> The devil is voted not to be; so of course, the devil is gone—
> But simple folks would like to know, "Who carries his business on?"[1]

The devil's business has been going on a long time. He has been able to study humanity for thousands of years and has focused his attacks through careful research. He is also aware of God's master plan. When God created us, He made us in His likeness. Unlike other creatures, we bear God's image (Genesis 1:27). Every woman and every man reflect the glory of the Creator. The more we reflect His image in our lives, the more glory God receives, and the more we are satisfied since we are fulfilling the very purpose for our existence.

But Satan doesn't want to go along with that plan. He has plans of his own. His scheme is to mar God's image by ruining God's chief creation—humanity. He has many tactics to accomplish his fiendish purposes.

Where do you fit into this story? Are you like the man? Are you living in the kingdom of darkness? Or is someone you love under the control of demonic forces? Are you fearful, convinced that the power of evil will never be broken?

This story offers hope, direction, and strength. Remember that while Satan is powerful—never underestimate his strength—Jesus' power and glory are even more powerful. Christ's death on the Cross has already broken Satan's power (see Colossians 2:15). We can take comfort knowing that our glorious Savior will save us from the kingdom of darkness.

Jesus Restores Us

The clash of the kingdom of darkness with the kingdom of light is dramatic. Satan is destructive; Jesus is constructive. Satan tears down; Jesus builds up. Satan takes life; Jesus gives life. Jesus summed it all up when He said, "The thief does not come except to steal, and to kill, and to destroy. I have come that they may have life, and that they may have it more abundantly" (John 10:10). What Satan stole from this man, Jesus restored.

Satan is destructive; Jesus is constructive. Satan tears down; Jesus builds up. Satan takes life; Jesus gives life.

The condition of the man before and after the encounter with Jesus is equally dramatic. He was once self-destructive; he is now self-controlled. He was once naked and intimidating; he is now clothed and gentle. He was once isolated from people; he is now integrated into society. He was once mentally and spiritually tormented; he is now in his right mind. He was once marred by hell; he is now made whole by Heaven!

It took years for Satan to whittle this man's life down to such a tormented state; it took Jesus moments to restore it. Just as He will restore all of creation one day in His glory, He demonstrated His glory that day in restoring this part of His creation. That's His business, you know. He knows that the enemy of God is a parasite, feeding off people's hopes. Jesus knows that we have a tendency toward spiritual entropy—losing the spiritual vitality that comes from being made in His image. Jesus' aim is to give back what Satan has stolen. God promised to His wayward people who had lost so much, "I will give you back what you lost to the stripping locusts" (Joel 2:25, NLT). That's Jesus' style—He is a giver. He is a restorer. He fixes what His enemy breaks.

You may be reading this right now with a sense of deep desperation. Your life has been marred by Satan's invasion. Maybe a certain sin in your life is so

Jesus' aim is to give back what Satan has stolen.

deeply rooted and so much a part of you that you've become convinced there is no deliverance possible. The hold on your life through possessive habits or even satanic oppression is so great that you can't imagine finding freedom. You are shackled and tormented by wickedness. It may have ruined your marriage, your occupation, and your relationships. You've tried everything, but you see no progress. Your life bears so many scars that you have all but given up. Maybe you *have* given up altogether.

Let me say that if that's your thinking, Satan has convinced you of his lies. He wants to keep you bound by having you believe that he's got you and there's no escape. He wants you to give up. He wants you to believe that you're trapped. But he's wrong! I have seen too many people who *have* been released. I know too many people who *are* whole. They are restored. Their hellish nightmare is over. The same Jesus who delivered the demon-possessed man also delivered me and a host of others. We sit in the camp next to Jesus; we are clothed with righteousness and in our right minds.

What is binding you? Is it a lifelong drug habit? Are you bound by a sexual perversion or pornographic obsession? Are discouragement and depression your constant companions? Listen—you are *not* beyond help! Jesus—the deliverer—knows your condition and has a plan. Don't let the lies in.

Jesus Holds Authority

Satan and the armies of hell have assaulted creation throughout history. The very name *Satan* means "adversary," and that is his principle role; he is against everything that God is for, including His people. Satan harasses people, attacking the mind and the will, polluting people with foul and destructive ideas. Satan is very resourceful. He uses whatever means he can to captivate people, whether through attitudes of the heart such as greed and lust or through forces like the media or addictive activities. Sometimes the Devil is subtle; other times he will make a frontal assault with no smoke and mirrors to cover up his actions. The lyrics of some modern songs unabashedly worship Satan's hellish power, using the sign of the pentagram and overtly displaying the biblically satanic figure 666. I've spoken to some researchers who have noted what they consider to be a link between satanic influence and suicide. The devil loves to cripple people with hopelessness and despair.

But Satan's power is limited. We must remember that.

Although Satan's power is not to be trifled with, we don't need to live in terror of it. Satan is restricted. He is not the opposite of God, as most people regard him. Rather, Satan was one of God's creations who rebelled and wanted more power as well as glory (see Ezekiel 28:12-19). Once known as Lucifer—which ironically means "the bearer of **But Satan's power is limited.** light"—he was one of God's highest ranking angels, but his pride consumed him. He wanted to be equal with God (see Isaiah 14:13-14). He has tried ever since to convince people that he is.

But the truth is that Satan and his minions can operate only under God's permissive counsel. The Devil's power is limited in scope. The demons inhabiting the man of Gadara begged Jesus not to torment them, and then they begged Jesus to *permit* them to go into the pigs. They were not able to make executive decisions on their own. They also did not consult with Satan, their supervisor. In the presence of the glorious Christ, their submission was to Him alone. Jesus held the reins of sovereign control.

Jesus, being God, is omnipotent; He has total authority. He is everlasting, while the Devil is finite—he has a definite time and place of his judgment and destruction. Jesus is the Creator; Satan is the creation. Jesus has unlimited power; Satan's power is definitely limited. Although we wonder why he is granted the power he does exercise, that power is restricted to stringent boundaries. Job in the Old Testament was the victim of satanic opposition, but behind the scenes God delineated the boundaries: "'All right, you may test him,' the Lord said to Satan. 'Do whatever you want with everything he possesses, but don't harm him physically.' So Satan left the Lord's presence" (Job 1:12, NLT).

Later on, after Job successfully withstood the onslaught of despair brought on by Satan, further negotiations were conducted. Satan again needed to gain God's permission before he could act. God granted permission, but again He set the parameters of the attack. "'All right, do with him as you please,' the Lord said to Satan. 'But spare his life'" (Job 2:6, NLT).

Satan has authority, but it is borrowed authority. God will allow Satan's evil attacks but will control them so that the subject, if he or she is a Christian, will not ultimately be destroyed. If you are struggling under Satan's power, you can rest in the fact that God is allowing the evil circumstance to strengthen your faith and cause you to be refined (see Romans 8:28). Be assured that you can find victory in resisting the Devil (see 1 Peter 5:8-9).

Basically we're in the same position that Europe was in when the Allies came in toward the end of World War II. At that stage the people knew the war was essentially over, although there would still be more skirmishes ahead. The end was in view. Similarly, through His death on the Cross Jesus has already won the war. As a result, Satan's end is also in view. The war is essentially over; it's the mop-up we're experiencing at this point! If the Lord lives in you, remember that you have within you a power that is mightier than all the forces of hell put together: "God's Spirit, who is in you, is greater than the Devil, who is in the world" (1 John 4:4, NCV).

The glory of divine authority was obvious that day at Gadara, and it was also a foreshadow of things to come. The demon-possessed man bowed before Jesus. How ironic but how predictive! One day it will be so for every person. In the end it will happen that "at the name of Jesus every knee will bow, in heaven and on Earth and under the Earth, and every tongue will confess that Jesus Christ is Lord, to the glory of God the Father" (Philippians 2:10-11, NLT).

The scene was also predictive of the punishment the Devil will one day receive at the hand of Jesus, Son of the Most High. The pigs ran down and were destroyed in the lake below. One day Jesus will return to establish His kingdom. When He does, He will imprison Satan for a thousand years. After a brief time of freedom, both Satan and his minions will be cast into the lake of fire, where "they will be tormented day and night forever and ever" (Revelation 20:2, 7-10).

The bottom line is this: Although you have a powerful enemy, you have an even more powerful deliverer. Don't attribute more power to Satan than he really has. The fact is, the God inside of you terrifies him. Believe that, and march forward in that confidence. You don't have to tremble before the minions of hell. They themselves tremble at the power, presence, and glory of God (see James 2:19). Walk in the light, and you have no need to fear the darkness. Remember that if the demons bowed, worshiped, and prayed in the presence of Jesus, we, His children, should do no less. Advance in this spiritual battle by prayer, for Satan trembles when he sees the weakest saint upon his knees!

Jesus Evokes Response

As is so often the case, the responses that day in Gadara were varied. Everyone marveled at what happened, but not everyone approved. Nothing has changed much since then. Christ's glory, as seen in His power against evil, is still controversial. Not everyone wants it. Not everyone welcomes Jesus. Not everyone wants to change sides.

Some fear Christ's glory and are repelled by it. The residents of Gadara didn't really want what Jesus had to offer. They chased Him away. This response is so different from what we see in the rest of the gospel narrative, isn't it? It seemed as if wherever Jesus went, people begged Him to stay, to touch someone else, to heal yet another. Not here. These people were afraid. His glory terrified them. His authority intimidated them.

Perhaps their fears were rooted in their materialism. The pig business was profitable, and Jesus' actions destroyed it. Could they trust Him? What else would He do?

Before we are too quick to judge the Gadarenes, we must realize that we respond in similar ways sometimes. So we need to ask ourselves, What do we value the most in life? Where do eternal things fit in? How vital is it to have radical change going on inside of us and around us? And what price are we willing to pay for it? Are such spiritual realities more important than income, status, and personal comfort? Jesus said, "For where your treasure is, there your heart will be also" (Matthew 6:21).

Some flock to Christ's glory and revel in it. The man who was once controlled by evil spirits is now under Christ's control. And in response, he wants to stay with Jesus. Who wouldn't?

199

He knew more than anyone else that he was in the presence of the glorious Son of the Most High. What a privilege to have encountered Him! He knew there was just no better place to be than just sitting at His feet.

But think for a moment what that meant on a spiritual level. Once the man had "defected" from Satan's kingdom and crossed over to the kingdom of light, he had a whole new relationship to the Devil. Once the man became a friend of God, he was an enemy of Satan and his demons. He was no longer on Satan's team. He belonged to Jesus.

It's true for you as well. When you come to Christ or are delivered from something by Christ, you enter into a new relationship not only with Him but also with the dark side. You become an enemy of the forces of hell and a target for attack. It may sound daunting to be considered an enemy of such a malevolent being, but don't forget the perspective. Satan is not God's opposite. He is not in competition in any real sense. Yes, these demons are real and antagonistic. But there is actually great joy in realizing this new relationship. Charles Spurgeon explained:

> There is something very comforting in the thought that the devil is an adversary. I would sooner have him for an adversary than a friend. Oh my soul, it were dread work for you if Satan were a friend of yours, for then with him you must forever dwell in darkness, shut out from the friendship of God. But to have Satan for your adversary is a comfortable omen, for it looks as if God were our Friend, and so far let us be comforted in this matter.[2]

Don't misunderstand. The demons of hell will do anything they can to oppose you, but take comfort in the truth that God protects you. Maybe the apostle John thought back to this event when he later wrote, "We know that those who have become part of God's family do not make a practice of sinning, for God's Son holds them securely, and the evil one cannot get his hands on them" (1 John 5:18, NLT). Don't do the Devil a favor by focusing too much on him as your enemy. He may roar and stalk. Let him. And let the one who purchased you with His own blood fight the battles as they come.

Jesus Commissions Us

Jesus flatly denied the man the opportunity to follow him. He sent him on his way with a job to do. Jesus was leaving the area and wouldn't be back; the residents wanted Him gone. But He wasn't about to go without leaving a witness. Jesus was making sure that the glory He manifested that day wouldn't end there. He commissioned this delivered one to tell people about the great things God had done for him. Since everyone around in the region knew about this man's history, Jesus' glory would spread through his testimony.

Jesus commanded him, "Return to your own house, and tell what great things *God* has done for you" (Luke 8:39, emphasis added). The grateful man immediately went out, not only to his home, but also through the whole region: He "proclaimed throughout the whole city what great things *Jesus* had done for him" (v. 39, emphasis added).

Note the subtle shift in terminology. Jesus instructs the man to tell what *God* had done; the man shares what Jesus has done. This is significant. The man realized that God and Jesus are one. The glory that Jesus shared with His Father was the glory of triumphing over the kingdom of darkness and of restoring life back to usefulness. Now everyone around that spiritually dark region would get the opportunity to understand that.

What a thought—Jesus' denial of the man's request became the avenue of greater glory. This delivered man became the first missionary Jesus ever sent out! Long before He commissioned the apostles to go into all the world (Mark 16:15) and before He sent out the seventy disciples to preach around Galilee (Luke 10:1), Jesus sent out this man to glorify the name of the Father and the Son.

Our purpose is to glorify our Creator and Savior. Peter noted that believers are "His own special people, that you may proclaim the praises of Him who called you out of darkness into His marvelous light" (1 Peter 2:9). The man who had lived so long in darkness was now basking in the light of Jesus' glory. Jesus wanted the news of what happened to spread around.

God reserves the right to plant us where He will derive the most glory. It may not be what we had in mind. He may ask you to leave your comfort zone and move to an area that needs to hear and see how God's glory works in your life. He may call you to a country far away from your home, or He may have you stay where you are and glorify Him in the place you were born and raised. The decision for our commission is solely His. God's plan goes beyond our narrow scope. Our desire may be for comfort or immediate gratification. But He wants His work to get mileage! If He says no to us, it may be because He has in mind something that will bring Him even more glory. Only eternity will reveal how God worked it all out. But the goal of the commission remains the same—tell people how great God is. Tell them that Jesus is the great deliverer who still invades lives with the light.

—

FOR REFLECTION AND DISCUSSION

1. What were some of your childhood images of the Devil? How did your view change as an adult? How has your view changed as a result of reading this chapter?

2. Make a list of the attributes of Satan's power and the attributes of Jesus' power. What are the similarities, and what are the differences? Is there a balance of power, or is there a huge difference?

3. Write out a personalized version of Joel 2:25-26, using your name and the description of the devastation you have experienced. Carry your "translation" around with you this week and use it in your daily devotions.

"[Your name], I will restore to you the years that the [drug use or infidelity or activity in the occult or whatever has bound you to the kingdom of darkness] has eaten.... You shall eat in plenty and be satisfied, and praise the name of the Lord your God, who has dealt wondrously with you."

4. Write out John 10:10, and keep it with you as a constant reminder of God's glorious power in your life. "The thief's purpose is to steal and kill and destroy. My purpose is to give life in all its fullness" (NLT).

5. Think of a prayer request that God has denied you. Step back from the trees of your situation, and try to imagine the forest of God's plan. What possible reasons could God have for not letting you have what you asked for? How might His glory be more powerfully displayed in other ways?

TWELVE

Transfiguration Glory

Three Men and the Mountain

*A*nd He said to them, "Assuredly, I say to you that there are some standing here who will not taste death till they see the kingdom of God present with power."

Now after six days Jesus took Peter, James, and John, and led them up on a high mountain apart by themselves; and He was transfigured before them. His clothes became shining, exceedingly white, like snow, such as no launderer on earth can whiten them. And Elijah appeared to them with Moses, and they were talking with Jesus. Then Peter answered and said to Jesus, "Rabbi, it is good for us to be here; and let us make three tabernacles: one for You, one for Moses, and one for Elijah"—because he did not know what to say, for they were greatly afraid.

And a cloud came and overshadowed them; and a voice came out of the cloud, saying, "This is My beloved Son. Hear Him!" Suddenly, when they had looked around, they saw no one anymore, but only Jesus with themselves.

Now as they came down from the mountain, He commanded them that they should tell no one the things they had seen, till the Son of Man had risen from the dead. So they kept this word to themselves, questioning what the rising from the dead meant (Mark 9:1-10).

*C*onfianza, a Spanish word, sounds a lot like our English word *confidence*. While the words are related, they mean different things. When we express confidence in others, we believe in them; we have faith in their friendship or promise. But *confianza* goes much deeper; it speaks of an unshakable reliance in others, of unconditional support for long-term friends and family members. To ask a person to speak *en confianza* would be asking that person to commit soul secrets to your trust.[1]

Peter, James, and John had confidence in Jesus. They knew Him as Messiah and Lord, and they had grown to love Him dearly. Every day was a delight to them as they lived in His presence. But when these three men encountered Jesus' glory up close, their confidence would grow to the level of *confianza*. The experience would be an anchor in future storms, when their lives were tossed by darker experiences.

The Last Year of School

At the time of the encounter recorded in this passage and in a parallel passage in Luke, Jesus had been training His disciples for over two years. It was a demanding curriculum. The Twelve had seen and heard remarkable things: lepers cured, dead people raised to life, people changed by profound and challenging teaching.

But time was short. In the near future Jesus would go to Jerusalem to face His ultimate challenge—His sacrificial death. In the final year with His dear friends, Jesus arranged some intensified teaching time. It was during one of these retreat times that this remarkable encounter occurred.

The past months had become hectic. Jesus' public ministry had been limited by a few developments. The crowds were growing so large that it was becoming risky for Jesus to move around in the cities. The people nearly mobbed Him when he stayed in one place too long. Also the controversy over His identity had intensified. The religious leaders were becoming more and more suspicious that He was an impostor. To make matters worse, some of the people who heard Jesus were organizing a maneuver to force Him into the political arena and make Him king (see John 6:15).

Jesus was concerned about the impact of these developments on His disciples. He had recently asked them what they had heard about other people's opinions of Him. "Who do men say that I am?" (Mark 8:27).

As they gave their answers, Jesus was even more direct. "But who do you say that I am?" (v. 29).

Peter spoke what they had all had come to know—Jesus was the promised Messiah, the very Son of God himself (Matthew 16:16; Mark 8:27-30).

The disciples had come to know the person of Jesus—He was divine. They had observed His *power*—He was omnipotent. Now three of these twelve men would see a glimpse of His *glory*.

Jesus made a strange statement to the Twelve: "*Some of you standing here right now will not die before you see the Kingdom of God arrive in great power!*" (Mark 9:1, NLT, emphasis added). What exactly was that supposed to mean? What glorious power did Jesus refer to, and who would be the select people to see the event? Within a few days those questions would be answered.

Intimate Friends

After spending several days with the whole group of twelve men, Jesus asked Peter, James, and John to accompany Him up the mountain. It was not unusual for Jesus to single out these three. They had been the select disciples with him on several other occasions as well. Here again they are chosen to be part of something unprecedented—an unveiling of Jesus' glory.

Who were these three men who would become prominent leaders for the church after Jesus left?

Peter—A Leader in the Making

Peter was a hardy fisherman whose nets were at home in the Sea of Galilee but whose heart was at home with Jesus. He was never far from Jesus' side. Peter was a man of action. In a kind of coarse simplicity Peter stumbled his way to spiritual maturity. He asked Jesus straightforward questions and gave even more straightforward advice, sometimes facing Jesus' rebuke for his brashness (see Mark 8:32-33). On another occasion Peter grabbed a sword and cut off an official's ear when Jesus was being arrested. Hotheaded but softhearted, Peter was always ready to respond out of love on behalf of his Master. He was a diamond in the rough.

Jesus early on changed this man's name from Simon to Peter, which means "a stone." The name was given as a signpost to what Peter could become rather than what he was. By nature he was unstable and unpredictable, but through contact with Jesus he would become solid as a rock. It would take time, but Peter would become a great spiritual leader and asset to the church.

James and John—Physical and Spiritual Brothers

James and John grew up in the same home; they shared a common name and a common business. Like Peter, they fished the waters of the Sea of Galilee, perhaps even as competitors to Peter and his brother, Andrew. James and John were known around the shores of the lake as the two sons of Zebedee (Mark 1:19). Jesus called them "Sons of Thunder" because they once wanted to call down fire from Heaven to destroy some Samaritans who wouldn't accommodate Jesus on His way down to Jerusalem (see Luke 9:51-56; Mark 3:17). The new name probably became a standing gag among the other disciples.

James and John were also ambitious. Probably at their prompting, their mother once asked Jesus to let her sons occupy the closest places next to Jesus in the future kingdom. It was no small request, and one that created quite a stir and even a rift among the other disciples (see Matthew 20:20-21, 24).

These three men—Peter, James, and John—were about to have an encounter that would shake them to their core, challenge them in their call, and later on propel them in their cause.

Summit on the Summit

The summit of Mount Hermon rises some ten thousand feet above sea level. We're not sure just how far this group went, but at some point they stopped to pray (Luke 9:28). As Jesus prayed, He was "transfigured" before His three friends. His appearance changed. His clothing dazzled—"white, like snow, such as no launderer on Earth can whiten them" (Mark 9:3). The men must have been stunned by such magnificence! It was both glorious and frightening at the same time.

These three wide-eyed disciples got a glimpse of Jesus' glory. The shroud of His humanity had been lifted, and they were seeing the manifestation of His royal splendor. This is what He would look like in the future kingdom!

Just a few days earlier Jesus had told the Twelve that some of them would see the kingdom of God before they died (Mark 9:1). In Scripture the word *kingdom* refers not just to God's future sovereign empire but also to His royal majesty or kingly manifestation.[2] The three disciples were seeing Jesus' kingdom, His royal majesty. This was what He had been talking about. This encounter fulfilled His promise.

If this were not stunning enough, the disciples were about to have an even more amazing encounter as Moses and Elijah appeared and joined the group. Moses and Elijah—two Old Testament heroes!

The disciples immediately understood the significance of the presence of these two men at this summit meeting with Israel's Messiah.

Moses was the giver of the Law and the one God used to establish the covenant with Israel. Moses had also written about Jesus, telling Israel that when He spoke, they should listen to Him: "The Lord your God will raise up for you a prophet like me from among your own brothers. You must listen to him" (Deuteronomy 18:15, NIV). Now Moses was standing with Jesus, giving testimony to Jesus' authority and glory. Elijah was Israel's bold prophet who defended the law to the nation. More than any other Old Testament prophet, Elijah performed great miracles to jar the nation back into remembering God's love for them. Now the two men who corporately represented the law and the prophets were confirming Jesus as the Messiah. In effect they were saying by their presence, "This is the one we've predicted; He is the one who has been the hope of our people from the beginning."

Luke's account of this encounter tells us that Jesus, Moses, and Elijah talked about "how he was about to fulfill God's plan by dying in Jerusalem" (Luke 9:31, NLT). The Crucifixion was the subject of this summit meeting. Jesus had told His disciples that He was going to die and rise again, but they hadn't wanted to hear it (see Mark 8:31-32). Now even the Old Testament "greats" are attesting to the divine plan of the Cross. It was as if all Heaven and Earth were waiting for this great moment of Jesus' death, resurrection, and ascension back into glory. Like figures in a surreal theater, Moses and Elijah were letting the spotlight point to Jesus as the only one who should occupy center stage. Peter, James, and John formed the small audience who would one day tell what they had seen and what it all meant.

Finally Peter, the bold one, broke into the conversation. "Rabbi, it is good for us to be here. Let us put up three shelters—one for you, one for Moses and one for Elijah" (Mark 9:5, NIV). It's safe to assume that Peter wanted to keep this mountaintop experience going as long as possible. It would take time to build those buildings; that would encourage Jesus, Moses, and Elijah to remain in this glorious state. Peter didn't want this to be over too quickly. He certainly didn't want to go to Jerusalem, where Jesus would suffer and die. Although Peter had good intentions, he really didn't know what he was saying (Luke 9:33).

Before the two heroes of the faith left the scene, something else happened—an overshadowing cloud engulfed the six men on the mountain. With the cloud came the unmistakable voice of God: "This is My beloved Son. Hear Him!" (Mark 9:7). Echoing what Moses had told the people in the Old Testament (Deuteronomy 18:15) and echoing His proclamation at Jesus' baptism (Matthew 3:17), the Father Himself added His endorsement of His Son.

Peter needed to hear those words. He needed to have Jesus' mission affirmed. Peter must know that Jesus' mission, which included the horrible death on the Cross, was on God the Father's eternal agenda. One day he would understand.

The three disciples had now seen and heard confirmed what they already knew—Jesus was the Son of the Living God, the Messiah promised throughout the Old Testament. The glory confirmed their theology.

The cloud was reminiscent of the way God attested to things in the Old Testament. The luminescent cloud was present in the wilderness to lead Israel (Numbers 9:17). The same cloud of glory overshadowed the tabernacle in the Sinai desert (Exodus 40:34-36). It showed up again when Solomon dedicated the Jewish temple to God (2 Chronicles 7:1-3). Here it was again, and only three disciples saw, heard, and felt the glory!

The Impact on the Three Disciples

As instantly as the glorious scene emerged, it also vanished. When the two visitors had gone, Jesus remained, and so did the adrenaline still pumping inside the veins of the three disciples. Jesus left them with clear instructions about how He wanted them to respond to what they had seen and heard: "He told them not to tell anyone what they had seen until he, the Son of Man, had risen from the dead" (Mark 9:9, NLT). They weren't to breathe a word of it! Imagine how difficult that must have been. Their natural impulse would be to process with the other nine disciples what had happened. But Peter, James, and John were sworn to silence until after Jesus had risen from the dead.

That time did come, and the men did discuss the Transfiguration, as the Gospel accounts reveal. But for these three men, the encounter was more than just a story to share. This encounter with Jesus' glory motivated them and prepared them for their future. What happened on the mountain that day would help them in the valleys of discouragement yet to come.

For example, the Transfiguration had quite an impact on Peter, for he wrote of this event as something that confirmed his own faith and prepared him for future effectiveness. "For we were not making up clever stories when we told you about the power of our Lord Jesus Christ and his coming again. We have seen his majestic splendor with our own eyes. And he received honor and glory from God the Father when God's glorious, majestic voice called down from Heaven, 'This is my beloved Son; I am fully pleased with him.' We ourselves heard the voice when we were there with him on the holy mountain. Because

211

of that, we have even greater confidence in the message proclaimed by the prophets" (2 Peter 1:16-19, NLT).

Peter went on to become a powerful preacher, one who heralded the gospel message to Jews and Gentiles alike. He became the first spokesman for Christ on the Day of Pentecost and then before the Jewish leaders in Jerusalem (Acts 2:14; 4:8). At the end of Peter's life, he even faced crucifixion himself—the very thing he so earnestly tried to keep Jesus from. According to historical records Peter was forced to witness the crucifixion of his wife, after which he insisted on being crucified upside down, saying he wasn't worthy to die as his Lord had.[3] Peter had learned to view suffering in this present life through the lens of future glory!

The Apostle James developed a thirst for the glories of the future. He was among four disciples who asked Jesus about the kingdom and His coming again (see Mark 13:3-4). Not long after Jesus died, James became the first martyr among the apostles. After being arrested by King Herod Agrippa I, James was executed by the sword (see Acts 12:1-3). Why he was singled out we are not sure, but perhaps it was the zeal for which he was always known. Being a vocal and intense sort, he may have been regarded as more threatening to the status quo of religious Judaism. He was a leader, he was an evangelist, and he was changed by what he saw that day on the mountain. He knew that facing death meant facing glory. Death was merely the threshold to the presence of the glorified Christ.

Finally, John would face Christ's death in a way none of the other disciples did. He is the only one of the apostles whom Scripture indicates was at the crucifixion scene. There at the foot of the Cross he was charged with the care of Mary, the mother of Jesus (John 19:26). After many years of fruitful service at Ephesus, where he fulfilled the charge of caring for Mary, John would be banished to the craggy isolated island of Patmos in the heart of the Aegean Sea. There, alone with his thoughts and with God, John received more glorious visions, which he faithfully described. His vision of future glory and especially of the glorious Christ comprise the last biblical book, the book of Revelation (see especially Revelation 1:9-18; 5:5-14; 19:11-16). John lived out the rest of his days getting glimpses of glory and looking forward to one day basking in it forever!

The Mountain Still Speaks!

At the Transfiguration, Jesus was not interested in showing off. He didn't take His three followers up to the mountain just so they could be dazzled with the visible display of His glory. This was an episode of accelerated learning for Peter, James, and John. Soon Jesus would leave them and ascend to Heaven; it was part of the plan of redemption. These soon-to-be-leaders and gospel writers needed this extra boost. They had seen and heard so much in the last two years, but none had experienced what the mountain encounter revealed to them.

What the three disciples discovered on the heights of glory has been recorded for us. Reading their accounts develops within us an anticipation of seeing and experiencing the glory of Christ. The Christian life is a series of changes and encounters with the living Jesus. Some of those experiences will seem mundane, while others will seem to lift us into a new awareness of possibility. What these few followers discovered that day was far different from anything else in their spiritual journey thus far.

What the three men learned through their encounter with Jesus provides us with some life-changing truths as well.

Jesus Wants to Reveal His Glory

The word disciple means someone who learns. As we follow Jesus, we are on a path of learning. Jesus instructed, "Take My yoke upon you and learn from Me" (Matthew 11:29, emphasis added). We do the learning while He does the revealing.

Jesus' goal with His disciples was to reveal His person, power, and glory. He shared his plans, disclosed His heart, probed with questions and challenges. He wanted to transmit truth to them, allowing that truth to transform them. Eventually Jesus was satisfied that He had completed this process of revelation: "Now they know that everything I have is a gift from you, for I have passed on to them the words you gave me; and they accepted them and know that I came from you, and they believe you sent me" (John 17:7-8, NLT).

But three disciples got to see His full glory. Jesus wanted to take these three men into a time capsule and experience what the Kingdom of Heaven is like in a microcosmic form. Perhaps Jesus had this episode especially in mind when He prayed to His Father: "I have given them the glory you gave me, so that they may be one, as we are.... Father, I want these whom you've given me to be with me, so they can see my glory.

You gave me the glory because you loved me even before the world began!" (John 17:22, 24, NLT).

What about today? How does Jesus reveal His glory to us now? We could cite several ways. However, for our purposes, let's simply say that He does so *through things that are bigger than we are.* There are times when part of the veil is pulled back, and we see more. Sometimes we see it in nature: "The heavens declare the glory of God; and the firmament shows His handiwork" (Psalms 19:1). Sometimes we see it in miraculous events: a terminally ill person is healed; a teenager is pulled back from the jaws of drug-induced suicide; a hate-filled couple is given the love and grace to reconcile. We see Jesus' glory in these events, and we are silenced, stunned by what they allow us to glimpse.

Not all of us will have the same experiences in life, of course. But we must not feel cheated. Only three out of twelve saw the Transfiguration. The rest were lingering below in the everydayness of life. We may cry that it wasn't fair for Jesus to do this, but He had His reasons. The others would get a glimpse of Jesus' glory after His resurrection and at His ascension. And they would also be ushered into His glorious presence when they died. Maybe Jesus knew that not all of them could handle this transfiguration experience at the time. There were times when Jesus would have liked to reveal more to His men, but they couldn't contain it. Jesus once declared, "Oh, there is so much more I want to tell you, but you can't bear it now" (John 16:12, NLT).

Jesus knows what you can handle and how faithful you have been to receiving other revelations He has given. Ask Him to help you to be open to what He shows you and content with what you have so far. As you seek to learn more about Jesus and encounter Him, realize that there is a biblical principle here. Jesus framed it this way: "To those who use well what they are given, even more will be given, and they will have an abundance. But from those who are unfaithful, even what little they have will be taken away" (Matthew 25:29, NLT).

What has God shown you about himself so far? Have you been obedient to it? Are you living in conformity to what Jesus has revealed to you? When it comes to truth, it seems we must either use it or lose it! Jesus is always faithful to reveal more of his person, power, and glory to those who have hungry hearts and who will use the information and experience in the right way.

Jesus Wants You to Respect His Glory

The voice from Heaven told the disciples to listen to Jesus. As we mentioned before, Peter especially needed to hear that. He was frightened by the transfiguration glory, and he just blurted out whatever came to mind. He expressed his plans for what he thought should happen next. Peter was trying to be the director over a heavenly script! Instead, he should have just taken it all in and listened.

Too often we do all the talking, the moving, and the planning while God is trying to get a message to us. When we should be listening for God's revelation, we are looking to give God instructions! But when God reveals himself to us, our ears should get more exercise than our mouths. James, the New Testament writer, counsels, "My dear brothers and sisters, always be willing to listen and slow to speak" (James 1:19, NCV). Let me suggest three practical ways that we can respect God's glory and listen to what He says to us.

1. Listen when you hear a message or read a book. During such "listening exercises," when there is spiritual input coming to your soul, don't be hasty with what you hear. If God is dealing with your heart about an issue, talk it over with Him. If He has opened your eyes to a spiritual truth, don't be too quick to react. Rather, ask Him how you are to respond. Mull over what He has revealed. Let it soak in. Think about what it might mean to you personally. Process the information carefully in the presence of God as you wonder about the possibility of what it requires of you. Such a moment of listening may become for you a threshold of a whole new level of spiritual experience.

215

This article by an unknown author offers good advice along these lines:

> At least one time in every sermon God breaks through the words of the preacher and speaks directly to the people. It may be in a single sentence or in just one phrase. We can well afford to listen to the entire discourse with care, lest we miss that one illuminated and searching sentence in which God speaks to us— a sentence that brings conviction, penitence, hope, strength, or renewed faith! So many of us miss that one special word from God because we are comparing the preacher's manner with that of some other preacher we have heard recently. From now on, just listen intently for that one portion God intends to be applied specifically to your heart![4]

2. Listen when a sudden and unexpected event occurs. Jesus' transfiguration was a planned event, from a divine perspective. But the three disciples didn't have a clue that it was coming. Their first reaction was hardly one of joy. The event startled them, and they hit the ground in fear. Jesus knew they were afraid and told them, "Arise, and do not be afraid" (Matthew 17:7). Only after the initial shock did the truth of what was happening began to sink in.

Things can happen to us in a similar way. Some of life's unexpected experiences are God's plans designed to reveal some aspect of His glory. It could be an accident. It might be an announcement of a fatal disease. At first we don't see how these things could possibly reveal God's glory. They seem intimidating and disorienting. That's why we need to slow down long enough to consider what else might be going on. Your first instinct is to be afraid. That's natural. But get past the fear, and look for the hand of God in the situation. It may be one of those rare occasions when God's glory will be revealed in an unusual way.

I have a friend whose father was given a short time to live. The news was a shock to the whole family, but it seemed to especially affect my friend Paul. Rather than pushing away such a painful experience, he pulled it into himself, embracing the

216

experience fully. His father was his closest earthly friend, and he was watching him die. Both father and son were believers, and both often discussed the splendors of heaven. They spent hours talking about the glory that would soon become reality for this parent. As Paul sat on his father's bed and watched him pass through the portals of death into heaven's glory, he became legitimately jealous of what his dad was now experiencing. God revealed His glory, and these two comrades in faith had slowed down to consider how this startling news might further their bond and whet their appetites for the grandeur of heaven.

Alexander Solzhenitsyn's account of *One Day in the Life of Ivan Denisovich* shows Ivan enduring all the horrors of a Soviet prison camp. On one particular day while Ivan is praying, a fellow prisoner watches him. With closed eyes Ivan doesn't notice his audience until the prisoner interrupts the prayer with a mocking remark. "Prayers won't help you get out of here any faster," the man said, sneering at Ivan.

Opening his eyes, Ivan answered back, "I do not pray to get out of prison but to do the will of God."[5] Ivan's story demonstrates how one can respect the glory of God by listening in prayer as well as speaking! It was Ivan's ears that were getting most of the exercise.

3. Listen in a worship service or a time of private devotion. At such times practice listening to God's voice. It was what the older saints referred to as practicing the presence of God. You are in divine company and should show divine respect. Listening is an art that must be deliberate. When we come to church to worship, we are often told to express our love to God, to tell Him how we feel. That is true, but there is a place for simply listening to His voice (Luke 10:39). When young Samuel was maturing in his calling he was instructed to pray, "Speak, Lord, for your servant hears" (1 Samuel 3:9). Practice the opening up of your spiritual senses.

In the earlier days of telegraphy a group of applicants were waiting to be interviewed as potential operators. Milling about the waiting room, most paid no attention whatsoever to the sound of the dots and dashes that began coming over a loudspeaker in the room. Then suddenly one of them rushed into the employer's office. After a few minutes he returned, smiling. "I got it!" he shouted, "I got the job!"

"How did you get it? You were behind us in line!" they angrily asked.

"Well, you might have been considered but you were all so busy talking that you didn't hear the manager's coded message over the loudspeaker," he replied. "It said, 'The man I need must always be on the alert. The first one who interprets this message and comes directly into my private office will be hired.'" Only one person in that jobless crowd was listening! Let's use the time we spend in worship to "tune in" to God's frequency and receive instructions.

Jesus Shows His Glory for Confirmation

Peter already knew that Jesus was the Messiah; he had confessed that publicly (Matthew 16:16). Yet the revelation of God's glory confirmed that confession of faith. What Peter knew as a personal discovery of faith became for him a crystallized experience. As he later would write about his day on the mountaintop, "And so we have the prophetic word *confirmed*" (2 Peter 1:19, emphasis added).

Glimpses into God's glory do that. It may be a miraculous healing or some significant way God makes His presence known. These experiences don't necessarily *produce* faith, but they do serve to *solidify* faith.

When I was in college, I had an old friend drop by my apartment for a prolonged visit. He arrived at my doorstep physically and spiritually exhausted, having injured himself in a work-related accident. Because of a compressed radial nerve in one of his wrists, the fingers in his hand were pinched together like a lobster's claw. He had little mobility on that side; his hand was rigid from the accident. Tony was a believer, but for several months he had fallen in with the wrong crowd and had made some poor choices. When he knocked on my door, he knew he didn't want to run from God anymore. So we talked and then prayed together that afternoon. I was privileged to watch as Tony ran back into his heavenly Father's arms.

Tony asked to spend the night. I let him have my bed while I opted for the couch. We had both enjoyed a Saturday of good fellowship, and now we needed rest. As my head hit the pillow, my mind was still whirring. I was thrilled that Tony had made the right steps that day; he was back in relationship with God. I knew nothing could be better. I also knew that God could do anything—nothing is impossible for Him. I began to wonder and pray all at the same time. "Lord," I prayed, "You could heal Tony right now, right here. I know you can. Nothing is too difficult for you. It may not be in your sovereign plan to do so, but it sure would be cool if you did," I continued. I knew God could heal. I had read the Bible stories, and though my faith wasn't built on miracles, I knew, at least theoretically, that God could still perform them if He chose to. With these thoughts in my mind, I started to drift off to sleep.

Within a few minutes I shot straight up in bed, awakened by shouting. It was Tony! He was calling my name feverishly and telling me to turn on the lights. *What happened?* I wondered. What kind of trouble was he in now? Was it a new pain sensation from the accident?

It was quite the opposite. There, sitting up in bed, was Tony, moving his hand effortlessly with complete freedom of motion. He had been healed! The next day he went back to his doctor, also a believer, who both confirmed the unlikelihood of such an event taking place on its own and verified that Tony had been healed quite apart from medical treatment. I had always known that God could do such things, but to see God's glory confirmed only bolstered my confidence all the more.

Jesus Shows His Glory as Preparation

When the splendor had ceased, Jesus told Peter and the two sons of Zebedee not to talk about what they had seen. After Jesus' resurrection they could tell what had happened. "So they kept this word to themselves" (Mark 9:10). As awesome as their peek into Jesus' glory was, the most useful thing about it would be what it would do for them in the future. What happened on that mountain was part of Jesus' investment in their future. He was depositing the riches of His glory into their lives so that they could face the fierce storms that would also be a part of their experience. Soon, dark days would eclipse the glorious moments as Jesus would be arrested and killed. The disciples would be severely tested. Even after the Resurrection and Ascension, when their hopes would be resurrected, they would face dark trials and even death. Peter would be crucified; James would be martyred in Jerusalem; and John would face the exile at Patmos. The dazzling light on that mountain was to prepare them for the darkness that would soon come.

It's great to "stand on top of the world" with God. Experiences of His glory cause us to surge with joy. But such encounters must do more than simply be enjoyed momentarily. They must prepare us. Any scintillating time of worship, any spine-tingling miracle, any special feeling we get from an encounter with God's glory serves its highest purpose when it carries us through the darker episodes of life. Just as Peter, James, and John were to latch on to the glory they had seen in the past and the glory that would come in the future, so must we. God's glory can become an anchor when trouble's waves sweep over us.

Embrace the revelation that God gives you about what lies ahead. In times of despair cling to it as you would cling to a life preserver in a storm.

As disciples of Jesus we are constantly learning. What we learn today prepares us for tomorrow; the lessons of tomorrow will then be the grist for the days ahead. But there is more to our relationship than just learning; we must also be involved in *sharing*. Jesus invested in these disciples so that they could reach others. Part of being prepared on the mountain was so that they *would* tell others when the time was right. Their experience of glory would help prepare others as well.

Peter wrote about the glory he had seen at the Transfiguration in his letters. John wrote a gospel, three letters, and the treatise of the book of Revelation. John wrote: "We beheld His glory" (John 1:14). Those writings have never ceased to be an encouragement for God's suffering people to go forward in the darkest times. Although the one-on-one time these disciples had with Jesus lasted only three and a half years, the learning and sharing continued. When Jesus left Earth, He told them to "go into all the world." And they did! As a result of meeting Jesus, these three fishermen became converts, then disciples, and finally apostles.

That's a healthy transition, I think. Allow your mountaintop experiences to add to your effectiveness as an ambassador.

Let Jesus use the glimpses of His glory to prepare you for your future, including the difficulties. Then use those same experiences to encourage others.

Step back and realize that every time Jesus reveals His glory to you— even if He gives you just a peek—He is committing His soul secrets to your trust. Your relationship to Him has become one of confianza.

— —

FOR REFLECTION AND DISCUSSION

1. What is your most recent "mountaintop experience"? What happened to you during the episode? How did you experience Jesus' glory?

2. Make a spiritual road map: Go back in your mind to when you first made a commitment to Jesus Christ. What progress have you made in seeing Jesus more clearly over the years? Write down a few notable experiences when God revealed himself through

a glorious moment;
a sudden and intimidating event;
a quiet place and time; or
a worship service filled with people.

3. How would you describe your present relationship to God (growing, slowing, dying, barely surviving, on a mountaintop, in the valley, in the desert, etc.)?

4. What makes you feel closer to God (nature, music, Christian fellowship, Christian service, etc.)? Has God ever taken you "off guard" by something that revealed His glory? Describe the situation.

5. Describe an experience with God that simply confirmed what you knew philosophically and academically. What did that experience do for your faith?

ENCOUNTER: FACE TO FACE WITH JESUS

6. Start carrying a notebook to record the lessons that God reveals to you. Use it also as a spiritual journal to record your life experiences. Make a commitment to pass on what you have learned about God to others who need encouragement.

THIRTEEN

Resurrection Glory

The Skeptic and the Risen Lord

*T*hen, the same day at evening, being the first day of the week, when the doors were shut where the disciples were assembled, for fear of the Jews, Jesus came and stood in the midst, and said to them, "Peace be with you." When He had said this, He showed them His hands and His side. Then the disciples were glad when they saw the Lord.

So Jesus said to them again, "Peace to you! As the Father has sent Me, I also send you." And when He had said this, He breathed on them, and said to them, "Receive the Holy Spirit. If you forgive the sins of any, they are forgiven them; if you retain the sins of any, they are retained."

Now Thomas, called the Twin, one of the twelve, was not with them when Jesus came. The other disciples therefore said to him, "We have seen the Lord."

So he said to them, "Unless I see in His hands the print of the nails, and put my finger into the print of the nails, and put my hand into His side, I will not believe."

And after eight days His disciples were again inside, and Thomas with them. Jesus came, the doors being shut, and stood in the midst, and said, "Peace to you!" Then He said to Thomas, "Reach your finger here, and look at My hands; and reach your hand here, and put it into My side. Do not be unbelieving, but believing."

And Thomas answered and said to Him, "My Lord and my God!"

Jesus said to him, "Thomas, because you have seen Me, you have believed. Blessed are those who have not seen and yet have believed" (John 20:19-29).

Certain things in life appear to be unbelievable. Take these following statements, for example. Listen to what the "experts" had to say about newer ideas that were being discussed during their lifetime:

"Everything that can be invented has been invented" (Charles H. Duell, U.S. Patent Office director, 1899).

"Sensible and responsible women do not want to vote" (Grover Cleveland, 1905).

"There is no likelihood man can ever tap the power of the atom" (Robert Millikan, Nobel Prize winner in physics, 1923).

"Heavier-than-air flying machines are impossible" (Lord Kelvin, president, Royal Society, 1895).

"The horse is here to stay, but the automobile is only a novelty" (The Michigan banker who advised Henry Ford's lawyer not to invest in the new motorcar company).[1]

Doubt is an integral part of human nature. We like to probe and question. Doubt is also part of the path to discovery. However, we may not always feel comfortable expressing our doubts. People can mistake our uncertainty for unbelief. With doubt also comes the fear that we will be misunderstood or even shunned.

That's why the story of the Apostle Thomas is a refreshing one. He was not afraid to say what he thought, even if he expressed doubts about things others readily accepted. Thomas wasn't content just to go along with the rest of the crowd. He didn't plod along, just nodding his head to everything and everyone.

It's time to take a closer look at Thomas. Unfortunately he gets a bad rap in almost every sermon preached about him. Castigated for being the arch patron of cynical doubt, he actually became one of the most ardent confessors of the faith! His story challenges the standards by which we judge spirituality.

Thomas: The Apostle from Missouri?

For centuries skeptics have found a friend in Thomas. "Doubting Thomas" is how almost everyone knows him. But a careful examination of his life discloses a man of supreme dedication and valor.

What made Thomas tick? What kind of a man was he? If he was such a doubter, how could he have lasted the whole three-and-a-half-year stretch of Jesus' earthly ministry?

A few noteworthy incidents give us a well-rounded picture of who Thomas really was. This man exhibited some admirable traits that are normally overlooked by people who think he had a question mark for a brain.

Chosen Friend

Before we consider any other point, we must remember that Jesus chose Thomas to be an apostle, a designation not given to every one of Jesus' disciples. *Disciple* was a broad New Testament term meaning follower or learner. There were many thousands of people who followed Jesus for different reasons. But an *apostle* was a person who followed at a deeper level. It was a designation for a representative. Jesus picked twelve men to be interns and commissioned them to preach and heal the sick. Thomas was one of these special representatives sent out by Christ.

It wasn't because Jesus had no other choice that He selected Thomas. It wasn't that Thomas talked Jesus into letting him tag along. No, Jesus had spent an entire night praying to His Father before He picked any of His men. Thomas was an apostle by prayerful choice, not by default (see Luke 6:12-13).

Actually none of the disciples were the best and brightest; they were astonishingly common and flawed. But Jesus understood Thomas, just as He understood Peter, James, and John. Thomas spent a lot of time with Jesus, listening to His messages, walking miles of dusty roads with Him, and watching His miracles. Thomas had the extraordinary privilege of just being with Jesus Christ.

It could have been that Thomas's attitude was set in a minor key and that he looked at life's darker side more than most. But perhaps Thomas was just a tad more honest than some of the others. But we should never forget that he was one of the few that Jesus assigned the privileged title *friend* (John 15:15). And Thomas would prove his friendship to Jesus on more than one occasion.

Loyal Follower

Thomas was a courageous and loyal follower, and he clearly expressed that loyalty in a conflict situation the disciples had with Jesus. When Jesus heard that his friend Lazarus was ill, He naturally wanted to go to Bethany to see him. But the disciples protested His decision, seeing some red flags. They adamantly reminded Jesus that during His last trip to Jerusalem, the Jews had tried to stone Him. They did not think it was a good idea to head south at this time. It was too risky. In fact it could be sheer suicide!

But Jesus was determined to go. When He wouldn't be dissuaded, Thomas stepped in and voiced his loyalty: "Let us also go, that we may die with Him" (John 11:16).

Was this pessimism? Was Thomas that much of a fatalist, or was this a brilliant show of courage—the willingness to follow to the point of making the ultimate sacrifice? It's hard to say, but one thing is clear: Thomas was a loyal friend. In fact, his willingness to follow Jesus to a possible death is markedly valiant. The other disciples were tentative; Thomas was tenacious. They didn't want the negative press; Thomas didn't seem to care what other people thought. He was not deterred by the prospect of trouble but was ready and willing to make the supreme sacrifice in following his Master.

The other disciples were tentative; Thomas was tenacious.

Honest Questioner

On the last night that Jesus spent with His twelve friends before His death, He shared a meal with them. The Upper Room, where they celebrated the Passover, was filled with the warmth of camaraderie as Jesus was preparing His men for the difficult days ahead. He would soon die the ignominious death of a common criminal on a Roman cross—something that He knew would throw them into despair. In the tenderness of that intimate setting Jesus sought to comfort His disciples. They huddled around the supper table, and Jesus spoke: "Let not your heart be troubled; you believe in God, believe also in Me. In My Father's house are many mansions; if it were not so, I would have told you. I go to prepare a place for you. And if I go and prepare a place for you, I will come again and receive you to Myself; that where I am, there you may be also. And where I go you know, and the way you know" (John 14:1-4).

It was a beautiful pledge. It was a sublime word of assurance. It was a statement that was intended to take them beyond their imminent pain and into future promise. But the promise was unclear to Thomas. He just didn't get it. All the pieces to the puzzle weren't on Thomas's mental table. Maybe the other disciples were wondering about the statement as well, but only Thomas voiced his confusion. So he interrupted Jesus' beautiful speech with an abrupt but very honest rebuttal: "Lord, we do not know where You are going, and how can we know the way?" (v. 5).

Although Thomas is often chided for this remark, he was merely asking an honest question. It was always easy to know what he was thinking. He lived his life with a kind of naked honesty.

Despondent Skeptic

By the time we see Thomas in his encounter with Jesus after His resurrection, we can better understand how Thomas processed his thoughts. All of the disciples were pretty drained emotionally and spiritually by the crucifixion of Jesus. They knew it was only a matter of time before they would be next in line for execution. That's why they were huddled behind locked doors, cowering in fear (John 20:19).

Thomas was determined to face life honestly. If Jesus was dead, then he would have to face it. As he had always done before, he would have to come to grips with the facts and just move on. He certainly wasn't eager just to jump back on the roller coaster and go for another spiritual thrill ride. Even though some of the disciples claimed that Jesus had appeared to them, Thomas needed to be more cautious this time. He would not give his heart away so quickly this time.

The other disciples had been adamant: "We have seen the Lord" (v. 25).

"Yeah, right!" Thomas probably mumbled. "They're tired and confused. We all are! They've been up a long time the last few days, and now they're seeing things!" But he knew that if he were ever going to invest any more faith in Jesus, he would have to have his own encounter with Him.

The band of disciples was now leaderless and directionless. Thomas wasn't the kind to follow just anyone, least of all a couple of his friends who thought they had seen someone who had just been executed!

A Visitor from Beyond!

Thomas wasn't in the room when Jesus arrived at the place where His followers were assembled. When Jesus appeared to this fearful bunch, He spoke words of peace and kindness: "Peace to you" (John 20:21). Those words were like fresh rain on parched soil. The disciples needed to hear this encouragement at such a chaotic moment, *but Thomas was not there to hear them*. Before the disciples could react, Jesus spoke again, this time words of commissioning: "As the Father has sent Me, I also send you" (v. 21). Such hopeful words, *but Thomas was not there to receive them*. Suddenly Jesus breathed on His disciples, who were now breathless from the encounter: "Receive the Holy Spirit" (v. 22). With these words came empowering to become strong in faith again, *but Thomas was not there for the strengthening*. And then without any delay Jesus gave His disciples authority: "If you forgive the sins of any, they are forgiven them; if you retain the sins of any, they are retained" (v. 23). What a responsibility, *but Thomas was not there for the instruction*.

Thomas should have been there, but he wasn't. We don't know why exactly. We could be hard on him and say that he deliberately isolated himself. Maybe he didn't want to be around anything or anyone who would remind him of the loss of Jesus' friendship. Maybe he was alone, pouting in despair. Maybe he was trying to escape a possible arrest. We aren't sure. But one thing is for sure—Thomas missed out on the encouragement, the commission, the empowering, and the instruction. By the time he came back to that meeting place, the other disciples were changed men. But Thomas was still chained to his disillusionment.

When Thomas arrived back at base, the other apostles gushed with excitement. But Thomas rebuffed their red-hot enthusiasm with icy words: "Unless I see in His hands the print of the nails, and put my finger into the print of the nails, and put my hand into His side, I will not believe" (v. 25). Why have any more hopes dashed to pieces? Why take any more chances?

The disciples were not necessarily surprised by this response. Thomas had expressed his honest feelings to them before. But the disciples weren't the only ones to hear the challenge. Thomas would soon have to face his words again.

From Gloom to Glory

Eight long days elapsed before anything happened. The disciples must have been growing tenser with every passing day. They were no doubt full of questions. Would He return? Was that the last they would ever see of Him? Were they just seeing things? What were they to do now? These thoughts surely tumbled through their minds as they lingered in the room. Thomas wouldn't budge. He may have even tried to rationalize with them—telling them that often after the death of someone significant, people sometimes imagine that they see their dead loved one.

Maybe it was at such a moment that Jesus arrived. When He did come, it was like the first visit—sudden and unannounced: "Jesus came, the doors being shut, and stood in the midst, and said, 'Peace to you!'" (John 20:26).

I can imagine that a gasp could be heard in the room when Jesus materialized. But then, because the greeting was such a reassuring and comforting one, everyone probably relaxed—except maybe for Thomas. He was very likely shaken. Looks of sheer joy covered the faces of the others in the room; Thomas, however, was probably as stunned as the others had been the first time they saw Jesus. *It's Jesus! It's really Him!* Thomas may have thought. *He is alive! What will He do next? What should I do now?*

Then Jesus looked directly into Thomas's eyes and spoke with deliberation. It was not a rebuke. There was no tone of anger or ill will. He didn't say, "Thomas, you unbelieving nitwit! Why did you doubt me? You've been with me for over three years. You saw my miracles. You heard my words. What's wrong with you?" Instead, Jesus' compassionate voice spoke precisely to what Thomas was struggling with. In a surprisingly humble way Jesus was acquiescing to the doubter's request. "Reach your finger here, and look at My hands; and reach your hand here, and put it into My side. Do not be unbelieving, but believing" (v. 27).

The writer doesn't tell us whether or not Thomas actually did touch those wounds. It would seem that he didn't have to. Just seeing Jesus and hearing Him was enough.

This is the Jesus that I knew up close!
This is the Jesus that was killed!
This is Jesus alive again!
This is none other than my Lord and God!

Why did Jesus come as He did, speaking words of grace and peace? Because these were friends. He came to restore to them the expectation and hope they all once had in Him, hope that was dimmed at the Cross. And He came to restore a fallen friend, a skeptically honest friend, a brokenhearted friend. Yes, even this chosen, loyal, seen-it-all-and-heard-it-all disciple needed his faith lifted. And Jesus was there to meet him on that level. Jesus "will not crush those who are weak, or quench the smallest hope, until he brings full justice with his final victory" (Matthew 12:20, NLT). Weakened by doubt and faltering in hope, Thomas needed an intervention of glory, and Jesus came to him.

Jesus met Thomas's honest doubt with honest evidence.

Obviously Jesus completely understood Thomas. He knew his mind.

He knew his heart. And Jesus met Thomas at his point of doubt and despair. Jesus met Thomas's honest doubt with honest evidence.

Thomas got the boost that he needed. He needed information. He needed evidence to settle his unstable heart. It couldn't be a secondhand encounter. It was great that his friends were all telling him about their experience with the risen Lord, but he must have his own. Thomas needed to encounter Jesus for himself. Nothing else would do.

Believing Thomas

Although Thomas is not known for his faith, it was magnificent. Once he saw Jesus for himself, he gave one of the clearest and grandest confessions in all of the New Testament: "My Lord and my God!" (John 20:28). Thomas didn't give some weak acknowledgment of his failure as much as a glorious and complete recognition of the person of Jesus. The evidence of the risen Christ was so powerful that Thomas knew he was in the presence of deity. It was a threshold moment as he boldly proclaimed his faith. In an instant Thomas went from faltering to faith, from skepticism to sincere trust. Earlier he was willing to brush off any notion that Jesus was alive; now he was making a great affirmation of faith.

And Thomas wasn't generic in his confession; he was precise. He didn't say, "You know, I now recognize that you are one of many good teachers in the world—a facet in the many-sided gem of deposited truth, one of many ways to God." Oh no! This was the recognition that Jesus was God. Why? Because Jesus hadn't even been *Thomas went from faltering to faith, from skepticism to sincere trust.* in the room when Thomas had expressed his doubts to the other disciples. Only an omniscient God could have known every thought and sentence that Thomas had said in private. Only an omnipotent God could materialize so suddenly in a room with locked doors. Thomas had no doubt. He finally understood that for three and a half years he had been walking with God!

The other disciples would come to this recognition as well. In the days ahead they would realize that Isaiah was referring to Jesus when he wrote: "For unto us a Child is born, unto us a Son is given; and the government will be upon His shoulder. And His name will be called Wonderful, Counselor, *Mighty God*, Everlasting Father, Prince of Peace" (Isaiah 9:6, emphasis added). Far from being a doubter at this point, Thomas was at the pinnacle of his faith.

Although Jesus never chided Thomas for his need for tangible evidence, He did gently follow up His appearance with a lesson about faith. "Thomas, because you have seen Me, you have believed. Blessed are those who have not seen and yet have believed" (John 20:29). Thomas's faith in Jesus was based on what he had seen. The evidence was indisputable. But millions more would never see what Thomas saw. Their faith is even better.

Restored to faith and fellowship, Thomas could honestly and loyally affirm his commitment to Jesus. Thomas became a restored believer.

And Thomas didn't stop with his Upper Room experience. Once the fires of faith had been fanned into flame again, he finished his course. Both history and tradition reveal that Thomas brought his unshakable faith eastward to Parthia (modern Iran), Babylon, China, and finally India, where it is supposed that he died. The people in these regions do not remember the doubting Thomas but the Thomas who believed and who then shared his rock-solid faith with them.

Does Thomas Have a Twin Today?

Thomas was known by his nickname, Didymus, which means "the twin" (John 11:16; 20:24; 21:2). However, his sibling is never mentioned in the New Testament writings. Maybe some of us are Thomas's "twins" in the sense that looking at his story is like looking into a mirror. Many of us can connect with his experience and struggles far more readily than we can with the experiences of other biblical heroes. If other "saints" appear to be too far out of reach, Thomas does not. Thomas isn't alone in his struggle. Countless other disciples have had to penetrate the barrier of doubt and discouragement in spiritual matters. Maybe you can relate to these four statements that emerge from Thomas's encounter with the risen Christ.

1. Faith Can Be Difficult

Some people never seem to have any difficulty believing. I have met a few like this. They hear about spiritual things and simply believe. God said it; I believe it; that settles it! is their motto.

This can be wonderful, but it can also have its drawbacks. As long as these eager believers get their information from reliable sources, there's no problem. But what if they hear things that aren't true? What if well-meaning cult followers teach them falsehoods? In this case the readiness to believe can be disastrous. Jesus spoke of those who believe almost too quickly and then later fall away (Matthew 13:5, 20-21). An eagerness to believe needs a healthy dose of discernment as well.

Others are more skeptical by nature. Their lives are filled with as many question marks as exclamation points. Although they are willing to believe, their experience is more like the man who said to Jesus, "Lord, I believe; help my unbelief!" (Mark 9:24). We shouldn't chide those who hesitate about matters of faith. Jesus didn't scold Thomas, and we shouldn't berate others who are like him. I agree with the writer who said, "The man who cannot live with doubts is a troubled person. For to have all the doubts settled is to have no mental pursuits taking place. And such a man, while of little trouble to himself, is also of little help to others. Doubts can be valuable if they force a man to search deeper and longer for answers. For to pursue the doubts is to come upon some exciting beliefs and truths."[2]

While we don't want to place doubt on a pedestal, we want to recognize that a sincere search for truth can be rewarding. Besides, Thomas wasn't the only skeptic in his group. All the disciples were doubters. When the women came to tell the disciples that Jesus had risen from the dead, the men were hardly an easy audience to win over. "And their words seemed to them like idle tales, and they did not believe them" (Luke 24:11). Not one of them was ready to believe the Resurrection.

Most people will admit that they've wrestled with a few doubts about spiritual things at one time or another. In fact, a sense of caution can be a wholesome thing. I consider myself to be a skeptic by nature. When I hear some astounding tale told by overzealous people, I almost always hesitate. I'm not eager to give away my trust. Although I have seen legitimate evidence of miracles, I've also seen enough phonies to maintain a holy skepticism. A few years ago a story circulated that the face of Jesus had appeared, of all places, in a tortilla! I was dumbfounded to see how many people flocked to see it.

When it comes to faith in God, many people struggle with doubt. It's not that they don't want to believe; on the contrary, they *do* believe. It's just that most of them are hungry to experience an honest faith—one that is based on something more than someone else's testimony. For some people this just doesn't come easily. For many it is a process. For Thomas it took his own experience with Jesus before his faith matured.

I appreciate Tim Stafford's honest confession of his struggles with faith. Raised in a Christian home, he knew that faith in God was a priority. But as his journey took him into the college years, he longed for something more than just the heritage of being told that God was important. Stafford wanted a faith awakening. In his book, *Knowing the Face of God*, he admits:

> When I looked for help, my eyes turned naturally to God. I needed His power and understanding, and I needed Him. But I could not find Him.
>
> I was supposed to "hear His voice" in a two-thousand-year-old book. I was supposed to "talk with Him in prayer." But when I read the Bible, I heard no voices, and my prayers often seemed more like talking to myself. My sense of His presence was never intense enough to form absolute proof of God. And other people's experiences were—other people's.
>
> One inky, blustery night when the wind blew the tree's arms high into the air, I walked for miles, asking God again and again to simply show Himself to me. I shouted to heaven to shatter the silence. I did not want to "work up" a feeling of God; I wanted God to break in on me.
>
> He did not.
>
> I heard no voice, saw no lights in the sky. I went home to my dorm room and went to bed. And I survived. I did more than survive; I grew. But I did not stop longing for God to be unquestionably real to me.[3]

Who doesn't want that? All of us, at the most basic level, desire to have a faith that is both dynamic and real. If you were honest with yourself, you'd have to say that you could never be content with something secondhand. You want to be sure; you want credible, reliable evidence that your commitment is well founded. There is no need to force ourselves into faith. Jesus will be patient with those who, like Thomas, are in a process that requires a bit more time.

2. Fellowship Can Be Dynamic

For whatever reasons, Thomas was not with the rest of his friends when Jesus appeared the first time. Had he been present, he could have experienced joy and certainty more quickly. And being together with his friends would have done him good.

When you go through difficult times or discouragement, how do you respond? If something shatters your lens of trust, do you pull away from people, or do you look to them for help? When you withdraw from other believers, you may feel perfectly justified. You may say, "I just need space" or "I have to process this alone, without distraction." You may rationalize, "I've been busy lately. Life can get that way, you know." Fair enough, but be careful. Faith requires spiritual input. Other people's faith perspective can keep us grounded. They can help direct us back to God. Thomas's pessimism about the validity of the disciples' claims was only accentuated by his absence. The erosion of faith can be a high price to pay for the mistake of being absent from fellowship.

The lesson is clear: The spiritual input of other believers is essential to maintain equilibrium during periods of doubt. Our first inclination may be to run away and stay cloistered. It is the very thing we must not do. We have been engineered by God to withstand the pressure of life best when we're together with other believers.

God designed us to be interdependent. Unless we are committed to togetherness, we run the risk of sliding further into disillusionment or simply missing out on hearing the truth and experiencing the joy that God has for us. Scripture instructs us: "And let us not neglect our meeting together, as some people do, but encourage and warn each other" (Hebrews 10:25, NLT).

By the way, that's the responsibility of *every* believer, not only the ones who are in need. When fellow believers isolate themselves from Christian fellowship, we mustn't just write them off. The early apostles lead the way in their example:

235

They initiated Thomas's initial recovery; they told him what they had seen and heard. Our friends who are missing from fellowship may simply need the loving pursuit of another Christian. Seek them out. Woo them back. Bring them back into the fold of faith. Paul knew the importance of such a pursuit when he wrote: "Brothers, if someone is caught in a sin, you who are spiritual should restore him gently" (Galatians 6:1, NIV).

3. Unbelief Can Be Dangerous

Probing a bit deeper into Thomas's heart reveals that he was struggling not only with doubt but also with unbelief. There is a difference. Doubt is honest; unbelief is obstinate. The disciples didn't tell Thomas just once what they had seen; they told him repeatedly. "The other disciples therefore said to him, 'We have seen the Lord" (John 20:25). The original word for said is in the imperfect tense, indicating repeated action. "They kept on saying" to Thomas that Jesus was alive. In spite of these repeated exhortations to believe, Thomas would not. His downward spiral was now well marked—going from doubt to isolation to unbelief. Thomas was becoming inflexible.

Listen to his attitude. He said, "I will not believe," rather than "I cannot believe." His words are the emphatic statement "I positively will not believe!"[4] That's the danger of unbelief. Doubt is one thing; it's an honest questioning. Unbelief digs in its heels in the presence of evidence and refuses to accept it. Unbelief is a willing denial mixed with an unreasonable prejudice toward God.

Have you ever encountered people who are caught in this kind of unbelief? I have on many occasions. "I just can't believe that stuff!" they insist. What they mean is "I won't believe." On one occasion I noticed this in a man who claimed to have "problems" with the Christian faith. I asked him that if I could show evidence that Jesus is the unique Son of God and that He rose from the dead, would he consider Him? "Absolutely not!" he replied. "I don't want anything to do with that!" That's not a problem with doubt. It's a much more advanced condition than that.

I know a man who goes to church every week with his family. He listens. He smiles. He sings the songs. But he has

236

built around himself a fortress of unbelief. This man is like Thomas, who was surrounded by followers of Jesus and still refused to believe. The man has told me honestly, "I won't believe it. I'll come to church, but I won't come to Jesus!" That's not doubt. That's obstinate unbelief.

Even true believers who wallow in doubt long enough can become like this. Unbelief can close the door to God's work in your life. The children of Israel did this repeatedly as they wandered through the desert for forty years. Recounting their story, the psalmist affirms, "Yes, again and again they tempted God, and limited the Holy One of Israel" (Psalm 78:41). Pretty amazing, isn't it? God, who is all-powerful and unlimited, could be limited by the response of His own people. Unbelief will do that.

Jesus once preached a sermon right out of the prophet Isaiah in His own hometown of Nazareth. His popularity had been on the rise, but not in that city. The hometown crowd that filled the Nazareth synagogue on that day was a skeptical one. After hearing His message, they responded cynically: "Hey, that's Joseph the carpenter's boy, isn't it?" Since they had known Him as a young boy, they felt that nothing of value could come from Him. Their doubts fermented into unbelief, which shut the door to any further blessing for them. "And because of their unbelief, he *couldn't* do any mighty miracles among them" (Mark 6:5, NLT, emphasis added).

What things about Jesus have you decided not to believe? What area of spiritual truth have you determined not to open up to? Unbelief can be a roadblock for Christians as well as for unbelievers. The writer of Hebrews warns, "Be careful then, dear brothers and sisters. Make sure that your own hearts are not evil and unbelieving, turning you away from the living God" (Hebrews 3:12, NLT). Even fellow Christian brothers and sisters can harden their hearts and solidify their doubts into brittle unbelief.

If you have discovered yourself meandering down a solitary pathway away from the fellowship of other believers and headed into the horizon of scoffers, stop now! Be reasonable enough to search out reasons for your dilemma and answers to your doubts. Unbelief can destroy the best of us; faith can save the worst of us! It may be that you need to doubt your doubts before you doubt your beliefs.

4. Doubt Can Lead to Development
While nurturing your doubt can be harmful, doubts can sometimes become the very pathway into vibrant faith. Periods of questioning can be for us a kind of watershed that drains our doubts in the right direction. This was the case for Thomas. His experience could have gone either way, but because of Jesus' glorious encounter with him, it went the right way.

A word to the spiritually uncertain. Jesus met Thomas at his point of unbelief. He came to revive the smoldering embers of shattered faith. It was a threshold moment for this doubting disciple. Although doubt and unbelief were warring inside of him, through his encounter with Jesus, Thomas faced them head-on. His doubt became his determining moment that would launch him into worldwide effectiveness.

Understand that your doubts don't intimidate God. The all-powerful risen Christ can handle anything our inquiring and doubting minds can conjure up. That in itself is liberating. Have you ever had troubling questions about God? Have you felt that such doubts just weren't welcomed around other Christians? You started to ask some friends about such issues, and they just looked at you incredulously, as if you were some subspiritual creature? Frustrating, isn't it?

Then take heart from this story of Thomas. I'll bet that those other disciples gave Thomas a few strange looks as well. But Jesus did not. He knew what Thomas was after, and He was there to help him get back to the place of strong faith. That's why Jesus graciously presented His wounds for Thomas to examine closely. Jesus had the same goal Thomas had— resurrected faith! After displaying the marks of His violent death, Jesus then insisted, "Do not be unbelieving, but believing" (John 20:27).

Do you need evidence regarding a spiritual matter? Don't be afraid to voice your concerns and uncertainties to God. Don't be afraid to search out the matter honestly and openly. God is more eager to reveal himself and His truth to you than even you are to encounter Him. God will graciously meet you at your point of need if you approach Him with an honest heart and an open mind. He is not daunted by intellectualism. He is never threatened by good solid questions. Just as He gave you a heart, He also gave you a mind. "'Come now, and let us reason together,' says the Lord" (Isaiah 1:18). If you are serious in your search, you will find plenty of resources that will provide solid answers to tough issues. Your issues and questions are probably not new; they've been asked and answered before.

Jesus once spoke of the importance of using the mind in our relationship to God. Using the law of Moses as His reference, He declared that we are to "love the Lord your God with all your heart, with all your soul, and with all your *mind*" (Matthew 22:37, emphasis added). When honest doubt is involved, Jesus will honor a person's mind. Sincere seekers need not be ashamed of spiritual questions around Jesus. He knows the value of bolstering one's faith by evidence, for it can be a launching pad for further spiritual growth. Wading through the marshes of uncertainty can lead to a genuine investigation that can result in solid faith. In fact, Jesus promised help from the Holy Spirit in such an endeavor: "When the Spirit of truth comes, he will guide you into all truth.... He will bring me glory by revealing to you whatever he receives from me" (John 16:13-14, NLT).

A word to the spiritually certain. The people who live, work, and go to school with you may have lots of questions about the Christian faith. These questions can become beneficial platforms from which to share the gospel. Don't minimize their curiosity or trivialize their pursuit of truth. Reasonable doubt must be met with reasonable answers. One of the apostles who watched this whole "Thomas episode" was Peter. His was one of the voices telling Thomas that Jesus was alive. Later, in his writings, Peter would expand on the need to provide solid answers for such people: "Always be ready to give a logical defense to any one who asks you to account for the hope that is in you, but do it courteously and respectfully" (1 Peter 3:15, AMP).

We don't want to encourage intellectual conceit, but we should partner with a person's intellectual concerns. Peter tells us to "be ready" to do that. That doesn't mean we all need to become theology professors wielding an apologetic sword with precision. But it does mean that we should be eager to share. As we gather the right information and demonstrate an enthusiasm about telling it, we're following the example of Jesus. As we hold out the evidence for the Christian faith and give people the opportunity to examine it, doubt will be short lived.

Jesus never told his followers to take a blind leap into a dark chasm, falsely calling it faith. Nor should we. Faith will often exceed reason, but it won't oppose it. I remember how impressed I was when I first met mature believers who had thought through some of the difficult issues of life and faith and could articulate them to me. The impact was profound and life changing.

You may be the kind of person who never required any help in believing. Perhaps you made a spiritual commitment the first time you heard about Jesus, and there were no roadblocks to your faith. If that's true, you are blessed! Jesus said so (John 20:29). But not everyone is like that, and we must be sensitive to them. We should also be excited about the prospects of an honest search. Learn what you can, and tell what you know! And don't underestimate the power of the Scriptures in revealing truth even to the skeptic.

The great spiritual communicator G. Campbell Morgan was already enjoying some success as a preacher when he was only nineteen years old. His career as a thoughtful minister looked promising. But then it seemed that he was attacked by doubts about the Bible. He began wondering if he could really trust it. The writings of noted agnostics such as Charles Darwin, John Tyndall, Thomas Huxley, and Herbert Spencer disturbed him. As he read their books and listened to their debates, Morgan became more and more perplexed. His perplexity blossomed into skepticism.

What did he do? He canceled all preaching engagements, put all the books in a cupboard, and locked the door. He went to the bookstore and bought a new Bible and reasoned with himself, "I am no longer certain that this Book is what my father claims it to be—the very Word of God. But of this I am sure: If it be the Word of God and if I come to it with an unprejudiced and open mind, it will bring assurance to my soul of itself." So he gave it another honest read. The result? "That Bible found me!" exclaimed Morgan. After this episode of wrestling with his doubts, Morgan emerged stronger and surer. The newfound assurance in 1883 gave him fresh motivation as a teacher of God's truth. G. Campbell Morgan devoted himself to the study and preaching of God's Word, for which we are still indebted. His uncertainty led him to the bedrock of unwavering faith![5]

— —

FOR REFLECTION AND DISCUSSION

1. Think about your own personal journey of faith. What things have you been prone to doubt? What have you done about those doubts? Which of the following responses are most helpful?

Keep them to myself, hoping they will go away on their own.
Pray about them, and ask others to pray for me.
Discuss them with other doubters.
Discuss them with a pastor or another mature believer.
Sift through good books to understand and articulate the issues.

2. If you could stand before God right now and ask Him one question, what would it be? How do you think He would answer you?

3. Practice the art of listening well. The next time an unbeliever or a struggling believer is asking questions, listen carefully. Rather than trying to formulate answers, let the questions sink in. Then silently ask God to give you wisdom to answer them well.

4. Think back to the time before your own conversion experience. What were the roadblocks that kept you from faith? How would you have completed this sentence then: "Unless _____ I will not believe!"?

5. How do you tend to process difficult issues of faith?

- In the presence of and with the help of others
- All alone with no one around

6. What things have convinced you of the reality of the risen Christ? How would you articulate that reality to those without faith? When was the last time you did?

FOURTEEN

Revelation Glory

Peeking Ahead

Then as I looked, I saw a door standing open in heaven, and the same voice I had heard before spoke to me with the sound of a mighty trumpet blast. The voice said, "Come up here, and I will show you what must happen after these things." And instantly I was in the Spirit, and I saw a throne in heaven and someone sitting on it! The one sitting on the throne was as brilliant as gemstones—jasper and carnelian. And the glow of an emerald circled his throne like a rainbow. Twenty-four thrones surrounded him, and twenty-four elders sat on them. They were all clothed in white and had gold crowns on their heads. And from the throne came flashes of lightning and the rumble of thunder. And in front of the throne were seven lampstands with burning flames. They are the seven spirits of God (Revelation 4:1-5, NLT).

I looked and I saw a Lamb that had been killed but was now standing between the throne and the four living beings and among the twenty-four elders. He had seven horns and seven eyes, which are the seven spirits of God that are sent out into every part of the earth.... And as he took the scroll, the four living beings and the twenty-four elders fell down before the Lamb. Each one had a harp, and they held gold bowls filled with incense—the prayers of God's people!

And they sang a new song with these words: "You are worthy to take the scroll and break its seals and open it. For you were killed, and your blood has ransomed people for God from every tribe and language and people and nation.

And you have caused them to become God's kingdom and his priests. And they will reign on the earth. (Revelation 5:6-10, NLT).

— —

The late bishop Richard Loring helped to put the past, present, and future into clear perspective. "While we have but one life, we, in fact, live three times," Loring once wrote.

The first "living" takes place in the womb. It is a simple but profound time of gestation in which things happen to prepare us for phase two— physical life outside the womb.

The second "living" is dramatically different. The transition from phase one into this phase must seem to the baby much like what we would call death, since everything that is known and familiar gives way to the different and unimagined. The arena is larger, but the purpose is the same—to prepare us for the next and culminating phase.

The third "living" is that for which we were made, that portion of life in which we become finally and forever what God intended us to be. We know the certainty of this in the heart's deep longing that pulls us forward, pulls us home![1]

Solomon was right: God has "planted eternity in the human heart" (Ecclesiastes 3:11, NLT). We will never be totally satisfied until the day when we are face-to-face with Jesus in Heaven—the place that He promised to prepare for us (John 14:2-3). One day it will be ours. Until then we can only take peeks into eternity. As we do, we are like moths drawn to a flame; we yearn to be home with our Savior.

One of those sneak previews is found in John's final writing, the book of Revelation. It is this peek forward that helps us prepare for the "third living." It is this final section that puts a bow on the whole package of Scripture. The Bible opens with the story of "Paradise Lost." Now it closes with the story of "Paradise Secured"!

The Contented Castaway

It was none other than John the apostle who wrote this final encounter with Jesus Christ and gave to generations to come this glimpse into the glory of Heaven. John began his life as a simple fisherman on the Sea of Galilee, but he would end his life as a special visionary in the midst of the Aegean Sea. On the first body of water he had seen Jesus in His earthly form. In the midst of this other body of water he would see Jesus in a form that no one else had seen Him.

A part of the inner circle of disciples, John referred to himself as "the disciple whom Jesus loved" (John 13:23; 20:2; 21:7, 20). It was John who leaned on the bosom of Jesus at the final Passover meal they all shared together. Now, only this special friend of Jesus would see a vision of eternity that would bring comfort to scores of believers in the midst of the trials of life on Earth.

John wrote from the island of Patmos, a rocky island some thirty miles off the coast of Asia Minor. But he wasn't on vacation. For two years John lived as an exile in this Roman penal colony. Rome saw him as a threat because of his beliefs and preaching. During the reign of Emperor Titus Flavius Domitianus, who demanded to be worshiped as "Lord and God," John was regarded as a dissenter. Like many of John's believing contemporaries, he refused to worship anyone except Jesus Christ as the Lord. So in A.D. 95 he was deported as a prisoner to this lonely land mass away from everyone.

John was hardly a young man at this point. In fact, some biblical scholars believe he was around ninety-five years old. In many ways the years on Patmos were the worst time of John's life. He had lost his freedom and was isolated from friends and family. Yet God met him there in powerful ways. In a Roman prison colony John would witness Jesus' glory once more in a unique experience.

The Jesus of the Future

John calls his extensive vision "the Revelation of Jesus Christ" (Revelation 1:1). It was as if God were pulling back the curtain so that John could see the glorified Jesus in Heaven, ruling over all His creation. As the phrase implies, John was seeing a revelation of *Jesus himself*. Jesus is the main character of the entire vision. The emphasis isn't on judgments, creatures, and cataclysmic phenomena but rather on Christ. The person of Jesus shines through every event and every prediction. The power of Jesus is made evident by the many judgments He enacts and the many commands He gives. The glory of Jesus is the overarching theme of the worship in Heaven and Earth. John's record, then, is a book that reveals by symbols the ultimate encounter we will have with Jesus in the future.

Sadly many people don't read Revelation because they are frightened by the terrifying events it depicts. That is unfortunate since the book contains a specific blessing to people who read it: "God blesses the one who reads this prophecy to the church, and he blesses all who listen to it and obey what it says. For the time is near when these things will happen" (Revelation 1:3, NLT). In some ways Revelation contains the "answers in the back of the book." In this last section of Scripture we look ahead to see Christ ultimately reigning and Satan eternally bound. We find not only God's complete judgment of the Earth and its inhabitants but also the fullness of Heaven.

The symbols the book employs shouldn't scare us but compel us. They are pregnant with meaning. There are lampstands, trumpets, bowls, thunderings, and strange creatures that spark the imagination. But why symbols? Symbols are not weakened by time; they transcend both culture and time so that all societies for centuries to come can be inspired by them. The symbolic language can also arouse strong emotions and create powerful mental images for the reader.

When my son was a toddler, I invented a game that I called "Say, play, and pray." It was a simple way for Nathan to grasp historical events from the Bible and then make them personal. I would read the Bible story to him; that was the "say" part. Next he and I would assume roles and act out the parts. For instance, I would be Goliath, and he would be David slaying me with the stone. We would even don costumes sometimes. This was the "play" part of it, and it was also the most fun. Finally we would "pray" together about the lessons we had just learned. The involvement in the story stimulated Nathan's understanding. The vivid imagery in Revelation does the same; it helps us grasp truth on a more stimulating level.

A Spiritual Time Machine

John's Patmos experience became the lens through which he was able to see Jesus' coming Kingdom. Visions transported

John into the future, where he glimpsed coming world events as well as the threshold of Heaven itself.

It's noteworthy that the voice John heard was the same trumpeting voice he had heard earlier as Jesus introduced Himself to John in this heavenly vision (Revelation 1:10-11). Jesus was calling to John from out of Heaven. It was the familiar yet regal sound of the Master he once followed around Galilee and Judea. The One who had once called John and the other disciples to encounter Him was calling again. John who once encountered Jesus in significant and intimate ways was being called to encounter Him again.

John's encounter with Jesus in this otherworldly experience foreshadows the encounter Jesus will have with all those who love Him. After all of the spiritual experiences we may have on Earth, it's far from being over for us. One day Jesus will call us to come upward for a further and much fuller meeting with Him. John's account here isn't a full description of the glories of Heaven but rather a sketch. We'll have to wait for the experience in order to have a full understanding of our future home.

Describing Heaven in earthly terms has some obvious limitations. John had the task of describing infinite realities in terms that finite beings would understand. It was like trying to explain to four-year-olds that they will really enjoy their honeymoon! Children lack the capacity to grasp the significance and fullness of such an event.

Nevertheless, even with its limitations, John's vision provides perspective for our present lives and whets our appetites for our future encounter with Jesus.

Our Worst Time on Earth
May Be Our Best Encounter with Jesus

It was while John was experiencing his loneliest episode of life that this revelation came to him. While Earth was closing its doors, Heaven was opening new ones. While this world had nothing more to say to John, the next world was beckoning him onward and upward. John once walked with Jesus in the flesh and witnessed His person, power, and glory, but this was by far the best encounter. John's period of painful separation from human contact brought him into contact with life on the next level.

I have seen this paradox in the lives of other suffering saints. Some of the most encouraging, cheerful, and optimistic believers I have met are those who have gone through intense suffering. Often those who have been confined to hospital beds or convalescent homes or even prison cells have told of God's special presence that sustained them in such places. I'll never forget going into the hospital room of a woman who was diagnosed with terminal cancer and was given only weeks to live. My visit was a surprise—to me! I turned the corner from the hallway into her room and found her sitting up in bed, beaming! She was encouraging a small group of friends who had come to mourn for her. Far from being in shock or remorse, she was helping all of us make sense out of this tragedy. She was so young and had been so full of life. Now her life was slipping away from her, and everyone was sensing the loss. As we were fumbling to make sense of it, she lucidly explained why she was looking forward to Heaven. She affirmed that Jesus had been more real to her during those final days of her illness than ever before. It was as if God was letting her peek beyond Heaven's threshold to see where she was going.

Learn to look for the richest experiences with Christ to come out of what might appear to be the worst experiences of life. Sometimes God can show His strength only while we are admittedly weak. Just as God spoke to Job "out of the storm" (Job 38:1, NIV), He will often reserve His best revelations for our most turbulent times.

The Ultimate Encounter Is Yet to Come

John's earthly experience with Jesus was great, but what he saw in the future promised to far outweigh it. Uniting with Jesus in Heaven will be the ultimate encounter. John is now in the Heaven he described, but he left for us the written record so we can know what to look forward to.

While paging through a magazine on a recent flight, I noticed an advertisement for a new Seattle hotel for business executives. It boldly promised "Good views! Good location! Good rates!" As I read it, I immediately thought of Heaven, our future home.

Good views. We will see God in His ultimate glory. It will be beyond our wildest dreams. It will outstrip what even Hollywood could conceive of on a good day. One evening as a father was strolling hand in hand with his young daughter, they watched the sun set. As the sky darkened and made millions of stars "come out," the little girl gave an audible gasp and blurted out, "Daddy, if Heaven looks this good on the wrong side of it, imagine what it must be like on the right side!"

Good location. Heaven will have something to delight everyone. What Heaven won't have is almost as important as what it will have. Heaven won't have any hospitals or pain clinics. Heaven won't have homeless shelters or homes for abused women and children. Heaven will have no death. "He will remove all of their sorrows, and there will be no more death or sorrow or crying or pain. For the old world and its evils are gone forever" (Revelation 21:4, NLT). That's something to anticipate.

Good rates. Heaven is the final ingredient of the free gift of salvation. It's all part of the package for being united with God's Son. The last invitation in Scripture invites people to take this free gift, saying, "Whoever desires, let him take the water of life freely" (Revelation 22:17). It will be the most excellent way to end our journey on Earth. When time stops here, eternity will begin there. Our final encounter with Jesus will be a happy ending—and a very happy beginning.

What will we see in Heaven? A better question is, *Whom* will we see? We shouldn't get hung up on the environmental issues of Heaven. Yes, we will see gold streets and pearly gates, but we will also see Jesus in all of His fullness.

We Will See Jesus' Person

We were created for fellowship with God, built to encounter Him. He wants our fellowship and our presence with Him. In Heaven that fellowship will be complete. John saw Jesus as He really is (see 1 John 3:2, NLT).

When you meet Jesus in Heaven, you will be able to communicate with Him personally and directly. It will be entirely different from the way you and I speak to Him now in prayer. Our communication is imperfect and waiting for fulfillment. Paul noted, "Now we see in a mirror, dimly, but then face to face" (1 Corinthians 13:12). Imagine looking into the face of Jesus and being able to say, "I love you, Jesus. Thank you for getting me here. Thank you for caring for me all this time."

When John saw Jesus in Heaven, he described Him as "a Lamb, looking as if it had been slain" (Revelation 5:6, NIV). Heaven is a place of brilliance, yet the Lamb is bearing the marks of a painful death! How could that be? It is only through the Lamb's suffering that we can be admitted into these eternal realms. When Jesus rose from the dead, He appeared to Thomas and invited him to touch those scars. He ascended into Heaven bearing them. They will be the evidence that our sins are eradicated by sacrifice. It humbles us to think that the only human work that will be visible in Heaven will be the marks of crucifixion on the Lamb of God! They will forever bear eloquent testimony that we didn't arrive in Heaven on our own merit but by His finished work.

The only human work that will be visible in Heaven will be the marks of crucifixion on the Lamb of God!

We Will See Jesus' Power

Only a limited number of people on Earth were ever able to see Jesus' miraculous power. But Heaven will broaden the audience. That power will be displayed in many ways. Part of Jesus' future power will be seen in His judgment as cataclysms are poured out on the Earth. The world will unmistakably know that it is Jesus' power they are experiencing (Revelation 6:16).

Many people are uncomfortable with Jesus the Judge. They prefer "gentle Jesus meek and mild." But both are true. He is both Savior and Judge. But we should think of His judgment in terms of the deep sense of satisfaction it will bring. God cannot turn His back on sin, and we wouldn't want Him to. We get livid when we read that another child has been raped or another innocent victim has been murdered. We feel the need for retribution. For God to sit back idly and never deal with those issues would give us cause for great concern. God is not amoral. He is loving but also just. In loving justice He will powerfully adjudicate over His creation.

Jesus the Lamb will carry out the judgment (John 5:22). That in itself is a powerful image. The Lamb who was slain *for* our sin will be the one executing judgment *on* our sin. He is the only one qualified to do so. I once read about a teenager who didn't notice an oncoming truck as he crossed a busy boulevard in New York City. But just before the young man darted in front of the speeding vehicle, a strong hand grabbed his shirt and pulled him back safely to the curb. Red with fear and adrenaline, the teen thanked the elderly man for saving him. Several weeks later the same teenager was in court to stand trial for stealing a car. When the boy looked up at the judge, he recognized him. "Hey, you're that man who saved me a few weeks back when the truck was coming," exclaimed the young man. "Surely you can do something now!" "Sorry, son," replied the magistrate. "On that day I was your savior. Today I am your judge!"

We Will See Jesus' Glory

Jesus wanted His followers to be able to see Him in the fullness of His future splendor. He prayed while on Earth, "Father, I desire that they also whom You gave Me may be with Me where I am, that they may behold My glory which You have given Me; for You loved Me before the foundation of the world" (John 17:24). When we encounter Jesus in the future, that prayer will be answered. John's first glimpse of Jesus in this vision was in brilliance as one with authority (Revelation 1:13-17). John's final picture is the city of the eternal state that radiates with the glory of God and the light of the Lamb illuminating it (Revelation 21:23).

When we get to Heaven, we will see more glory than the demon-possessed man saw when Jesus came into his town. We will see His glory much longer than the brief glimpse the three disciples had on the mountain as Jesus was transfigured. We will be even more in awe than Thomas, who viewed the resurrected Christ. This will be an eternal encounter, and we will revel in His glory.

We Will See Jesus' People

Too often we wonder about pragmatics in Heaven: What will we do? Once again think in terms of relationships. Think of those who will be there with us. All those who have known God throughout history will be present. You will be able to walk around with Moses and discuss the Red Sea event. Esther, Deborah, David, Enoch, Stephen, and Peter, as well as countless others will be enjoying the same experiences in the eternal Kingdom. We've only *read* about some of the encounters that people had with Jesus while on Earth. In Heaven we'll be able to be with these people and together encounter the glorious Christ. You'll be able to meet the leper who was cured. You'll be able to talk with Moses and Elijah yourself about the transfiguration incident. You can spend some time with Jonah and discuss fishing! You should keep your eyes open for a few more as well:

John the Baptist will be there—enjoying the fulfillment of his purpose.

Nicodemus will be there—having all his questions about the Kingdom answered at last.

The Samaritan woman will be there—drinking freely from the River of Life.

The prostitute will be there—singing loudly of the forgiveness she received.

Saul of Tarsus will be there—adoring the Jesus who pursued him.

The former leper from Galilee will be there—worshiping Christ with great fervor.

The nobleman will be there—standing with his healed son and other family members who believed in Jesus through his testimony of faith.

Matthew will be there—enjoying Jesus' eternal home—tax free!

The former paralytic will be there—enjoying the eternal benefits of forgiveness and probably standing arm in arm with his four friends.

The former cripple from Bethesda will be there—leaping and praising God.

The demon-free man from Gadara will be there—sharing his story with others.

Peter, James, and John will be there—following the Lamb.

Thomas will be there—basking in the certainty of his glorious Lord.

Besides seeing our biblical brothers and sisters, you will see all your relatives and friends who followed Jesus. What a reunion that will be!

Each day you live brings you closer to that gathering. The future looks incredibly bright, wouldn't you say? It promises to be filled with encounters all centered on Jesus Christ.

The Future Encounter Will Include a Variety of Activities

Heaven will be much more than a hug-a-thon reunion with loved ones and saints. We will be busy there.

We Will Worship Him Directly

Our worship in Heaven will be unbelievably full and complete. We will have no more veil, no more silence, no more darkness in our worship. We will no longer sing and pray to the invisible God. We will worship the visible ruler of Heaven and Earth while being in His presence. We will sing sweetly and boldly. No more mumbling. No more imperfect praise. No more fumbling around for the right words and the right melodies. Every redeemed person will celebrate with the combined chorus of thousands upon thousands of people (Revelation 5:11-12). The music will be impressive! Yes, pure song will flourish in the future Kingdom.

I remember as a child thinking that church was boring. Sometimes I still do, depending on where I am. That will never happen in Heaven. The experience of worship in Heaven will be so fulfilling, we will want to do it all the time (Revelation 4:8-11; 5:8-14). Jesus informed the woman at the Samaritan well that God wanted His creation to "worship in spirit and truth" (John 4:24). The capacity to do so will be fully realized in the Kingdom of Heaven.

I have on occasion experienced moments in worship that seem to lift me out of myself and transport me directly into the throne room of God. Those were times I felt I could touch Heaven itself. But these experiences all ended, of course, and I went back to life as usual. Yet I never stop yearning for experiences like that. When they come, I am grateful, but I must never try to manufacture such a worship experience. Rather I now see these are spiritual *hors d'oeuvres* designed to get my appetite ready for the future, when such worship will be constant and complete.

We Will Serve Him Gladly

Forget those ideas about sitting around on a cloud dressed in a white sheet and playing a harp. That happens only in the movies—bad movies. We will be busy in Heaven, and I'm glad because I don't like to sit still. Our business won't all be spent on praise. We will also be serving the Lord. "His servants shall serve Him," John declares (Revelation 22:3). What an encouragement to us that in Heaven our service will be perfect. So many times on Earth in trying to serve the Lord, we find ourselves handicapped by sin and weakness. But in Heaven all obstacles to our service to Christ will be gone. Perfect service in a perfect environment!

We will occupy ourselves as servants of God in the purest and highest sense. Think of the people Jesus healed. They were so willing to serve Jesus. Some were ready to travel with Him throughout the countryside. But Jesus limited their scope of service, often telling them to stay put or go back home and share what happened with their own families. In Heaven they will all be able to serve unrestricted. Think of the father who received his son back to life. How grateful he must have been. His occupation was being a royal official for an earthly government. But in Heaven he will be able to work for the Lord to his heart's content. Think of the apostles who were killed for their faith and were thinking that their time of service was cut short. Eternity will give them every opportunity to do things for Jesus.

We Will Reign with Him Jointly

It's difficult to imagine, but it's true just the same—we will share in Christ's glory by reigning with Him. The bond between Jesus and His followers is so strong that it will be demonstrated even in the sharing of His eternal authority. Jesus assured His Church, "To him who overcomes I will grant to sit with Me on My throne, as I also overcame and sat down with My Father on His throne" (Revelation 3:21). It is a staggering thought that we redeemed sinners will share such a lofty position with Christ.

Once we get to Heaven, we will receive rewards. When Paul was ready to die, he wrote: "Finally, there is laid up for me the crown of righteousness, which the Lord, the righteous Judge, will give to me on that Day, and not to me only but also to all who have loved His appearing" (2 Timothy 4:8). It seems that these rewards are tied to what we do here and now in service for Jesus (2 Corinthians 5:10). Our lives will be evaluated so that God might reward us for what we've done for Him before we made it to Heaven.

As a child I remember the joy of getting simple rewards for work well done. Some of my teachers would place little gold stars at the top of my homework if they felt I did a good job. It always made me feel great inside. It motivated me to keep trying hard to do well in future assignments. Picture what the reward session will be like in Heaven. Just thinking about it creates both excitement and incentive. In one of the parables Jesus told, He used the conversation of a master's rewarding his servants as an analogy of what it will be like. The ruler declared, "Well done, good and faithful servant; you were faithful over a few things, I will make you ruler over many things. Enter into the joy of your lord" (Matthew 25:21). It will be great to hear those words from the lips of Jesus one day.

Humbling, isn't it, to think that God will hand us a reward. For what! He chose us. He arranged the circumstances of our lives so that we would respond to His call. He saved us and let us serve Him while on Earth. He provided for our needs every step along the way. He did it all! Yet, as it is His delight to be with us, it is also His delight to make the eternal experience as rewarding (literally) as possible for us. So get ready for a royal welcome! And it will last forever. Paul referred to our reward as "an imperishable crown" (1 Corinthians 9:25).

Encountering Christ presently will assure your encountering Him eternally. Or, to use the words of Richard Loring, making sure the "second living" is done right will ensure that the "third living" is in order. That's the perspective Jesus had when he encouraged His followers to "lay up for yourselves treasures in Heaven" (Matthew 6:20). It only makes sense. We'll spend the rest of our lives there! Don't let anyone put a damper on your excitement for your future home with remarks like, "You're so heavenly minded that you're no earthly good." Live responsibly, but live with the thought that an eternity with Jesus awaits us at the finish line.

We are thankful to John for writing about his vision. It is only a glimpse, a peek, a window that will one day lead into a vast Kingdom. We have a description of what lies ahead, but it's like watching a black-and-white movie of a place, then visiting it and seeing it in magnificent color and glory. The two can't really be compared.

I heard of a toddler who got onto an elevator in one of the tall buildings in New York City. His dad pushed the button to go to the top. The young boy stared at the indicator buttons flashing as they went up past the floors: the tenth floor, twentieth, fiftieth, and higher. Up the boy went. It seemed as if the ride would never end. The little boy started to get nervous. He had never had such an experience and wasn't sure where they were going. Suddenly, thinking this might be a trip to Heaven, he took his daddy's hand and blurted out, "Daddy, does God know we're coming?"

The future awaits us, and it is good. One day Jesus will call you to come to Him. It may be by your death; it may be by the direct intervention of His coming. But He will call; you will go to be with Him. Heaven is a very real place, a wonder-filled place—designed just for you (see John 14:1-4). There, in that final and eternal meeting together with Jesus, you will be forever changed. It will be instantaneous, and it will be complete. The personal fellowship with your Creator and Savior will never end. Yes, He does know you're coming, and He wants you to be ready for that ultimate and eternal meeting. Are you?

FOR REFLECTION AND DISCUSSION

1. Which describes your attitude about Heaven? Which attitude is the best? Why?

I don't have time to think about Heaven; I'm too busy here!

Heaven sounds pretty boring to me, but it beats the alternative!

Heaven will mean I don't have to be responsible any longer (no rent payments, tax filings, book reports, dishes to clean up, kids to feed).

Heaven will be so much better than here on Earth. I want to get out of this place. I'm tired of my daily routine.

Heaven is my ultimate goal, and being with Jesus will be the ultimate payoff, but I want God to use me for His glory as long as He can. This Earth will be the last chance I get to witness to anyone.

2. One of the most helpful ways to think about Heaven is to think about what it will not have. Take a sheet of paper and write down a list of some of the sorrows, disappointments, and painful experiences that you've been through. Then read Revelation 21:4 aloud as you crumple up the paper and toss it away!

3. Of all of the people we've discussed in this book, who (besides Jesus) intrigues you the most and with whom would you like to spend some concentrated time with in Heaven once you get there?

4. Since so much of our future in Heaven will be spent in worship, why not develop some creative ways to expand on your worship experience here and now (to get into practice a bit). Here are some suggestions:

Write your own simple song of praise, and sing it to God (Revelation 5:9).

The next time you have personal devotions, try bowing in prayer (Revelation 4:10).

Sing a familiar song but with new meaning. Think about the words carefully (Revelation 15:3-4).

5. Name three things that you've considered doing for God here on Earth but lacked the time, money, or talent. Read Revelation 7:15; 22:3; and John 12:26. Be encouraged that one day you'll be able to serve the Lord without any of those restrictions.

6. What things do you expect to be rewarded for once you get to Heaven? Ask a close friend to help you on this one—it just may encourage you!

Meeting Jesus Yourself

The journey through the Gospel accounts of Jesus' encounters with people is nothing short of remarkable. So individual! So personally tailored! So full of surprises! Everyone who met Him up close was profoundly changed after spending time with Him. That's the common thread through all these New Testament cameos. Although the people whose lives Jesus touched were different from one another, their common ground was the fact that He changed them. Jesus took them as they were but loved them too much to leave them that way. Some were changed by His message; for others it was a miraculous event; for still others it was a glorious manifestation. But for everyone Jesus Christ was the one person who made their lives full and forever different.

We have met Jesus through the pages of Scripture—the real Jesus, the historical Jesus. This is not the Jesus of the Hollywood set or of the heady divinity student's systematic theology. This is the incomparable Son of God.

Jesus took them as they were but loved them too much to leave them that way.

We have seen Jesus' magnificent person. He was not what people expected Him to be. John the Baptist was stunned that He would so readily identify with common sinners. Nicodemus found Him to be much deeper, more probing, and more personally demanding than simply a "teacher come from God." The Samaritan woman spoke of her hope for the coming Messiah, while the Messiah she hoped for stood there ready to refresh and restore her broken life. Simon the Pharisee found Jesus to be an unpredictable dinner guest, while the prostitute found Him to be an unprecedented forgiver! Saul of Tarsus thought

Jesus was dead but then realized that He was not only alive but also the Lord of life and death—for everyone!

We have seen Jesus' amazing power. His power was coupled with a strong dose of compassion as He touched an untouchable leper. The power of His word extended over many miles to heal a dying young man and bring a nobleman and his family to faith. The power of His loving call and presence redeemed an outcast tax collector. His forgiving power restored a paralytic's heart and body. The power of His mercy touched a hopeless cripple and not only cured his body but also gave his life new meaning. It wasn't Jesus' power alone that made the difference. It was the way He used His power that so incredibly altered people's lives and the way they viewed God.

We have seen Jesus' unspeakable glory. The dark underworld of demons shuddered in respectful terror before the mighty Son of God and fled from a man they held under their sway for many years. Three of Jesus' disciples *We must have* caught a glimpse of His glory and *our own encounter* weren't allowed to talk about it until much later on—an experience that *with Jesus.* readied them for any suffering that might come their way in the future. Thomas and the other disciples, though once shaken to the core over Jesus' death, were completely reenergized in faith when they saw Jesus in all His resurrected glory. And finally John, an old man waiting out his time on an isolated island, was able to pull back eternity's veil and glimpse his future and ours in the glory that is to come.

This is the real Jesus. Through Him Heaven was made near. This was "God with skin on." Those who met Him knew it. And most of them became loyal followers, committed to His Kingdom of transformation. They joined the team. They furthered the cause. The impact on their lives was unmistakable.

But so much for their story. So much for their journey. It is your journey and mine that completes the course. We must have our own encounter with Jesus.

Their experiences may be similar to ours in many ways. But their stories provide only the templates. Their encounters show the model of how a religious person or a brokenhearted person or an outcast meets Jesus. And their example inspires us to have our own relationship with Jesus. The personal relationship we have with Him must indeed be personal! One relationship is never exactly like another. Each is unique, and each is based on the person's individual characteristics and experiences.

The New Testament encounters with Jesus are not blueprints; they are guidelines. They have been preserved and given to us by the God who created us and craves our fellowship and wants us to crave His.

At the beginning of this book I expressed my desire that your reading about how Jesus met with these men and women would create in you a deep yearning to meet Him too. You are now faced with the question: Have you met Him yet? Have you met the real Jesus? Not the pale, passive Jesus you may have learned about when you were a child. Not the ineffective, unapproachable Jesus you may have heard about from others. Have you met the Jesus whose revolutionary love radically changes people? Are you ready to meet Him? If you have already met Him, are you ready to meet Him in a new way? Are you prepared to have Him astound you, restore you, forgive you, heal you, give you purpose?

Jesus wants to meet with you. He wants to make you whole and give your life direction. Are you willing to get in step with His plan for you? Do you walk with Him and hunger to see more of His person, power, and glory in your daily life?

I hope, to some degree at least, that this book has pointed you in that direction. I hope that seeking Jesus and His transforming presence will become your daily preoccupation. I expect that if this turns out to be the case, your life will be both full and empty. It will be full because of the satisfaction that comes with such a relationship. It will be empty because you have glimpsed eternity, and you will never be fully satisfied until you see Him face-to-face!

ENDNOTES

Introduction: Will the Real Jesus Please Stand Up?
1. Bruce Barton, *The Man Nobody Knows: A Discovery of the Real Jesus* (Indianapolis: Bobbs-Merrill, 1925), 27–33.

Chapter 1: A Messenger in the Middle of Nowhere
1. John F. MacArthur, *Matthew 1–7*, vol. 1 of *MacArthur New Testament Commentary* (Chicago: Moody Press, 1985), 80.
2. Many scholars who have "harmonized" the Gospels— that is, who have placed the events recorded in the New Testament into chronological order—agree that Jesus went into the wilderness for forty days after his baptism. Therefore, when the Gospel of John says, "The next day John saw Jesus coming toward him, and said, 'Behold! The Lamb of God who takes away the sin of the world!' "(1:29), the phrase "the next day" refers not to the day of the baptism but to the day after John's response to the Jerusalem leaders who had come to confront him. For a further explanation of this phrase in John 1, see John F. MacArthur, *Matthew 1–7*, vol. 1 of *MacArthur New Testament Commentary* (Chicago: Moody Press, 1985), 103; and for more detailed clarification of this timeline, see Harold W. Hoehner, *Chronological Aspects of the Life of Christ* (Grand Rapids: Academie Books, 1977), 44; and A. T. Robertson, *A Harmony of the Gospels for Students of the Life of Christ* (San Francisco: Harper San Francisco, 1950), 22–3.
3. For a fuller view of this, see G. Campbell Morgan, *The Great Physician* (Westwood, N.J.: Revell, 1937), 12–5.
4. Howard Hendricks, The Bible Illustrator for Windows (Parsons Technology, Inc.), 1997–1998. All rights reserved. Illustrations copyright © 1998 by Christianity Today,

263

Inc. All rights reserved. Portions copyright © 1984–1995 Faircom Corp.

Chapter 2: Religion Gets a Makeover
1. "Items to Use in Illustrations," *Leadership* (Fall 1991): 89.
2. Merrill C. Tenney, *The Zondervan Pictorial Encyclopedia of the Bible* (Grand Rapids: Zondervan, 1975), 4:434.
3. Roy Gustafson, *What Is the Gospel?* (Minneapolis: Billy Graham Evangelistic Association, 1980).
4. Charles Colson, *Born Again* (Old Tappan, N.J.: Spire Books), 116–7.
5. Ibid.

Chapter 3: Mender of Broken Hearts
1. Herbert Lockyer, *All the Women of the Bible* (Grand Rapids: Zondervan, 1967), 236.
2. F. M. Lehman, *The Love of God: Hymns for the Family of God* (Nashville: Paragon, 1976), 17–8.
3. *INFOsearch™*, Illustrations data and database, search word: "Gypsy," vol. 1997.2. The Communicator's Companion™, P.O. Box 171749, Arlington, Texas 76003. Web site: <www.infosearch.com>.

Chapter 5: Voted Most Likely Not to Convert
1. "Tarsus," *Wycliffe Bible Encyclopedia* (Chicago: Moody, 1975). Logos Library System.
2. Ibid.
3. W. J. Conybeare and J. S. Howson, *The Life and Epistles of Saint Paul* (Grand Rapids: Eerdmans, 1978), 27.
4. Ibid., 47.
5. Ibid.
6. Adapted from Kenneth W. Osbeck, *Amazing Grace: 366 Inspiring Hymn Stories for Daily Devotions* (Grand Rapids: Kregel, 1990), 170, and Kenneth W. Osbeck, *101 Hymn Stories* (Grand Rapids: Kregel, 1997).

Chapter 6: The Power of His Touch
1. William Barclay, *The Gospel of Matthew*, The Daily Bible Study series, vol. 1 (Philadelphia: Westminster, 1975), 295.
2. Ibid., 296.

3. Dr. Paul Brand and Philip Yancey, *Fearfully and Wonderfully Made* (Grand Rapids: Zondervan, 1980), 139–40.
4. Quoted by John Stott, *Involvement: Being a Responsible Christian in a Non-Christian Society* (Old Tappan, N.J.: Revell, 1984), 41.
5. *INFOsearch™*, Illustrations data and database, search word: "Humanitarian." The Communicator's Companion™, P.O. Box 171749, Arlington, Texas 76003. Web site: <www.infosearch.com>.
6. Ibid., search word: "Evangelist."

Chapter 7: The Power of His Word
1. Merrill C. Tenney, ed. *The Zondervan Pictorial Encyclopedia of the Bible* (Grand Rapids: Zondervan, 1975), 5:745.
2. Alan Redpath, *A Testimony to Divine Healing* (pamphlet).
3. William Barclay, in *Inspiring Quotations Contemporary and Classical* (Nashville: Nelson, 1988), 67.
4. Dwight L. Moody, quoted in Edythe Draper, *Draper's Book of Quotations for the Christian World* (Wheaton, Ill.: Tyndale House, 1992), entry 3735.

Chapter 8: The Power of His Love
1. William Barclay, *The Gospel of Matthew*, The Daily Bible Study series, vol. 1 (Philadelphia: Westminster, 1975), 329–30.
2. John F. MacArthur, *The MacArthur New Testament Commentary*, vol. 2 (Chicago: Moody Press, 1987), 61–2.
3. William McBirnie, *The Search for the Twelve Apostles* (Wheaton, Ill.: Tyndale House, 1978), 174–5.
4. *INFOsearch™*, Illustrations data and database, search word: "Carnegie." The Communicator's Companion™, P.O. Box 171749, Arlington, Texas 76003. Web site: <www.infosearch.com>.
5. George MacLeod, quoted in Edythe Draper, *Draper's Book of Quotations for the Christian World* (Wheaton, Ill.: Tyndale House, 1992), entry 2131. Taken from The Bible Illustrator for Windows (Parsons Technology, Inc.), 1997–1998. Entry 891. All rights reserved. Illustrations copyright © 1998 by Christianity Today, Inc. All rights reserved. Portions copyright © 1984–1995 Faircom Corp.

Chapter 9: The Power of His Forgiveness

1. Lloyd Cory, *Quotable Quotations* (Wheaton, Ill.: Victor, 1985), 304.
2. William Barclay, *The Gospel of Matthew*, The Daily Bible Study series, vol. 1 (Philadelphia: Westminster, 1975), 327.
3. Even the disciples reacted this way when they saw a blind man. Probing Jesus, they asked, "Why was this man born blind? Was it a result of his own sins or those of his parents?" (John 9:2, NLT).
4. W. Phillip Keller, *Rabboni* (Old Tappan, N.J.: Revell, 1977), 116.
5. James S. Hewett, *Illustrations Unlimited* (Wheaton, Ill.: Tyndale House, 1988), 218.
6. Phillip Yancey, *The Jesus I Never Knew* (Grand Rapids: Zondervan, 1995), 174–5.
7. Patrick Morley, "When You Need a Friend," *Moody Monthly*, November 1990, 62–5.
8. Charles R. Swindoll, *The Tale of the Tardy Oxcart and 1501 Other Stories* (Nashville: Word, 1998), 92.

Chapter 10: The Power of His Mercy

1. William Barclay, *The Gospel of Matthew*, The Daily Bible series, vol. 2 (Philadelphia: Westminster, 1975), 22.
2. James S. Hewett, *Illustrations Unlimited* (Wheaton, Ill.: Tyndale House, 1988), 346.
3. Donald W. Brenneman, quoted in *Leadership*, vol. 12, no. 2. Taken from The Bible Illustrator for Windows (Parsons Technology, Inc.), 1997–1998. All rights reserved. Illustrations copyright © 1998 by Christianity Today, Inc. All rights reserved. Portions copyright © 1984–1995 Faircom Corp.
4. Edythe Draper, *Draper's Book of Quotations for the Christian World* (Wheaton, Ill.: Tyndale House, 1992), entry 4498.

Chapter 11: Restoration Glory

1. Quoted in Albert M. Wells Jr., *Inspiring Quotations Contemporary and Classical* (Nashville: Nelson, 1988), 57.
2. Tom Carter, *Spurgeon at His Best* (Grand Rapids: Baker, 1988), 57.

Chapter 12: Transfiguration Glory

1. Howard Rheingold, *They Have a Word for It* (New York: Saint Martin's Press; Los Angeles: Jeremy Tarcher, 1988), 28–9.
2. John F. MacArthur, *The MacArthur New Testament Commentary*, vol. 3 (Chicago: Moody, 1983), 59.
3. Ibid., vol. 2, 142–3.
4. *INFOsearch*™, Illustrations data and database, search word: "Illuminated." The Communicator's Companion™, P.O. Box 171749, Arlington, Texas, 76003. Web site: <www.infosearch.com>.
5. Ibid., search word: "Denisovich."

Chapter 13: Resurrection Glory

1. James S. Hewett, *Illustrations Unlimited* (Wheaton, Ill.: Tyndale House, 1988), 408.
2. Neil C. Strait, *Quotable Quotations: Compiled by Lloyd Cory* (Wheaton, Ill.: Victor Books, 1985), 108.
3. Tim Stafford, *Knowing the Face of God* (Grand Rapids: Zondervan, 1986), 13.
4. Kenneth S. Wuest, *The New Testament—An Expanded Translation* (Grand Rapids: Eerdmans, 1961), 265.
5. Warren Wiersbe, *Wycliffe Handbook of Preaching and Preachers* (Chicago: Moody, 1984), 211.

Chapter 14: Revelation Glory

1. Taken from Marle Hank, *Forward Day by Day*, August 17, 1991.

ABOUT THE AUTHOR

S kip Heitzig is the pastor of Calvary of Albuquerque in New Mexico—one of the twenty largest churches in America. This vital congregation has over 13,500 adults and their children, and the church has spawned over forty churches internationally.

Skip hosts a nationwide radio program and television show, "The Calvary Connection," and he reaches out to people all over the world through his multi-media ministry.

Skip attended Victor Valley Community College in California and UCLA. He received a degree in radiology. Later, he earned BA and MA degrees from Trinity Seminary and an honorary doctorate from G.F.A. Biblical Seminary in India. He is the author of more than twenty books. He lives with his wife, Lenya, in Albuquerque, New Mexico.